The International Design Yearbook 1995

The International Design Yearbook 1995

editor **Jean Nouvel**

general editor **Paul Jodard**

assistant editor **Jennifer Hudson**

Laurence King

The editor and the general editor particularly want to thank the assistant editor, Jennifer Hudson, the Japanese researcher, Junko Popham, and Joanne Lightfoot at Calmann & King for their help during the preparation of this book.

Special thanks go also to Jon Turner and Jason Claisse at Imagination for their work on the design and layout.

Published 1995 by Laurence King Publishing

A catalogue record for this book is available from the British Library.

ISBN 1 85669 059 8

Based on an original idea by Stuart Durant
Designed by Jason Claisse at Imagination, London
Printed in Singapore

contents

design for the present

Jean Nouvel

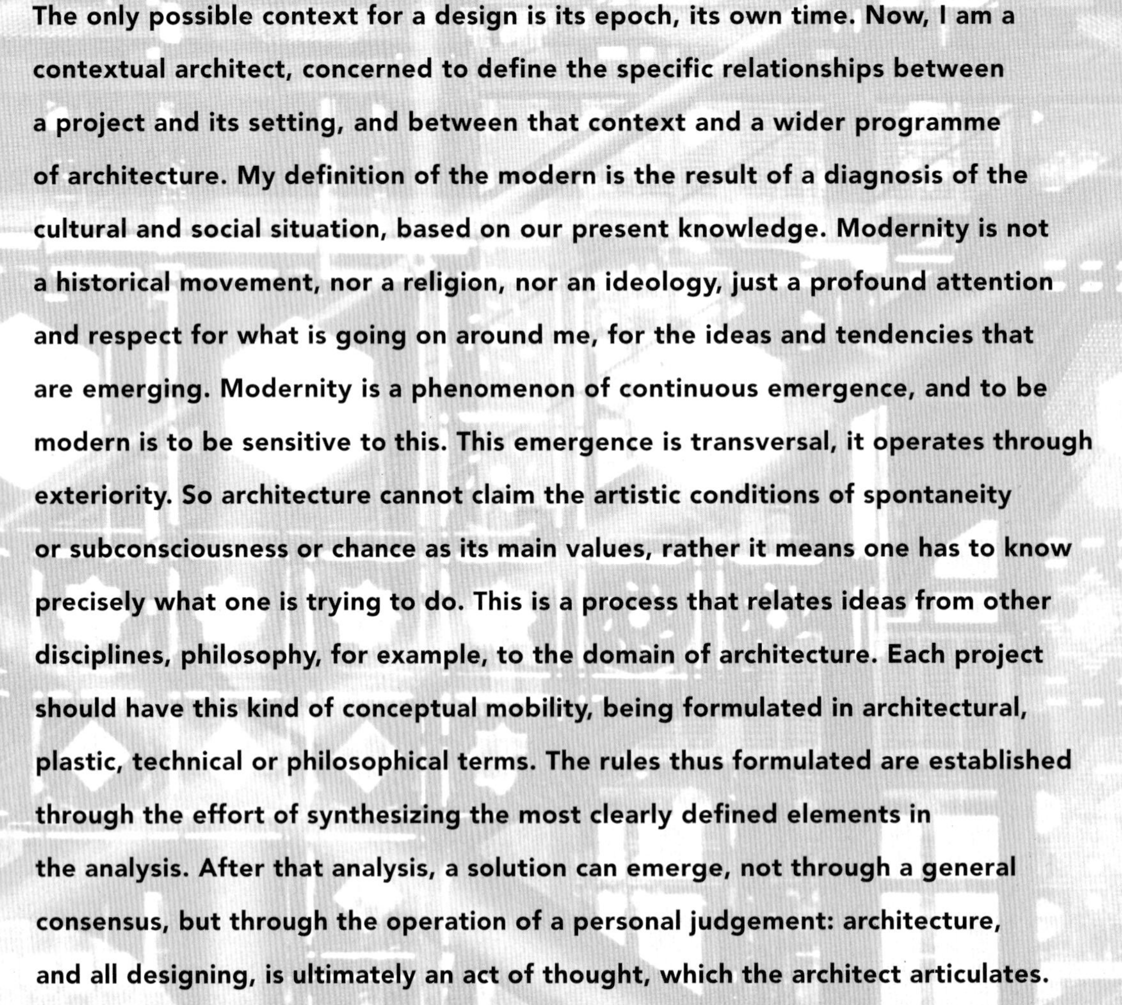

The only possible context for a design is its epoch, its own time. Now, I am a contextual architect, concerned to define the specific relationships between a project and its setting, and between that context and a wider programme of architecture. My definition of the modern is the result of a diagnosis of the cultural and social situation, based on our present knowledge. Modernity is not a historical movement, nor a religion, nor an ideology, just a profound attention and respect for what is going on around me, for the ideas and tendencies that are emerging. Modernity is a phenomenon of continuous emergence, and to be modern is to be sensitive to this. This emergence is transversal, it operates through exteriority. So architecture cannot claim the artistic conditions of spontaneity or subconsciousness or chance as its main values, rather it means one has to know precisely what one is trying to do. This is a process that relates ideas from other disciplines, philosophy, for example, to the domain of architecture. Each project should have this kind of conceptual mobility, being formulated in architectural, plastic, technical or philosophical terms. The rules thus formulated are established through the effort of synthesizing the most clearly defined elements in the analysis. After that analysis, a solution can emerge, not through a general consensus, but through the operation of a personal judgement: architecture, and all designing, is ultimately an act of thought, which the architect articulates.

That doesn't mean that there is no room for individuality, wit or humour, but what I detest in post-Modern architecture, for example, is the absence of any analysis, and the elevation of superficial wit to the level of a general principle. Architecture is a durable statement, and it has to be about the nature of the present: it has to be a witness of its time, signed by an individual architect. The analysis I describe is the starting point, but there comes a moment of synergy when the argument is in place, when it is essentially possible to fix the concept. The work, miraculously, almost, becomes plastic rather than verbal; memory and attention take over, and everything learnt fuses its plastic and connotatory values into a new object, more ambiguous, more mysterious, an oeuvre d'art.

top View of the interior of the Institut du Monde Arabe, Paris, the building that brought Nouvel's work to a world audience.
below Two views of the Hotel Les Thermes, Dax.

For these reasons, architects should take designing furniture or lighting or products as a serious matter. Some classic designs - for chairs, for example - can last fifty, seventy or even a hundred years or more. A piece of antique furniture is still a witness to its age, can still make a true statement, even if in terms of use it is more appropriate to the age of Louis XII, XIV or XV! But the only valid reason for changing the design of an object has to be based on a change in need, in purpose, in the social and temporal situation. Nothing fills me with more horror than seeing someone try to change the design of a wine glass, for example, to fit a new and more fashionable style. The shape of a traditional Bordeaux glass has evolved over time to meet its own rationale. Any change in its form has to come from outside, not from the whims of a designer. So we can talk about a category of design basics, objects which keep their own function, which have been developed through a craft process through the years, unmarked by style. They should not be changed, not out of reverence for the past but because there is no need to change them. Modifying them for commercial, marketing or economic reasons is a dilution of their content, a banalization of design.

But there exists another category, of objects which are designed as part of their time, as contemporary statements, and where the personality of the designer can and should show through the object. I have no problem with that kind of design, provided that it meets the criterion of responding to its own epoch, and not being indulgent or superficial. It's around these two opposite poles that the work here has been selected. There are, if you like, two definitions of serious design, both valid - and neither about design that is dull. One is design that is serious because it respects and understands the cultural and historical context of the present, the other earns its seriousness from the commitment and attitude of the designer. In the best design, as in the best architecture, these two qualities fuse. The designer's personal vision, on the one hand, and an understanding of context, on the other, fuse into the final design.

top Night-time view of the Nemausus housing project.

centre Roofline of the Hotel Les Thermes, Dax.

bottom Exterior of the Hotel Hauterive, near Bordeaux.

Columns in the main hall
of the Institut du Monde Arabe.

One reason why the designer, as opposed to the architect, has room for this degree of expression is that designing does not demand the same exterior resources, the same complex and structured environment, as architecture. Design has to have the same awareness as architecture, of course, but can often be in advance, because it doesn't suffer from the time-lag involved in building. And so design can be experimental, allowing the designer a freedom to innovate and to try out ideas in the same way as an artist.

The aesthetics of modern product design can be seen in terms of awareness, of function, and of the inspirational. I say inspirational - miraculous, even - because we have long got past the point when the function of objects and machines was clearly visible, when you could lift the lid and look inside to find out how something was made and how it worked. So one of the functions of design is to make us aware of how the black box works, of making its functions accessible, of explaining the miraculous in what it does.

A major tendency, especially in product design, is towards a certain kind of minimalism. What appear to be simpler and simpler objects are capable of performing more and more complex tasks. This isn't just because of miniaturization and the use of light-weight materials, it's a true paradox between simplicity and complexity. This paradox design has to help resolve. It's to do with the rate of change, the challenge of opportunity, the fact that a computer that used to fit into a large room is now the size of a postcard, that a television set can also be a video output, a computer screen, an active interface with new communication media. This change is not visually evident; objects appear simple, but are not simplistic; in fact they are more and more capable and complex. In the late 1980s some designers tried to reduce such products to brute banality, using decoration to disguise the object. That approach was clearly ridiculous, even if it produced some things with an artistic validity. But design has to be about problem-solving, not problem-avoidance.

Some of the main areas where this pressure of change is at its most extreme are in military hardware, aerospace projects, medical and scientific equipment and high-performance sports. The military world, above all, is a premonitory world, it has the greatest financial and technical resources: every invention has come down through the military. There is nothing quite as beautiful as a weapon, in the abstract, as an area of research continually defining new forms. And I'm fascinated by space vehicles, medical scanners and fighter planes, and I think Formula One cars and Olympic racing bikes are among the most beautiful objects of the last few years. This is design under pressure, at such an extreme that is almost anti-design. But technological innovations percolate down from these areas, which are themselves important in defining the contemporary aesthetic and material matrix of design. The evolution of this performance-based aesthetic is one of the defining parameters of the modern, and any philosophy of design needs to take it into account.

A further development in design is the empowerment of the user, whether in terms of modular furniture or modular phones. More and more people are becoming aware of the potential of design. Perhaps, as Joseph Beuys suggested, 'every man is now an artist.' This doesn't mean that they are good artists, unfortunately, but this level of sensibility does impose more challenges, even duties, on the designer. This raises the question of the intelligence of the object, even if it isn't the guarantee of good design. The only place left for the absurd or incomprehensible object is in the field of artistic design, where poetry and theatre have their part to play. True design must neither terrorize or theorize, or impose itself, but simply explain, accommodate and welcome the user. Making the complex simple, making the intelligent object intelligible, making the object express its time, is very complicated, and is also the most exciting challenge faced by the designer today.

Window detail at the Hotel Les Thermes.

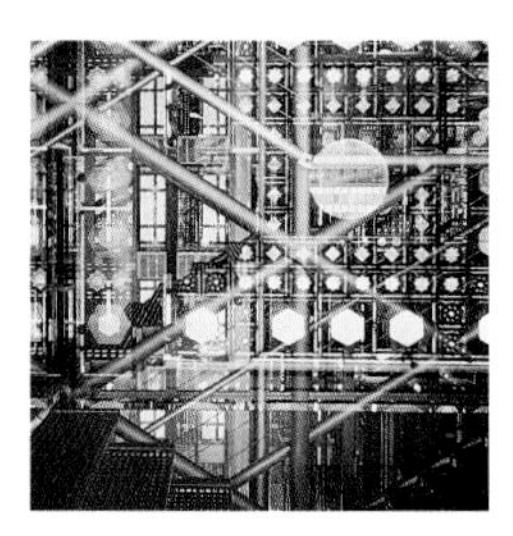

design and the future

Paul Jodard

' Architecture cannot be but a very specific reflection on external conditions that are increasingly powerful and unavoidable. Architecture becomes therefore a mutation, a transformation of given conditions. We can only operate through alteration, through adjunction, through iteration... enhance certain traces, identify them out of the chaos...'

Jean Nouvel, interview in *El Croquis*, 1994

facing City-side exterior wall of the Institut du Monde Arabe: the size of the shutters is photoelectrically controlled, creating a dense and variable interior light, supplemented by the light passing through the translucent alabaster cladding of the interior courtyard.

right The Tour Sans Fins project is intended to stand by the Grande Arche at la Défense, Paris, and serve as a French World Trade Center. The external cladding is glass, with the interior armature progressively less visible, so that at its summit the building will merge into the sky.

A survey published by Architektur und Wohnen during the 1994 Milan Furniture Fair named Jean Nouvel as one of the two architects most cited in creating the classic designs of the future (the other was I.M. Pei, creator of the Louvre pyramid). For an architect who is on record as saying that 'the future of architecture will no longer be architectural' there is a certain irony in this accolade. For Nouvel's architecture, and his furniture design, is especially concerned with confronting the problems of the present.

Take, for example, his Institut du Monde Arabe in Paris, completed in 1987 (the year he was also voted Furniture Designer of the Year at the Paris Salon). It is a building that was embroiled in controversy even before construction began, and which has divided opinion on its merits ever since. (To set the record straight, it is certainly the finest contemporary building in Paris, both intellectually and aesthetically.) Like all great buildings, its style defies simple categorization. It has been called Historicist, because of the deliberate echoes of Muslim architecture. It has been called Modernist, because of its use of glass walling on a steel frame. It has been called High-tech, because of the installation of electronically-controlled lighting and communication systems. None of these parts, however, even approach the sum of the whole, as the building's critics fail to understand the nature of Nouvel's design process.

For Nouvel, the only preconception in starting on a new project is that of the present: how is this building going to confront and respond to its own time, and fulfil its proper function. This involves a process of analysis and discussion, the identification of intellectual as much as visual strategies for defining the project. Only once that definition is in place does the process of visualization begin. In the case of the Institut du Monde Arabe, this meant arriving at an understanding of the inner nature of Arab architecture, and finding a form for that understanding that would be valid in a Western context. This does not mean visually translating Arab motifs into modern materials, but finding a new paradigm between the principles of East and West. In the Institut, this intellectual synthesis has led on to forms of profound complexity and visual density. The process of reduction does not stop there, but provides a foundation for technical and aesthetic virtuosity, that leads in turn to exquisitely contemporary statements in architecture.

For the same reason, the similarities between his buildings are only superficial. Certainly, Nouvel uses steel, glass, aluminium and concrete regularly, but not from some pre-conceived High-tech principle, but because they are to hand, the materials of today. The only linking theme is his own quest for the expression of a contemporary aesthetic defined by the final architectural form, and aware of the lack of independence for architecture - it has to exist in a social, physical and historical context. So architectural expression is inevitably as complex as the society we live in, the world that the building is for: hard-wired chaos theory, if you like. The spatial density of the Institut, for example, is radically different from the light and space of the Fondation Cartier building or the Tour Sans Fins project. Yet the same intellectual force can be discerned at work in all three. The Occam's razor of Nouvel's approach has left its bright cutting edge on each.

The Elementaire chair designed by Nouvel for Ligne Roset, in polyurethane foam and black leather.

In his furniture design the same process of reduction and rebuilding can be seen. Furniture should be simple, functional and direct, at one with the spirit of its time. It should be created for use, not for disposal, an enduring rather than a fashion object. His Elementaire chair was designed for the French company Ligne Roset, and he described its conception and design in these terms: 'it's about what I call basics, elementary things. The degree zero of design. Elementaire is a black armchair, dumb, cubic, minimal. It's well made but it's nothing else. "Move on, there's nothing to see here," it says. It's the kind of furniture I need because I've no time for furniture caricatures that dislocate and travesty the meaning of a place. Let me make this clear: I hate all furniture as fashion, created like styles, overdone, over-referential. I need simple things, so I set about making simple things. Anti-design, free of imagination. Elementaire is black and square, it works ergonomically. It's neither very comfortable or very uncomfortable. It's normal. And Roset simply said "Done" when they saw it.'

His new furniture for the Fondation Cartier comprises desking and storage systems, in grey-lacquered steel. A desk, said Nouvel, is simply a supported surface. So the Cartier desk (called Lss, Nouvel dislikes vowels) is a minimal surface on narrow legs. The skill of the design lies in the way the steel surface has been reinforced to maintain its rigidity as well as its narrow profile. The elegance of the solution derives from its simplicity. So with the storage units, which are carefully-proportioned boxes on swivelling stands. The function of the furniture has been taken down to essentials, and the result evolved from there. One Cartier employee I met inspecting his office at the opening of the Fondation called the furniture 'pure Tati,' comparing his new workplace with the wit and charm of the interiors in Tati's film 'Mon Oncle'. He was delighted.

The office furniture designed by Nouvel for the Fondation Cartier in Paris. The desks and rotating cupboards are made of sheet steel, and Nouvel's intention was to create an almost invisible piece, with narrow legs and a thin top. The whole building is intended to be as transparent as possible: it is set in a historic garden in Paris, and the furniture needed to follow the same logic.

Despite the discipline that Jean Nouvel brings to designing, whether for buildings or furniture, wit and individuality do have their place. The Pierre chair he created for the Hotel St Pierre near Bordeaux has just that lightness of touch: four chromed steel legs support a round white seat, with arms and back fitted with simple white pads. The whole effect is both relaxed and jaunty: it is made for a place in the sun. But the humour and the wit have to spring from the original conception, not be tacked on afterwards. Nouvel detests post-Modernism, perhaps even more in furniture than in architecture: he has a low regard for the work of Graves, Stern and Bofill. He recently described Memphis design as 'purely anecdotal, based solely and always on witticisms and absurdities', yet he admires the design of Ettore Sottsass, whose new lamps and wrist-watches are included here, and he respects the individuality of Michele de Lucchi's lighting and industrial design. Just as his own work is infused with his own broad culture, determination and

left The Hotel Hauterive sits among vineyards in a quiet village near Bordeaux. The furniture, for the restaurant and for the hotel rooms, had to be elegant and relaxed without being formal. The St James chair has a foam seat, arms and backrest, covered in white leather, on a simple chromed tubular frame.

right Nouvel's new chair for Sawaya & Moroni plays an intellectual game with Mies's Barcelona chair, not only twisting the legs of the design but re-inforcing this new tension with openwork seats made of twisted straps, instead of the plain leather of the original.

direction, Nouvel is open to personal jeux d'esprit: he has a profound admiration for the work of Ron Arad, for example. His own new chair for Sawaya & Moroni deliberately plays games with a classic, the Mies van der Rohe Barcelona chair. 'Suppose you took one and pulled its leg!' he explained. And that is what he did, twisting the legs, rather than extending them. The result is neither absurd nor fanciful, but a restatement of the dynamic tension in the original chair, as well as being a new object, lively and nervous in its own right. Putting the idea of the Barcelona chair to the test has wrought from it a new definition, just as in Nouvel's architecture new definitions continually emerge. For the Nemausus housing project in Nîmes, for example, he showed that you could use industrial building elements such as steel stairways and aluminium wall-cladding successfully in a domestic matrix - and beyond that, by using such materials the habitable space of each apartment could be increased by up to sixty percent more than in conventional solutions. Nouvel's choice here shows the same challenging attitude: conventional solutions are not rejected - though decoration for its own sake is - rather what attracts him is the evidence that the conventional and the possible solutions have been worked through, thought out, refined and redefined.

'Time for reflection can sometimes be more important in a career, or in the development of a design attitude, than time spent in active production.' This was one of the comments Nouvel came up with while selecting work for this Yearbook. It can be read on a number of levels: a wry reflection on the present state of the design industry, a sober insistence on thought before action, or a determination that content is more important than style. The selection he has made indeed shows the design profession in a period of reflection. With the darkness of the recession seeming to lift, the mood has changed to contemplating a future in which the exuberance - some might say the excess - of the 1980s is no longer appropriate. This chimes with calls at recent design conferences for longer-term design, for green design, for energy-efficient and environmentally-friendly design. Statements from designers as diverse as Rolf Sachs ('the basic idea is to get away from the subjective addiction to design of the last few years'), Bang Design ('producing new ideas is not an attempt to prolong a disposable society') and Philippe Starck ('we're moving into the "moral market"') show how widespread these concerns have become. But this spirit of restraint has only rechannelled the output of designers, not reduced the flow. The level of submissions for this Yearbook, for example, remained comparable to earlier years, even if the balance between different areas has changed.

One reason for this may be that while the recession has affected some areas of design (furniture is a good example), in others, such as product design, the continued development of technology has created a growing, not a reducing, series of challenges and opportunities. New technologies, new materials, new techniques have fuelled an expansion of designs available for the home, as well as for the office and workplace. As Nouvel points out in his own text, these technologies demand the designer's full participation. Thus as one part of the market offers fewer opportunities, another part of the market is expanding, not only in terms of volume but in terms of the way designers are employed. For there is growing evidence that more and more companies are taking heed of the pioneering example of firms such as Olivetti and Philips, Sony and IBM, and involving designers throughout the development process for new products. The long-term spread of this approach will, in time, put designers at the centre of the creative process in industry. It links them with the marketing and economic bases of modern production, and with developments in engineering and technology. Bringing the design discipline into a team with the other main partners in industry is an opportunity not a constraint, provided the added value created by design is fully appreciated.

This familiar argument now has an added urgency and relevance. After the uproar of the 1980s, the consumer can no longer be defined as a predictable entity. Not only are considerations from the past no longer valid (it can be argued that the past has been rejected, even the immediate past), the present itself is shot through with obscurity, crisis, and *anomie*. The proliferation of tactics between global branding, niche marketing, stratified sectors, total quality control and so on shows how much industry is itself uncertain. Market research no longer produces clear answers, only further and more enigmatic questions. In Andrea Branzi's words 'this is a particular period, squeezed between a rejected past and an improbable future, in which the system of post-industrial capitalism has run out of alternatives.' He also points out that 'while information is lacking on what kind of future people are seeking, this does not mean that there will be no future. If the future cannot be "forecast" it must be "designed"; it cannot be researched, it must be proposed. Today more than ever, business, if it wants to get out of crisis, must be capable of designing, of autonomously proposing new scenarios.' This is a strong statement of what many designers feel about the importance of design, that it is not a business that exists only for industry or for a market, but a global social activity in which the market, industry, technology and the environment are seamlessly connected, one and the same, not opposing but complementary factors. There is no difference between maker and consumer, between industry and society. In this new social matrix, design and designers have a key role in proposing new definitions of living.

left Table design by Nouvel for Sawaya & Moroni,1993. The deliberately thick aluminium top contrasts with the slim metal legs.

below The seating for the CLM/BBDO offices near Paris; slabs of foam covered in red leather that also serve as impromptu desks.

If the distinctions between business and marketplace are eliding, so too are traditional definitions of home, family and work. Changing demographic patterns, different life expectancies, new patterns of family grouping, both through divorce and changing customs, are all challenging the perceived definitions of the house. Themes of modesty and transience are to be found: the refusal to adopt a single, permanent living space runs in parallel to the ending of life-time single employment. The idea of residence is replacing that of home for many young people, for whom a fixed location is no longer a pre-condition of success. The phenomenon of active retirement, often involving re-location, varies the historical perception of birthplace. Such changes force new obligations on designers to create new opportunities of self-expression through design in society.

At the same time the nature of work is changing. In the 1970s we were offered a future in which work would disappear in favour of endless leisure: we have inherited a present in which work, for those who have it, is all-pervasive, not only through technology but also through business, with its insistence on achievement and competitiveness. Even if there is some evidence that this pressure is easing in favour of wider social goals, the traces of the endemic greed of the last decade have cut deeply into society, and it is for designers to propose remedies.

So Nouvel's choices for the Yearbook, marked by his insistence on the total involvement of design, come at an opportune moment. Through them, he demonstrates an alternative approach to the subjective, consumerist over-design of the 1980s, one which responds to the diverse, iterative and complex nature of the present. This synergetic approach is analytical without being reductive, dynamic though tentative, contextual and yet personal. It represents a classic view of design in the best sense of those words, and a manifesto for the future.

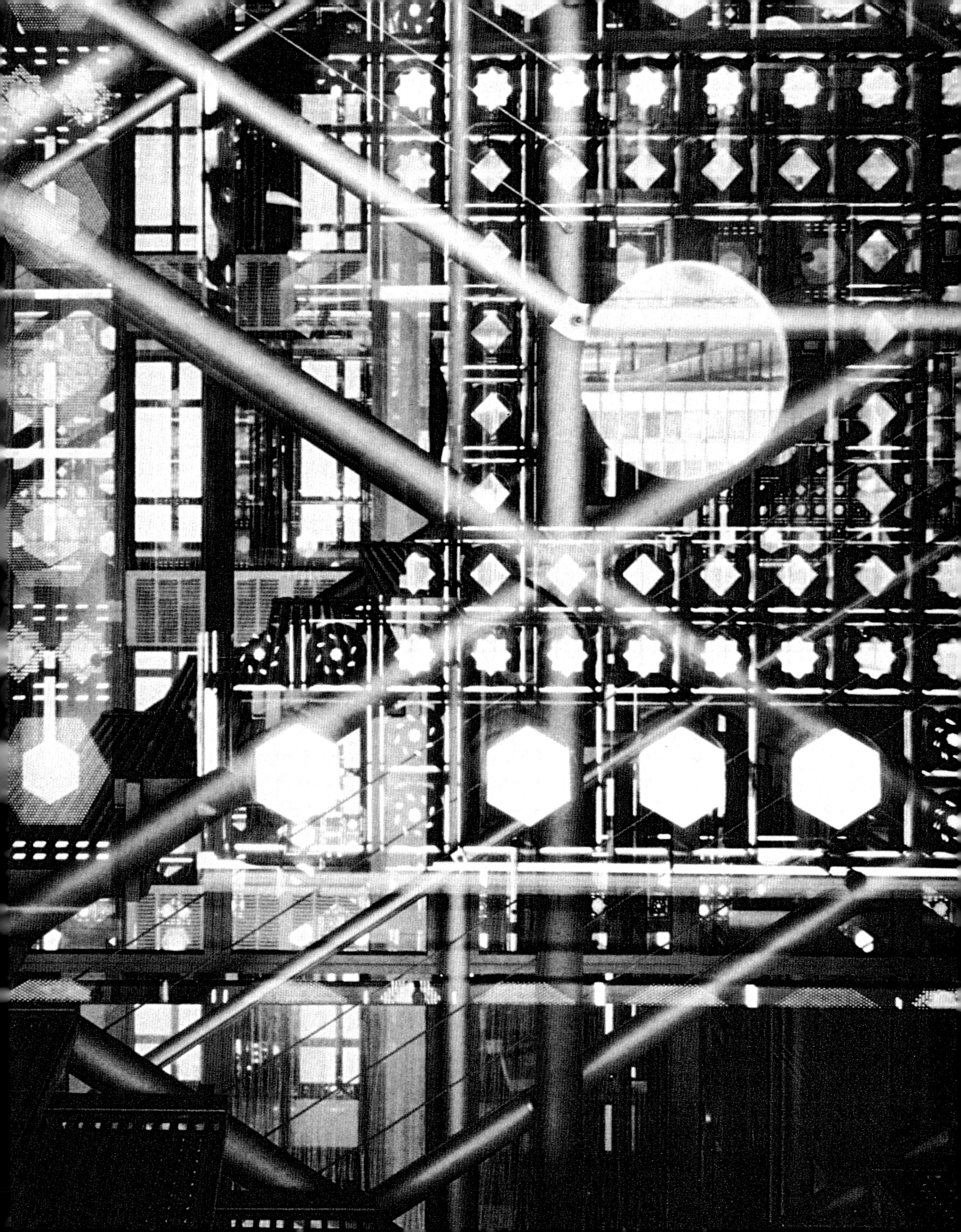

furniture

Recently Jean Nouvel showed me the prototype seating furniture for the offices he has designed for CLM/BBDO in Paris. A large red leather two-seater sofa, with a broad top, had been cut from a single block of foam. You could sit on it conventionally, Nouvel explained, or sit at an angle and use the top as an impromptu desk. The design seemed to be symmetrical, and if so, I asked, would it reverse? Nouvel's response was simply to push the sofa over. The angles didn't match, and I sprawled gently down onto the floor when I tried the new arrangement. But Nouvel's way of answering the question was instructive. Just as his test of the quality of architecture is the finished work, rather than the model or drawing for it - 'a building that isn't better when built than as a design isn't much of a building' - so his gauge of furniture design is a hands-on, practical one. 'Does this design work?' was a regular question he posed during the selection of work for the Yearbook.

The themes that emerge from the selection also echo Nouvel's concerns in his own architecture. These are appropriateness to purpose, contemporaneity, clarity and directness. Sometimes these values have been expressed through a choice of simple forms, such as Rolf Sachs' minimal desking, Starck's new stacking chairs or Enzo Mari's Novecento shelving. But direct design also embraces such advanced work as Ron Arad's boxed chairs, Ingo Maurer's bed, and Marc Newson's chair and table. Indeed Arad's forms, for which Nouvel has a deep appreciation, can be seen as pivotal in his selection, standing between simple and clear designs and more complex, personal solutions such as Chérif's Homage à Aalto or Borek Sipek's Tak-Tak. Just as Nouvel's own architectural design moves from the abstract process of analysis to the more personal one of visualization, so he respects the same process in others.

Nouvel's preference for the thought-out design rather than the decorative has also emphasized modest designs, expressed through portable and pack-flat furniture, furniture from recycled and recyclable materials, as well as through simple forms.
The theme of modesty - a motif of the 1994 Paris Salon du Meuble - is not only a reflection of the pressures created by the recession, or a reaction against the gaudier tastes of the 1980s. It is also a response to changing patterns of living and society, with fewer large families, more social mobility and different perceptions of permanence. Nouvel himself is against an attitude to furniture that treats furniture as fashion, to be dumped in favour of the next season's model, but he is equally against programmatic furniture that imposes solutions rather than choices. He would encourage furniture designers to use an 'invasion strategy', to be aware of the opportunities for empowerment and identity choices in furniture offer the user.
'The house is nothing more than a framework. It is a work in progress that will change with the generations, the evolution in mentalities and the people that live in it, with the forceful penetration of certain pieces of furniture, objects or art.
All those whose work touches on the cultural side of living can open doors to another way of living.'

1 Werner Aisslinger
design Endless shelf
materials MDF, cherrywood, aluminium
dimensions h 36cm w 36cm d 36cm
h 14⅛in w 14⅛in d 14⅛in
manufacturer Porro Industria Mobili, Italy

Werner Aisslinger's Endless Shelf is a modest, though elegant, solution to a problem he himself encountered when moving home. What he needed was a storage system that could adapt to any new space, and be used for books, records, CDs or other objects. It is based on a module of 36cm square panels, joined with steel-bolted aluminium cross and T units, and so it can be extended and planned at will. Vertical separators can be omitted, giving an alternative shelfspan of 74cm, and the recommended maximum height is just over three metres. The supporting feet can be set to give between 100 and 140mm of clearance from the floor.

2 Jasper Morrison
design High/low stool Orb I & II
materials Steel, birch plywood
dimensions h 41cm, 75cm w 45cm d 39cm
h 16⅛in, 29½in w 17¾in d 15⅜in
manufacturer Noto-Zeus, Italy

4 Jasper Morrison
design BB Basic Bookshelf
materials Lacquered wood
dimensions h 190cm w 130cm d 40cm
h 75in w 51⅛in d 15¾in
manufacturer Cappellini SpA, Italy

3 Jasper Morrison
design Shelving system Alpha
materials Aluminium, laminated board, plated steel
dimensions h 202cm, 118cm, 86cm w variable d 32cm
h 79½in, 46½in, 33⅞in w variable d 12½in
manufacturer Alias, Italy

left **5** Erik Magnussen
design Table Click
materials Chipboard, honeycomb cell, firwood laminate, veneer or plywood, plastics, steel
dimensions h 73cm L 90cm, 135cm, 150cm, 210cm d 80cm, 100cm
h 28¾in L 35½in, 53⅛in, 59½in, 82⅝ d 31½in, 39⅜in
manufacturer Fritz Hansen A/S, Denmark

6 Katsuhihoko Ogino
design Desk
materials Plastic
dimensions h 100cm w 100cm d 65cm
h 39½in w 39½in d 25⅝in
manufacturer Iris Ohyama Inc., Japan

7 Carlo Colombo
design Bed Archimède
materials Varnished metal, beech plywood
dimensions w 179cm d 204cm
w 70⅝in d 80⅜in
manufacturer Cappellini SpA, Italy

Jean Nouvel liked the simple but effective folding legs on Erik Magnussen's table for Fritz Hansen. The hinge acts as a locking device as well, and the legs can be mounted on a series of different surface materials, giving a range of styles and prices. Carlo Colombo's bed for Cappellini was admired for its re-statement of a traditional form in traditional materials (metal and beech ply) and with keen proportions.

9 Achille Castiglioni
design Tray with folding base Super Mate
materials Beechwood
dimensions h 42cm w 49.5cm L 59cm
h 16½in w 19½in L 23in
manufacturer é de Padova, Italy

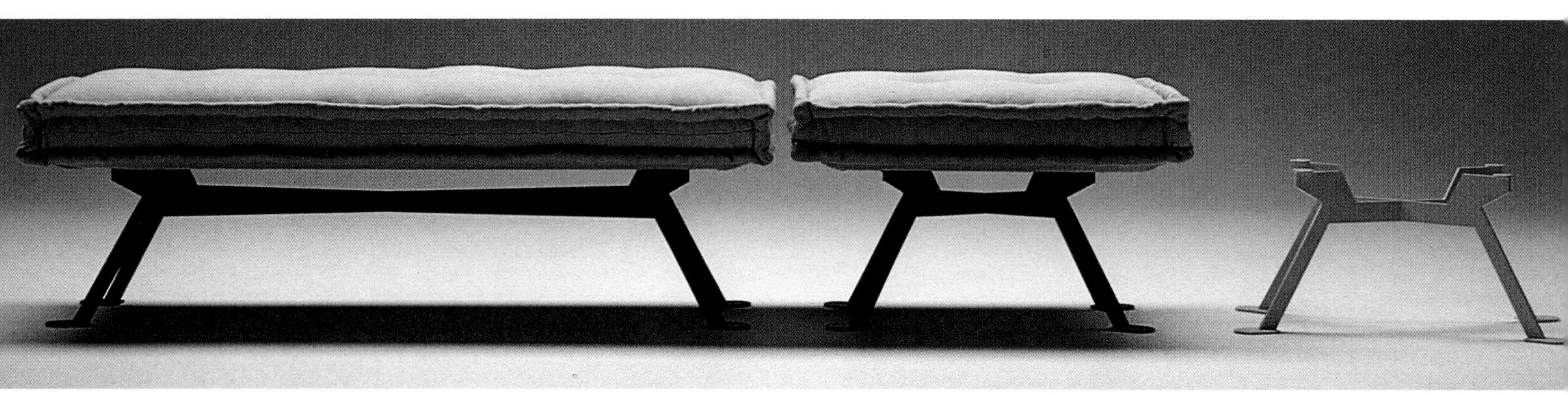

10 Achille Castiglioni
design Bench Fix
materials Painted steel, polyurethane powder, metal, cotton canvas
dimensions h 42cm w 50cm L 75cm
h 16½in w 29½in L 29½in
manufacturer é de Padova, Italy

Scalandrino, manufactured by Zanotta, is a new genre of object. It takes the concepts of the folding table, the ladder shelf and the extensible table and marries them up. The extensions of the table become slats in a shelving system, just by swinging the table top from the horizontal to the vertical. And as the slats do not move out of the horizontal in the transformation, it is theoretically possible to make the change with the shelves filled - or the table laid. But the exercise that Scalandrino really demonstrates is Castiglioni's mental agility in linking the three concepts with such a restrained solution, in which the neatness of the engineering adds to the wit.

11 Achille Castiglioni
design Table/shelves Scalandrino
materials Steel, beech, linoleum
dimensions Table: h 72cm w 151cm d max 91cm
Table: h 28⅜in w 59⅜in d max 35⅞in
Shelves: h 120cm w max 91cm d 80.5cm
Shelves: h 47in w max 35⅞in d 31½in
manufacturer Zanotta SpA, Italy

left **12** Enzo Mari
design Flower stand Pollice Verde
materials Natural teak, galvanized steel, ABS
dimensions h 36cm L 80cm d 60.5cm
h 14⅛in L 31½in d 23⅞in
manufacturer Zanotta SpA, Italy

13 Enzo Mari
design Secrétaire
materials Fibreboard, scratch-resistant embossing
dimensions h 70cm L 100cm d 40cm-72cm
h 27½in L 39½in d 15¾in - 28¼in
manufacturer Zanotta SpA, Italy

14 Nazanin Kamali
design Nest of tables
materials Epoxy coated flattened wire rod
dimensions h,w,d, cubes 43cm, 37cm, 31cm
h,w,d, cubes 17⅞in, 14½in, 12¼in
manufacturer Aero Ltd., UK
(Limited batch production)

Enzo Mari's designs now often make directness their prime quality, and so it is with the Novecento and Wunderkammer series of storage/shelving units for Zanotta. If his work some years ago had a strong graphic and decorative element, this has been replaced recently with cleaner forms, such as those of his Danubio armchair or the Flores boxes shown in the 1994 *International Design Yearbook*. There is almost a return to the very simple forms of the 1970s, the plain metal and canvas stacking chairs and unadorned *wood brut* storage units. This year's new pieces are straightforward glass-fronted shelved boxes, available in a series of different sizes, in a coloured particleboard finish. Jean Nouvel liked their efficiency and restraint, and found the Teca CD holder (overleaf) one of the best objects submitted: 'it says what it does and it does it' was his comment.

left **17** Enzo Mari
design CD holder Teca
materials Anodized aluminium
dimensions Various sizes
manufacturer Robots, Italy

18 Luciano Pagani, Angelo Perversi
design Bookcase Laima
materials Steel, aluminium, glass
dimensions Shelving module h 190cm w 95cm d 45cm
Shelving module h 35⅜in w 37⅜in d 17⅝in
manufacturer Zanotta SpA, Italy

19	Paolo Lomazzi
design	Shelf Spider
materials	Steel wire, steel sheet, aluminium
dimensions	h 100cm, 200cm w 50cm d 41.5cm
	h 39½in, 78¾in w19⅝in d 16in
manufacturer	Zerodisegno, Italy

right **20** Niels Gammelgaard,
Lars Mathiesen of Pelikan Design
design Screen Wing
materials Aluminium
dimensions h 180cm L 94cm d 13cm
h 70⅝in L 37in d 5⅛in
manufacturer Art Andersen & Co, Denmark

21 Pierluigi Cerri
design Table Naòs
materials Aluminium, wood or glass
dimensions h 74cm L 250cm d 100cm
h 29½in L 98⅜in d 39½in
manufacturer Unifor SpA, Italy

right **23** Matthew Hilton
design Bookshelf
materials Lacquered plywood and chipboard
dimensions h 192cm w 90cm, 150cm
h 75⅝in w 35½in, 59in
manufacturer Alterego, Italy

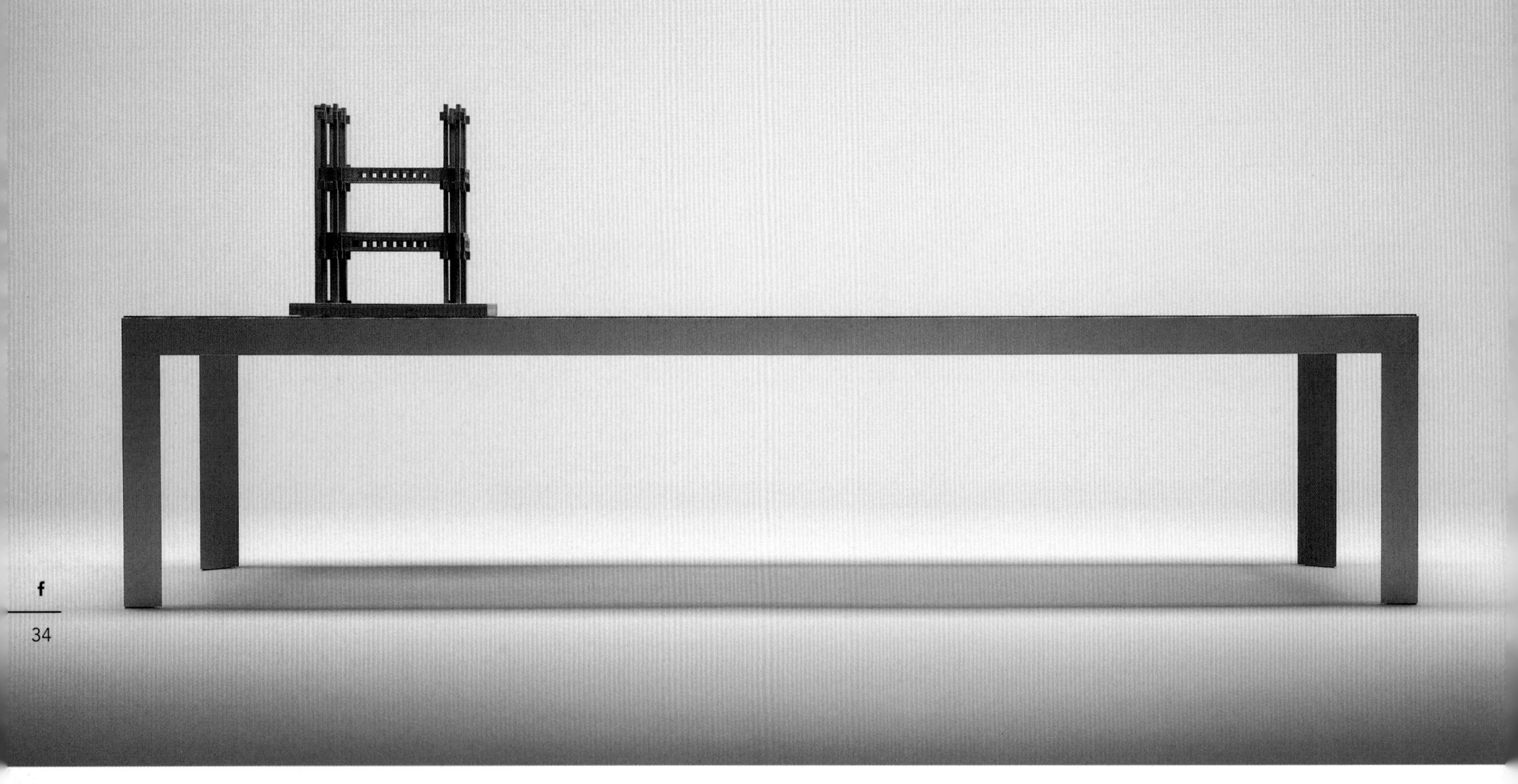

22 Pierangelo Caramia
design Storage system Screen
materials Natural wood
dimensions Various sizes
manufacturer Arredaesse, Italy

24 Piero Gilardino
design Storage units 50
materials American cherrywood, transparent tempered glass, white opaque glass or mirror
dimensions h 175cm, 79cm w 120cm d 45cm
h 68⅞in, 31in w 47¼in d 17in
manufacturer USO, Italy

25 Enzo Mari
design Table Lapo
materials Crystal
dimensions h 40cm L 120cm-140cm d 60cm-70cm
h 15¾in L 47¼in-55⅛in d 23⅝in-27½in
manufacturer Fiam Italia SpA, Italy

26 Vittorio Livi
design Screen Esse
materials Beechwood, sand-blasted crystal
dimensions h 168cm w 52cm d 14cm
h 66½in w 20½in d 5½in
manufacturer Fiam Italia SpA, Italy

Droog Design is based in Delft, in the Netherlands. They produce works by a number of young designers, (those included here are Martyn Hoogendijk, Gijs Bakker, Henk Stallinga and Djoke de Jong). The company's name could be seen as a pun on 'dry design', and there is a strong element of ascetic 'non-design' often present, blended with a subtle re-evaluation of design concepts, and executed in basic materials and plain colours. Here Martyn Hoogendijk has taken the simple loading pallet and stretched and bent it into a different, ambiguous genre. Because the humour is not forced, the work remains a proper piece of furniture, not just a design statement.

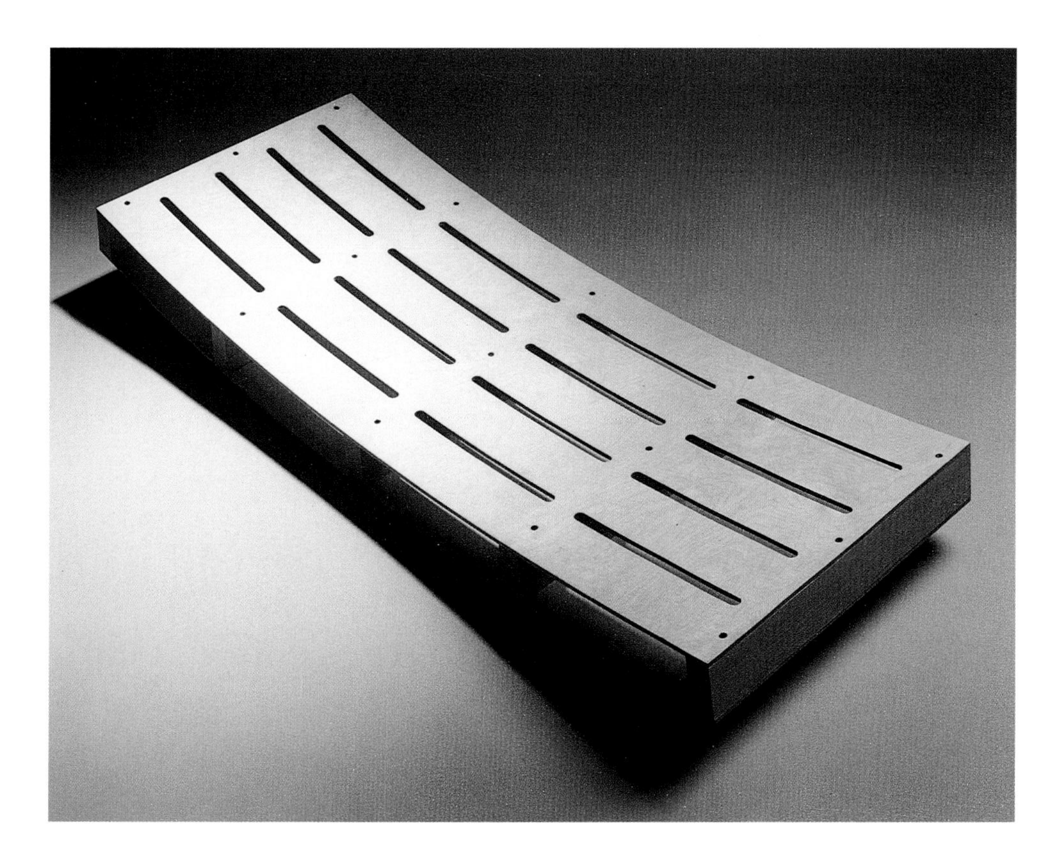

27 Martyn Hoogendijk
design Pallet Bed
materials Birch wood
dimensions h 12cm L 170cm d 68cm
h 4¾in L 66⅞in d 26¾in
manufacturer Droog Design, The Netherlands

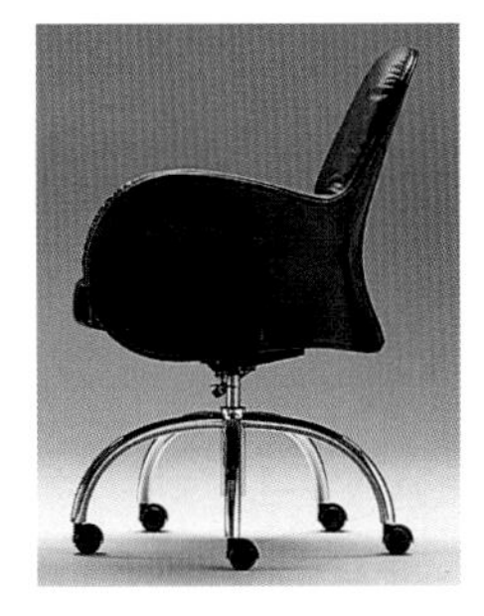

28 Vico Magistretti
design Armchair Serbelloni
materials Metal, expanded polyurethane, leather, fabric
dimensions h 85cm w 60cm d 54cm
h 33½in w 23½in d 21¼in
manufacturer é de Padova, Italy

29 Vico Magistretti
design Table Beyle
materials Cherry or beechwood
dimensions h 76cm L 200cm d 100cm
h 30in L 78¾in d 39½in
manufacturer é de Padova, Italy

30 Vico Magistretti
design Table Betulla
materials Aluminium, birch
dimensions h 40cm L 86cm d 41cm
h 15¾in L 33⅞in d 16⅛in
manufacturer é de Padova, Italy

31 Vico Magistretti
design Sofa Tuareg
materials Steel, expanded polyurethane, dacron, cotton fabric, rhombo-fe
dimensions Chaise: h 74cm L 150cm d 84cm, h 29⅛in L 59in d 33in
2-seater: h 74cm L 168cm d 84cm, h 29⅛in L 66⅛in d 33in
3-seater: h 74cm L 234cm d 84cm, h 29⅛in L 92⅛in d 33in
manufacturer é de Padova, Italy

32 Vico Magistretti
design Armchair Louisiana
materials Leather, polyurethane, metal
dimensions h 86cm L 80cm d 87cm
h 33⅞in L 31½in d 34¼in
manufacturer é de Padova, Italy

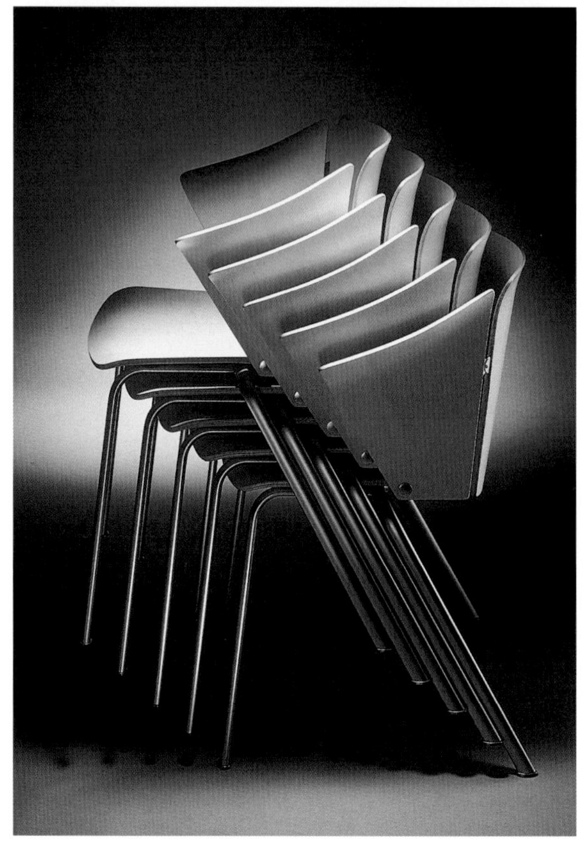

33 Vico Magistretti
design Vico Chair
materials Laminated wood, steel
dimensions h 78cm w 64cm d 45cm
h 30¾in w 25½in d 17¾in
manufacturer Fritz Hansen A/S, Denmark

34 Ross Lovegrove
design Eight Chair
materials Polyurethane, metal
dimensions h 78cm w 54cm d 50cm
h 30⅝in w 21¼in d19⅝in
manufacturer Cappellini SpA, Italy

35 Christopher Connell
design Chair Oak
materials American oak
dimensions h 80cm w 42cm d 47cm
h 31½in w 16½in d 18½in
manufacturer Map Pty Ltd., Australia

left **36** Bang Design
design Stacking chair Tim
materials Moulded plywood, tubular steel frame
dimensions h 81cm w 47cm d 54cm
h 31⅞in w 18½in d 21¼in
manufacturer Anibou Pty Ltd, Australia

37 Aldo Rossi
design Chair
materials Maple
dimensions h 83.5cm w 42cm d 45.5cm
h 32⅞in w 16½in d 17⅞in
manufacturer Molteni & Co. SpA, Italy

38 Thierry Poubeau
design Stacking chair Pauline
materials Wood
dimensions h 87cm w 35cm d 53cm
h 34¼in w 13¾in d 20⅞in
manufacturer Soca Line, France

39 Ninaber\Peters\Krouwel
design Stacking chair Quin
materials Chromed steel, laminated beechwood
dimensions h 77.5cm w 55cm d 50cm
h 30½in w 21¾in d 19⅝in
manufacturer Kembo bv, The Netherlands

40 Philippe Starck
design Stacking chair Olly Tango
materials Curved plywood, lacquered finish, chromium plated metal
dimensions h 90cm w 42cm d 58cm
h 35½in w 16½in d 22⅞in
manufacturer Driade SpA, Italy

Philippe Starck said in a recent interview that 'furniture still interests me but right now I have the happy chance of working on electronic products and on transport - motorbikes, planes, boats. And in those fields there is a lot to be discussed anew, to be reinvented.... As a result of that I probably won't be designing much furniture for the next two years.... It's as if for the next few years it'll be enough to do "maintenance work". 'That Starck has by now set out a full programme of work in furniture, which therefore needs consolidating rather than expanding, is true, but that is no consolation to those who have followed the bright trace of his wit and invention over the last fifteen years. The new stacking chairs for Driade, with their subtle range of colours and nicely judged forms, show his talent is still as strong as ever, as does his new bed Soeur Jeanne, for Cassina (overleaf).

42	Philippe Starck
design	Bed Soeur Jeanne
materials	Beech/cherrywood, aluminium
dimensions	h 80cm w 280cm L 236cm
	h 31½in w 110¼in L 92⅞in
manufacturer	Cassina, Italy

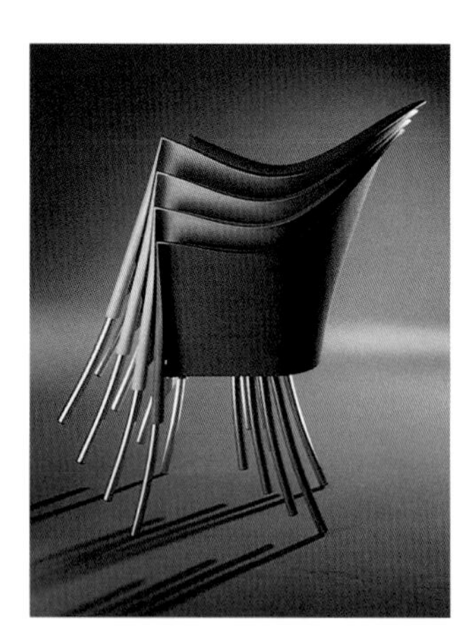

41	Philippe Starck
design	Stacking armchair Lord Yo
materials	Polypropylene, aluminium, anodized wirework
dimensions	h 94.5cm w 64cm d 66cm
	h 37⅛in w 25½in d 26in
manufacturer	Driade SpA, Italy

43 Michele de Lucchi
design Folding table
materials Maple wood, laminate, metal, aluminium
dimensions h 75cm di 140cm
h 29½in di 55⅛in
manufacturer Vitra International AG, Switzerland

44 Piero Lissoni
design Table Ferro
materials Iron
dimensions L 180cm-240cm d 85cm
L 70⅞in-94½in d 33½in
manufacturer Porro Industria Mobili, Italy

45 Sottsass Associati
design Cabinet Anteo
materials Varnished beech and kiln-dried beech veneer
dimensions h 186cm w 114cm d 64.5cm-86.5cm
h 73¼in w 44⅞in d 25⅜in-34in
manufacturer Zanotta SpA, Italy

46	Sottsass Associati
design	Stacking chair Elena
materials	Steel, aluminium alloy, plastic laminate
dimensions	h 76cm w 51cm d 49cm
	h 30in w 20⅛in d 19¼in
manufacturer	Zanotta, SpA, Italy

47 Sottsass Associati
design Bookshelf Giorno
materials Wood
dimensions h 225cm L 240cm d 40cm
h 88⅝in L 94½in d 15¾in
manufacturer Schopenhauer SpA, Italy

48 Berkhard Vogtherr
design Small room
materials Beechwood
dimensions Table: h 75cm w 150cm d 73cm, h 29½in w 59in d 28¾in
Chair: h 80cm w 36cm d 46cm, h 31½in w 14⅛in d 18½in
Bed: h 110cm w 90cm d 208cm, h 43⅜in w 35½in d 81⅞in
Armchair: h 78cm w 46cm d 62cm, h 30¾in w 18⅛in d 24⅜in
manufacturer Cappellini SpA, Italy

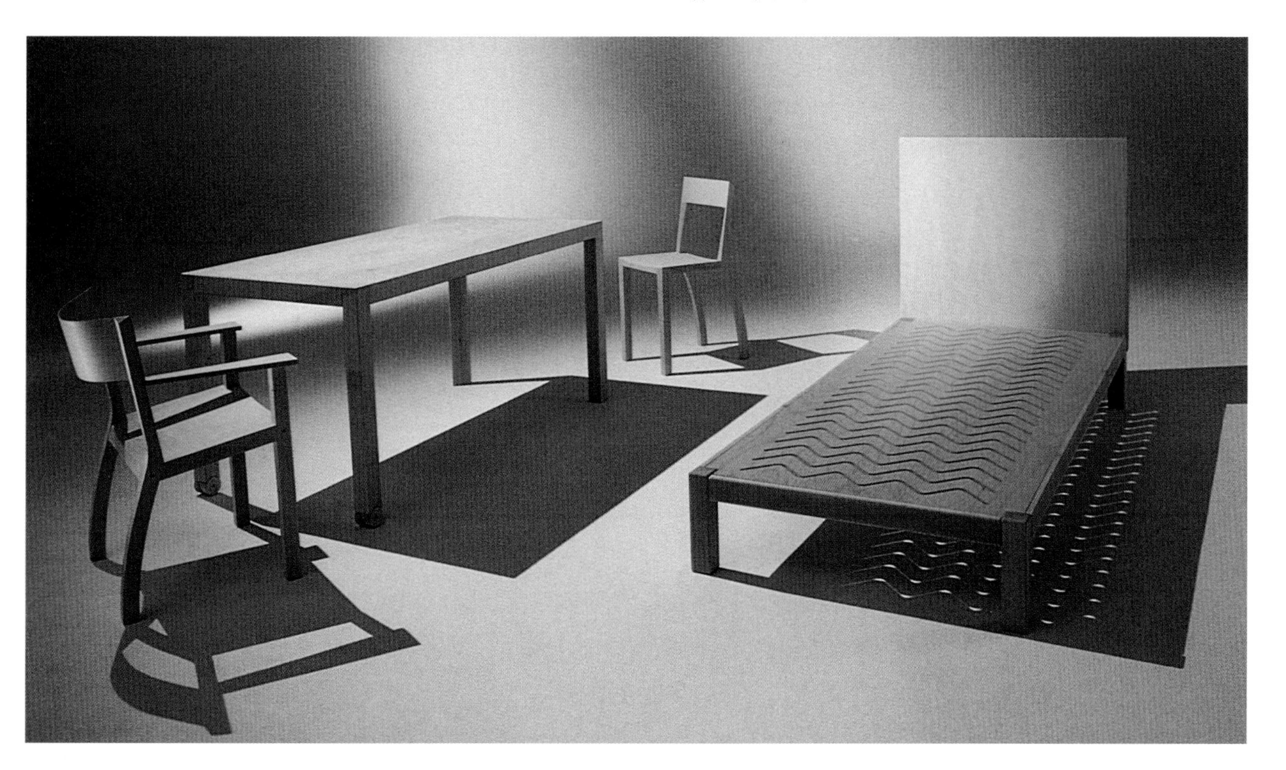

49 Luke Pearson
design Rise & fall table Lolly Pop
materials Steel tube, birch plywood
dimensions h 60cm - 85cm di 50cm
h 23½in - 33½in di 19⅝in
manufacturer Royal College of Art, UK
(Prototype)

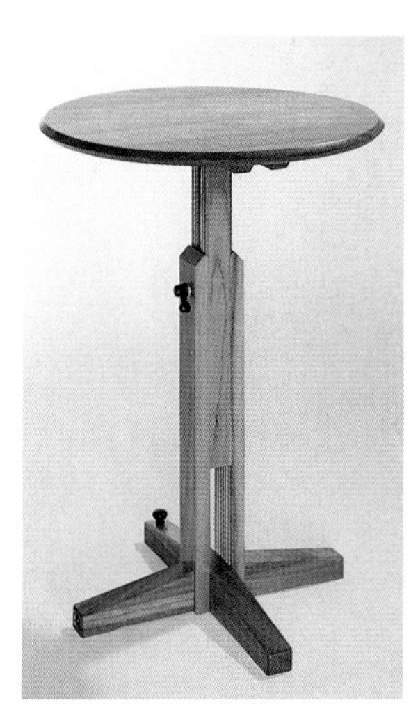

50 Bernard Vuarnesson
design Table
materials Solid wood, birch wood, beechwood
dimensions h 64cm - 110cm di 62cm
h 25⅛in - 43⅜in di 24⅜in
manufacturer Sculptures-Jeux, France

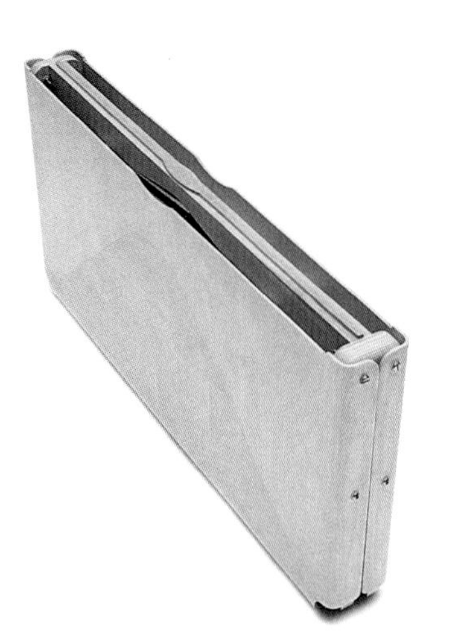

51 Julia Leakey
design Portable table with benches
materials Birch plywood, ash, aluminium
dimensions Table: h 72cm w 90cm d 90cm, h 28⅜in w 35½in d 35½in
Folded: h 45cm L 90cm d 9cm, h 17¾in L 35½in d 3½in
manufacturer Royal College of Art, UK
(Prototype)

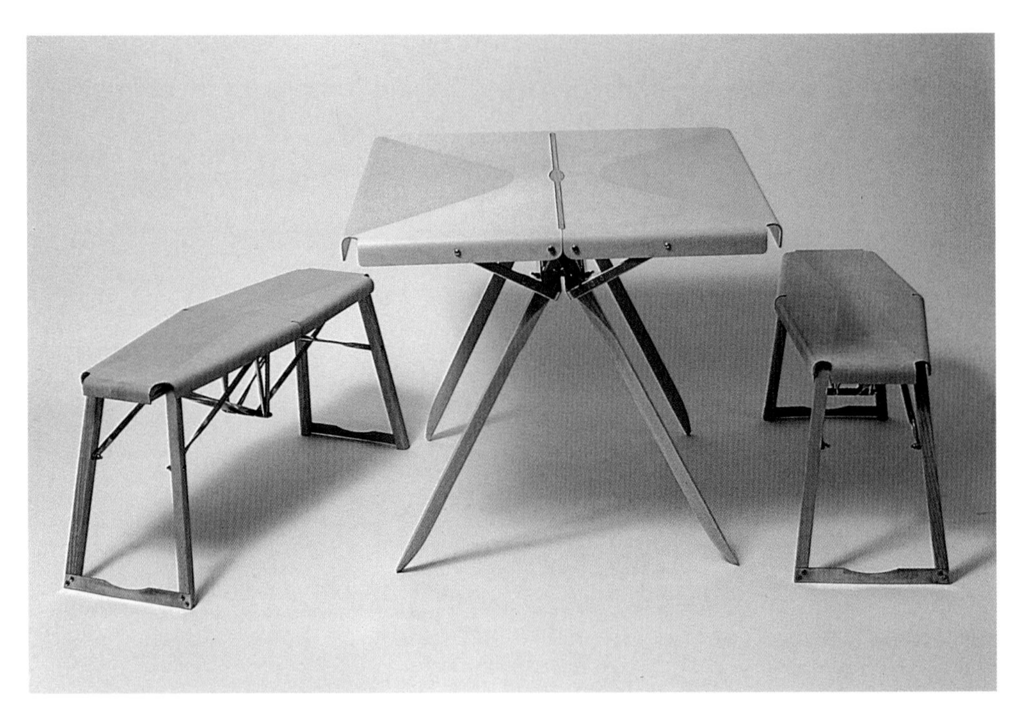

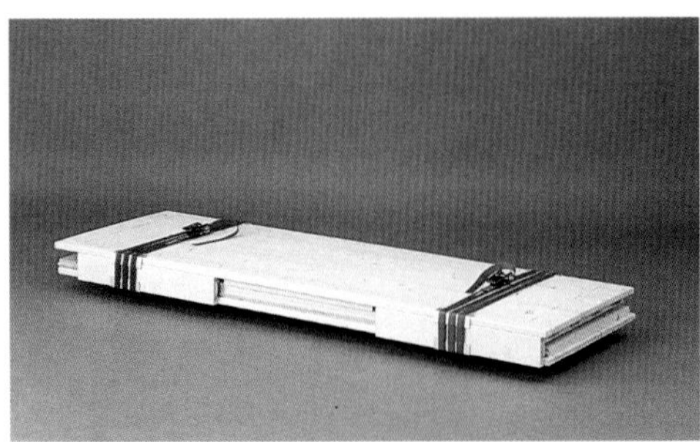

52 Heinz Baumann
design Wardrobe Nomad
materials Wood, steel, nylon
dimensions h 184 cm w 60cm d 60cm
h 72⅜in w 23½in d 23½in
manufacturer Möbelmanufaktur, Switzerland
(Limited batch production)

53 Olivier Leblois
design Suite Cardboard Family
materials Cardboard
dimensions Chair: h 67cm w 73cm d 76cm, h 26⅜in w 28¾in d 30in
Table: h 33cm L 100cm d 33cm, h 13in L 39½in d 13in
Bookshelf: h 184cm w 89.5cm d 29.5cm, h 72⅜in w 35½in d 11⅝in
manufacturer Quart de Poil', France

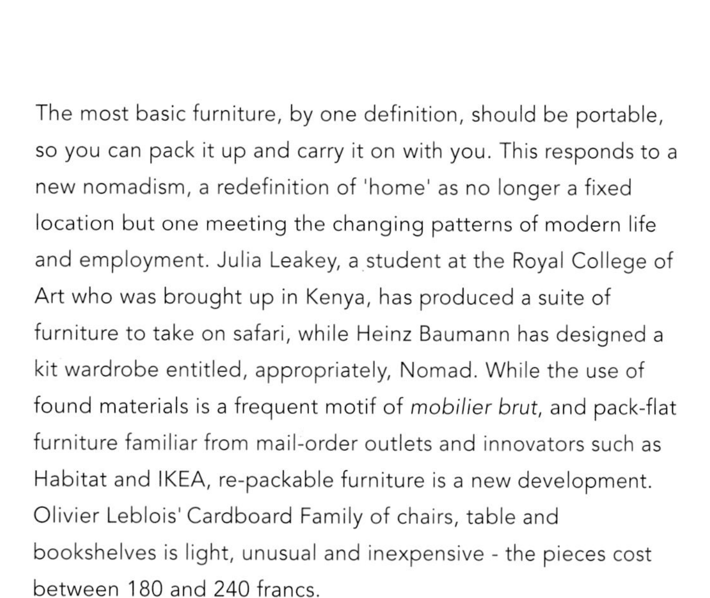

The most basic furniture, by one definition, should be portable, so you can pack it up and carry it on with you. This responds to a new nomadism, a redefinition of 'home' as no longer a fixed location but one meeting the changing patterns of modern life and employment. Julia Leakey, a student at the Royal College of Art who was brought up in Kenya, has produced a suite of furniture to take on safari, while Heinz Baumann has designed a kit wardrobe entitled, appropriately, Nomad. While the use of found materials is a frequent motif of *mobilier brut*, and pack-flat furniture familiar from mail-order outlets and innovators such as Habitat and IKEA, re-packable furniture is a new development. Olivier Leblois' Cardboard Family of chairs, table and bookshelves is light, unusual and inexpensive - the pieces cost between 180 and 240 francs.

54 Rolf Sachs
design Bookcase Q-bus
materials Untreated artificial wood
dimensions h 80cm, 60cm, 40cm w 40cm d 40cm
h 31½in, 23½in, 15¾in w 15¾in d15¾in
manufacturer Rolf Sachs Furniture GMBh, Germany

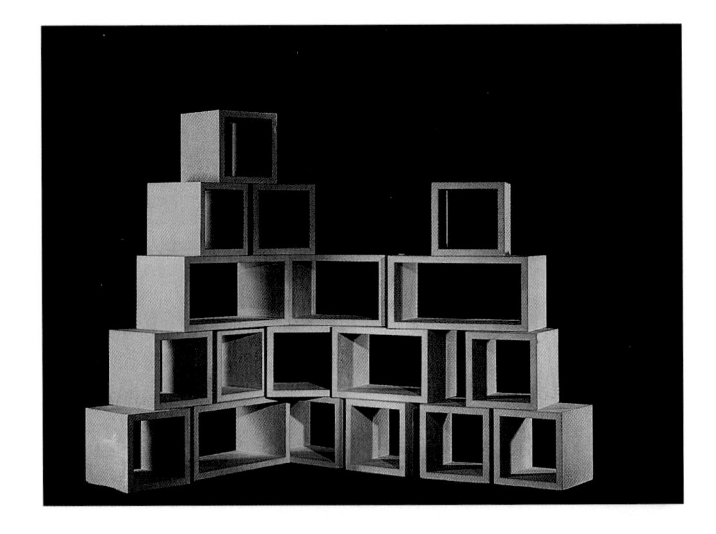

55 Rolf Sachs
design Chair Säss elle
materials Cherry wood and felt
dimensions h 68cm L 190cm d 84cm
h 26¾in L 74⅞in d 33in
manufacturer Rolf Sachs Furniture GMBh, Germany

56 Rolf Sachs
design Couch e geil
materials Felt
dimensions h 1cm w 60cm L 400cm
h ⅜in w 23⅝in L 94½in
manufacturer Rolf Sachs Furniture GMBh, Germany
(Limited batch production)

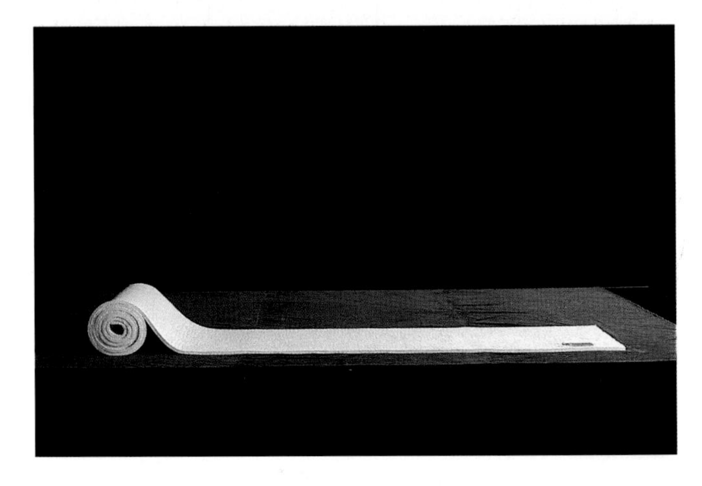

Rolf Sachs' new collection is called, graphically, !m-ob ili ape zzi; one level of translation is 'furniture in pieces'. Such a process of deconstruction is central to Sachs' approach, which seeks to get back to simple forms, away from the subjectivity of the last decade. He describes these pieces as 'non-fixed, open constructions... each individual part fits together naturally to form a whole: its strength derives not from complicated construction or extravagant design. Matter-of-fact and functional, it serves the user.' The cube that forms the base of a chair is also the support unit for the desk, the couch e geil is a simple length of re-cycled felt with a securing strap that doubles it into a cushion, and so on. But simplicity and flexibility need not exclude subtlety and innovation. The Ha-all unit is the first in a new series of function-images, in which function and appearance combine, in this case to both decorate and sound-proof a wall.

57 Rolf Sachs
design Sound absorbing picture Ha-all
materials Foam
dimensions w 300 x 300cm d 6cm
w 118in x 118in d 2⅜in
manufacturer Rolf Sachs Furniture GMBh
(Limited batch production)

58 Rolf Sachs
design Desk with stool Schreibtisch für M
materials Maple wood
dimensions h 72cm L 310cm d 140cm
h 28⅜in L 122in d 55⅛in
manufacturer Rolf Sachs Furniture GMBh

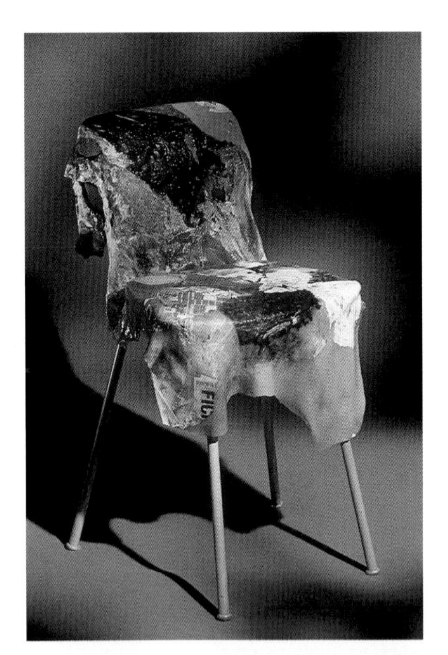

59 Beata Bär, Gerhard Bär, Hartmut Knell
design Chair Series of Mixed Plastics
materials Recycled mixed plastics
dimensions h 80cm w 45cm d 45cm
h 31½in w 17¾in d 17¾in
manufacturer Bär + Knell Design, Germany
(Limited batch production)

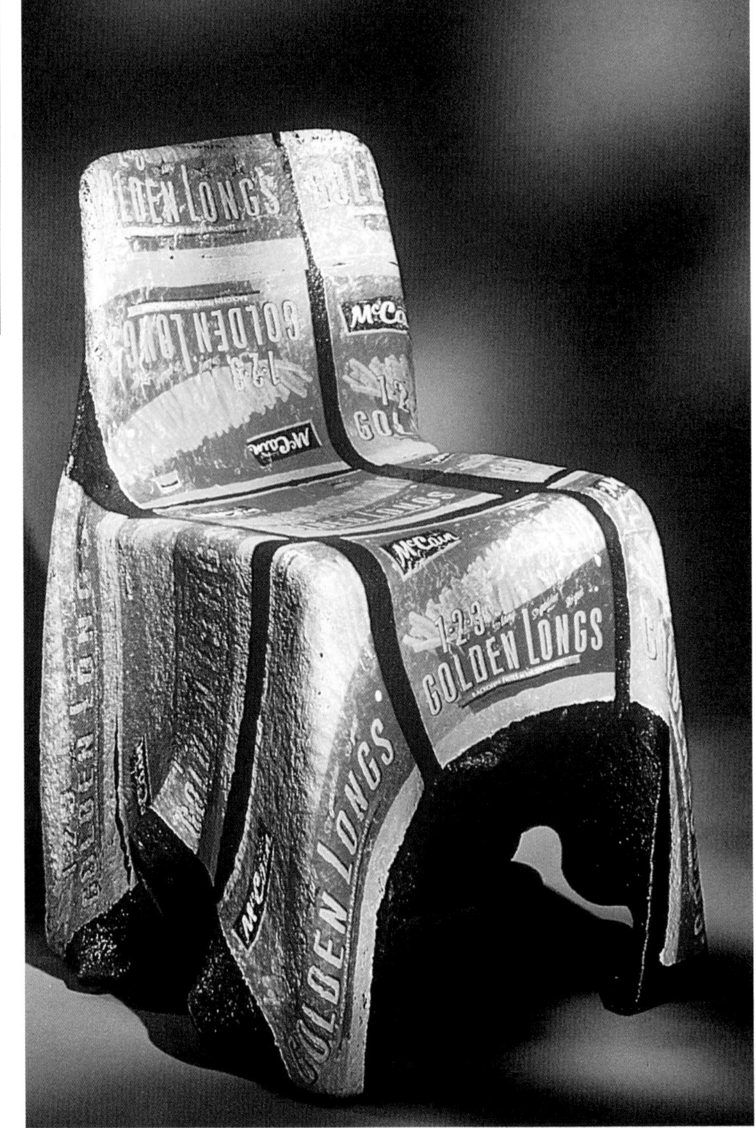

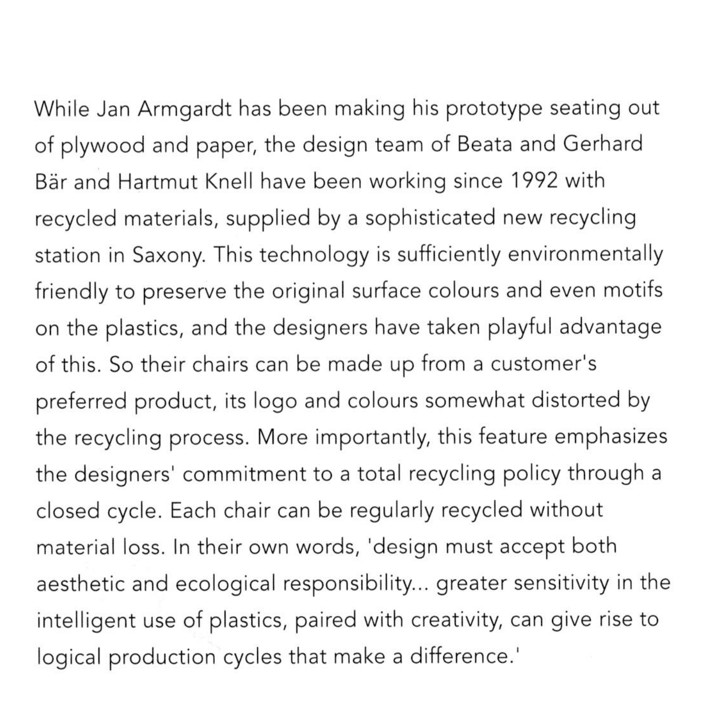

While Jan Armgardt has been making his prototype seating out of plywood and paper, the design team of Beata and Gerhard Bär and Hartmut Knell have been working since 1992 with recycled materials, supplied by a sophisticated new recycling station in Saxony. This technology is sufficiently environmentally friendly to preserve the original surface colours and even motifs on the plastics, and the designers have taken playful advantage of this. So their chairs can be made up from a customer's preferred product, its logo and colours somewhat distorted by the recycling process. More importantly, this feature emphasizes the designers' commitment to a total recycling policy through a closed cycle. Each chair can be regularly recycled without material loss. In their own words, 'design must accept both aesthetic and ecological responsibility... greater sensitivity in the intelligent use of plastics, paired with creativity, can give rise to logical production cycles that make a difference.'

below **62** Jan Armgardt
design Easy chair JA 30P
materials Plywood, paper
dimensions h 75cm w 75cm d 70cm
h 29½in w 29½in d 27½in
manufacturer Prototype

63 Jan Armgardt
design Chair JA 26P
materials Plywood, paper
dimensions h 90cm w 45cm d 55cm
h 35½in w 17¾in d 21⅝in
manufacturer Prototype

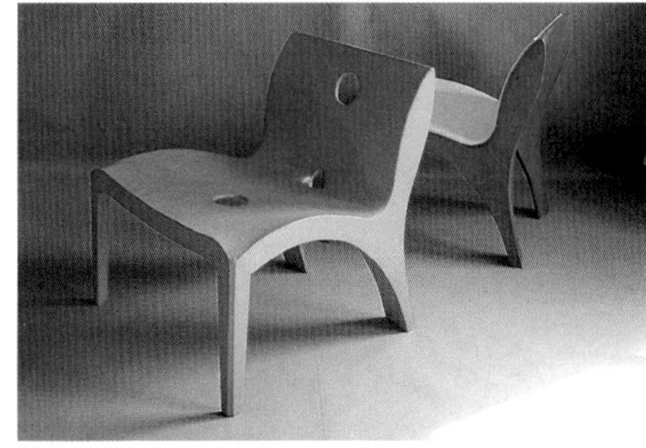

60 Jan Armgardt
design Easy chair JA 33P
materials Plywood, paper
dimensions h 67cm w 60cm
h 28½in w 25¾in
manufacturer Prototype

61 Jan Armgardt
design Chair Für Brigitte
materials Plywood, paper
dimensions h 47cm w 40cm d 40cm
h 18½in w 15¾in d 15¾in
manufacturer Prototype

64 Francesco Pascali
design Chair Lola
materials Plywood
dimensions h 77cm w 40cm d 40cm
h 30⅜in w 15¾in d 15¾in
manufacturer Targa Italia, Italy

66 Andrée Putman
design Stacking tables Gigognes
materials Varnished oak, lacquered metal
dimensions h 55cm, 48cm w 44cm d 44cm
h 21¾in, 18⅞in w 17½in d 17½in
manufacturer Ecart Design, France

65 Andrée Putman
design Suite Rue des Minimes
materials Beechwood, lacquered finish
dimensions Bench with backrest: h 45cm L 140cm d 35cm, h 17¾in L 55⅛in d 13¾in
Chair: h 63cm w 40cm d 50cm, h 24⅞in w 15¾in d 19⅝in
Armchair: h 63cm w 38.5cm d 54cm, h 24⅞in w 15⅛in d 21¼in
manufacturer Ecart Design, France

67 Roger Bateman
design Trans Shelving
materials MDF, aluminium
dimensions h 37cm w 26cm d 120cm
h 14½in w 10¼in d 47¼in
manufacturer Viaduct, UK

69 Alberto Meda
design Chair Highframe
materials Aluminium, polyester net covered in PVC
dimensions h 83cm w 52cm d 45cm
h 32¾in w 20½in d 17¾in
manufacturer Alias, Italy

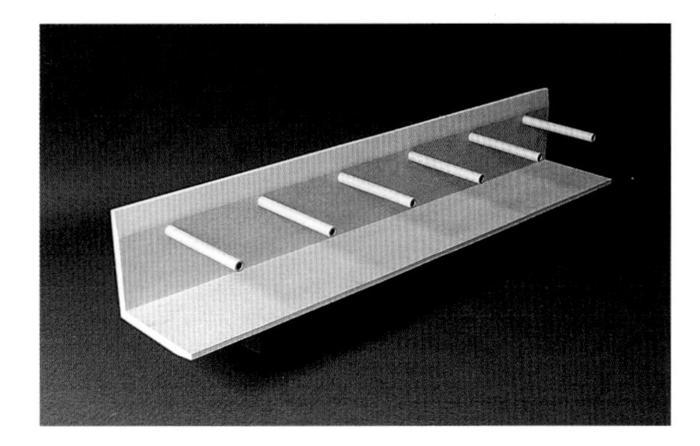

68 Ciatti SpA
design Stacking chair Isetta
materials Coloured thermoplastic, technopolymer
or lacquered/veneered plywood
dimensions h 79cm w 41cm d 49cm
h 31⅛in w 16⅛in d 19⅜in
manufacturer Ciatti SpA, Italy

70	Thomas Sandell
design	Armchair
materials	Birch wood, wool fabric
dimensions	h 70cm di 60cm
	h 27½in di 23½in
manufacturer	CBI, Sweden

below **71** Ron Arad
design Table Fly Ply
materials Walnut coloured wood, aluminium
dimensions h 52cm, 75cm L 210cm d 95cm
h 20½in, 29½in L 82⅝in d 37½in
manufacturer Driade SpA, Italy

bottom left **72** Ron Arad
design Folding trolley T Four 4
materials Aluminium, walnut coloured wood
dimensions h 71cm w 55cm L 118cm
h 28in w 21¾in L 46½in
manufacturer Driade SpA, Italy

bottom right **73** Ron Arad
design Chair Empty Chair
materials Walnut coloured wood, satinized stainless steel
dimensions h 90cm L 57cm d 57.5cm
h 35½in L 22⅜in d 22⅝in
manufacturer Driade SpA, Italy

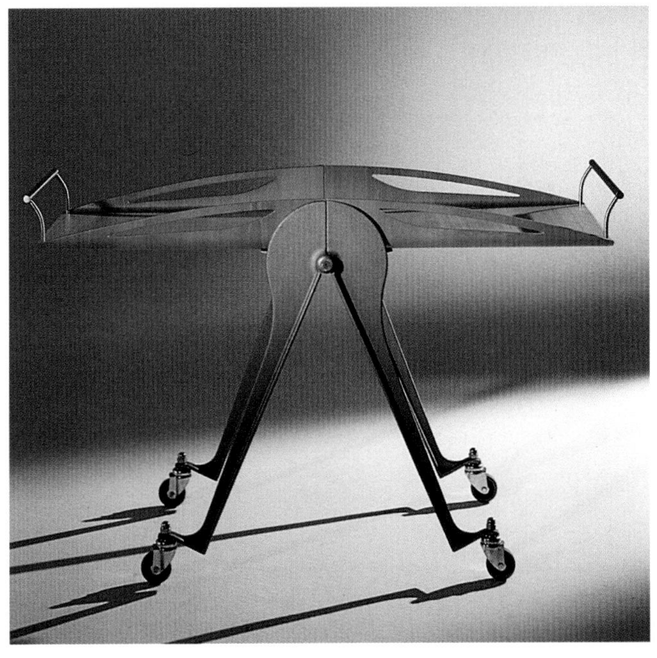

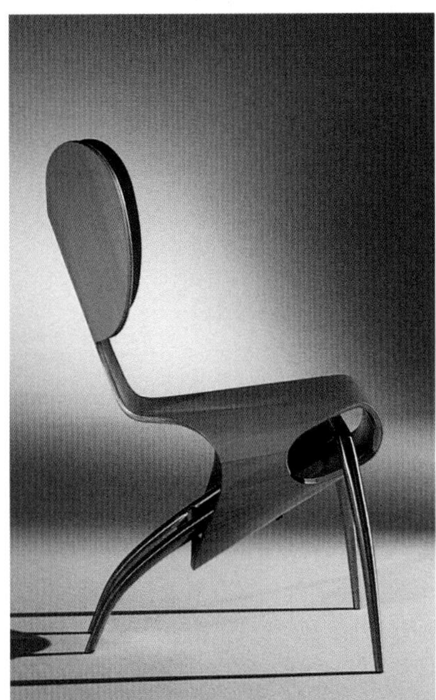

74 Ron Arad
design Table and chair Anonimus
materials Steel, glass, elm wood
dimensions Table: h 50cm - 57cm di 46cm
Table: h 19⅝in - 22⅜in di 18⅛in
manufacturer Noto - Zeus, Italy

75 Ron Arad
design Chair Box in Four Movements
materials Bronze, steel or wood
dimensions h 40cm w 40cm d 40cm
h 15¾in w 15¾in d 15¾in
manufacturer Ron Arad Studio, UK
(Made to order)

76	Ron Arad
design	Shelving system Fly on the Wall
materials	Cherrywood, bronze or stainless steel, patinated steel
dimensions	30cm cube, 11⅞in cube
manufacturer	Ron Arad Studio, UK (Made to order)

77 Ron Arad
design Chair Equal Partners
materials Wood, steel
dimensions h 100cm w 130cm d 75cm
h 39½in w 51⅛in d 29½in
manufacturer Ron Arad Studio, UK
(Made to order)

78 Ron Arad
design Chair Appropriate
materials Mirrored stainless steel, steel, wood
dimensions h 110cm w 90cm d 90cm
h 43⅜in w 35½in d 35½in
manufacturer Ron Arad Studio, UK
(Made to order)

79 Ron Arad
design Bookshelves Bookworm
materials Thermoplastic polymer
dimensions L 320cm, 520cm, 820cm
L 126in, 205in, 323in
manufacturer Kartell SpA, Italy

'Risk (of failure) is an essential ingredient in the experimental. One never knows for sure if intuition is to be trusted, yet there is nothing else to follow. Experience is even more fickle. If there are any questions, it is better to ask after, when it is definitely too late, and not before when the answers are not yet known. The new need is not to worry about their *raison d'être*. Any questions?'

Ron Arad's comments on his new pieces give both the flavour of the man and something of his approach to his work - personal, open-ended, inquisitive, visual, unregulated by fallacies such as markets and movements. The contrast, superficially at least, with Jean Nouvel's approach - contextual, analytical, verbal, reasoned, then synthesized into formal and visual expression - could not be more radical. Yet each has a huge admiration and appreciation for the other's work.
For Nouvel, Arad's new furniture was one of the central choices in his selection. The qualities that they both share are singleness of purpose, a profound understanding of their crafts, and the inner certainty that it is the rightness of the final work that matters, not the ideological route which leads there.

80	Ron Arad
design	Chair And the Rabbit Speaks
materials	Aluminium, alcantara, plywood
dimensions	h 95cm w 40cm d 55cm
	h 37½in w 15¾in d 21¾in
manufacturer	Ron Arad Studio, UK
	(Made to order)

81	Ron Arad
design	Chair A Suitable Case
materials	Cherrywood, plywood
dimensions	h 110cm w 45cm d 105cm
	h 43⅜in w 17¾in d 41⅜in
manufacturer	Ron Arad Studio, UK
	(Made to order)

82	Ingo Maurer
design	Table Once in a Blue Moon
materials	Corian, glass, metal
	Light source integrated in base shoots
	against a glass mirror with frosted surface
dimensions	h 45cm L 270cm d 140cm
	h 17¾in L 106⅜in d 55⅛in
manufacturer	Ingo Maurer, GmbH, Germany
	(Limited edition)

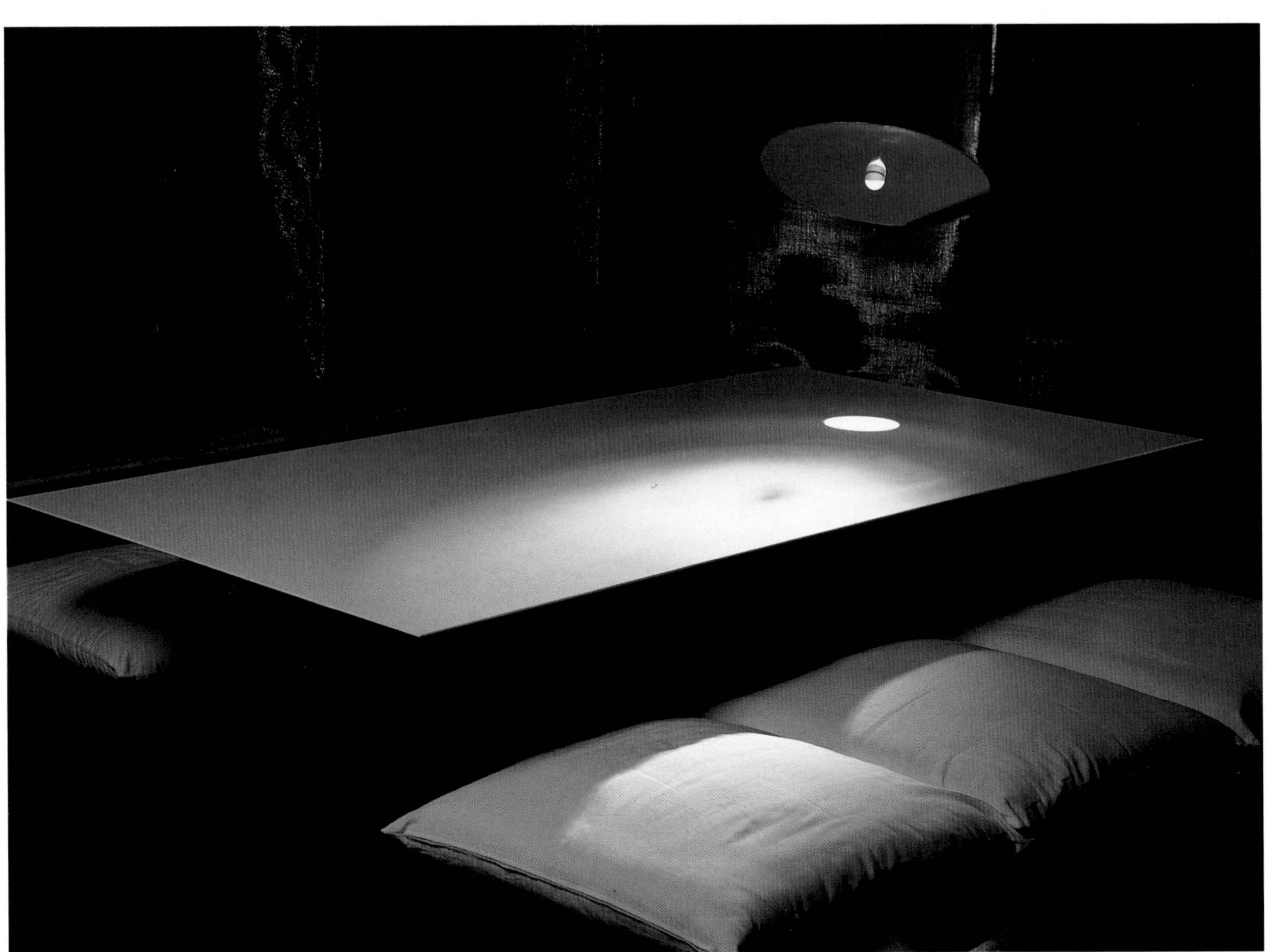

83	Guy Dyas
design	Television Tall Boy
materials	Maple wood
dimensions	h 100cm w 69cm d 60cm
	h 39½in w 27¼in d 23½in
manufacturer	Idée Co. Ltd., Japan

Guy Dyas is a British designer who has worked in Japan. His commission from the Idée Company in Tokyo was for a television set that would be a radical alternative to the 'black box' approach so common elsewhere. The average television, he realized, did not integrate into most domestic interiors, other than High-Tech ones, and the Tall Boy, using a compact 11-inch tube with remote control, is available in a natural maple finish or in orange, green or blue stained wood. The piece is one metre high, so that this 'interior friendly' set can be watched either standing or sitting.

84 Yves Behar
design Bookshelf Jules & Jim
materials Steel, steel floor tile
dimensions h 225cm w 90cm d 55cm
h 88⅝in w 35½in d 21¾in
manufacturer One-off

85 Yves Behar
design Bookshelf A Thin Blue Line
materials Steel, birch wood
dimensions h 30cm w 110cm
h 11⅞in w 43⅜in
manufacturer One-off

86 Trix & Robert Haussmann
design Mirror-inlay cabinet Wogg 14
materials Steel, mirrors, laminate
dimensions h 184.5cm w 108cm d 55cm
h 72⅝in w 42½in d 21¾in
manufacturer Wogg AG, Switzerland
(Limited batch production)

above left **87** Trix & Robert Haussmann
design Table Model 7010
materials Pear, maple and nut wood
dimensions h 72cm w 270cm d 90cm
h 28¾in w 106⅜in d 35½in
manufacturer Draenert Studio GmbH, Germany

88 Gijs Bakker
design Fruit table
materials Maplewood
dimensions h 105cm w 35cm d 80cm
h 41⅜in w 13¾in d 31½in
manufacturer Droog Design, The Netherlands

89 John Rantanen, Dwight Huffman of Haute House
design Chair Trash or Treasure
materials Pallet, wood, poplar, castors
dimensions h 99cm w 76cm d 71cm
h 39in w 30in d 28in
manufacturer Haute House, USA
(Limited batch production)

90 Constantin Grcic
design Chair Quick
materials Beech plywood, anodized aluminium
dimensions h 83cm w 42cm d 42cm
h 32¾in w 16½in d 16½in
manufacturer Cappellini SpA, Italy

91 François Bauchet
design Pear chair
materials Pear wood
dimensions h 91cm w 38cm d 41cm
h 35⅞in w 15in d 16⅛in
manufacturer Néotù, France
(Limited batch production)

92 Menguzzato-Villis-Nascimben Arch Ass.
design Stool CIP
materials Metal frame, epoxy lacquer, chrome
dimensions h 89cm, 96cm w 46cm d 46cm
h 34¼in, 37⅞in w 18⅛in d 18⅛in
manufacturer Casamania by Frezza, Italy

93 Katsuhihoko Ogino
design Chair
materials Plastic
dimensions h 67.5cm w 54cm d 47cm
h 26⅝in w 21¼in d 18½in
manufacturer Iris Ohyama Inc., Japan

94 Pol Quadens
design Carbon Fiber Chair
materials Carbon, kelvar, glass fibre, epoxy
dimensions h 82cm w 41cm d 57cm
h 32¼in w 16⅛in d 22⅜in
manufacturer Pol International Design Co. SPRL, Belgium

Pol Quadens is a Belgian designer, whose work in lighting has previously appeared in the *International Design Yearbook*. Here his fluid and graceful sense of form has found expression in a new medium, carbon fibre. This material, originally developed for military purposes (not only is it light-weight and extremely strong, but also it creates no radar echoes), has now, in the way Jean Nouvel describes in his introduction, filtered down into general manufacturing. Quadens' chair is comfortable and resilient, and remarkably light - to the extent that one doubts it can carry a normal body-weight, at first sight.

96 Ciatti
design Trolley Tappabucchi
materials Plywood, beechwood, polished steel
dimensions Module: h 60cm w 150cm
Module: h 23⅝in w 59in
manufacturer Ciatti, Italy

95 Köbi Wiesendanger
design Bookcase Presence Imperfetto
materials Natural fir, lacquered books
dimensions h 173cm w 140cm d 30cm
h 68⅛in w 55⅛in d 11⅞in
manufacturer Avant de Dormir, Italy

below **97** Köbi Wiesendanger
design Bookcase Presence Imperfetto
materials Natural fir, ceramic cups and saucers
dimensions h 210cm w 140cm d 30cm
h 82⅝in w 55⅛in d 11⅞in
manufacturer Avant de Dormir, Italy

98	Thomas Krause, Philip Ludvigsen
design	Bench Mega Ant
materials	Aluminium, steel
dimensions	h 75cm w 200cm d 45cm
	h 29½in w 78¾in d 17¾in
manufacturer	The design is based on a computer remodelling of a chair design by Arne Jacobsen. (One-off)

99	Jorge Pensi
design	Chair Lauro
materials	Injected aluminium, steel tubing, chrome, enamel
dimensions	h 85cm w 55cm d 62cm
	h 33½in w 21¾in d 24⅜in
manufacturer	Kron SA, Spain

100 Mario Mazzer
design TV stand Jumbo
materials Painted metal
dimensions h 73cm, 59cm w 59cm-86cm d 46 cm-73cm
h 28¾in, 23in w 23in-33⅞in d 18⅛in-28¾in
manufacturer Morphos (division of Acerbis Int. SpA), Italy

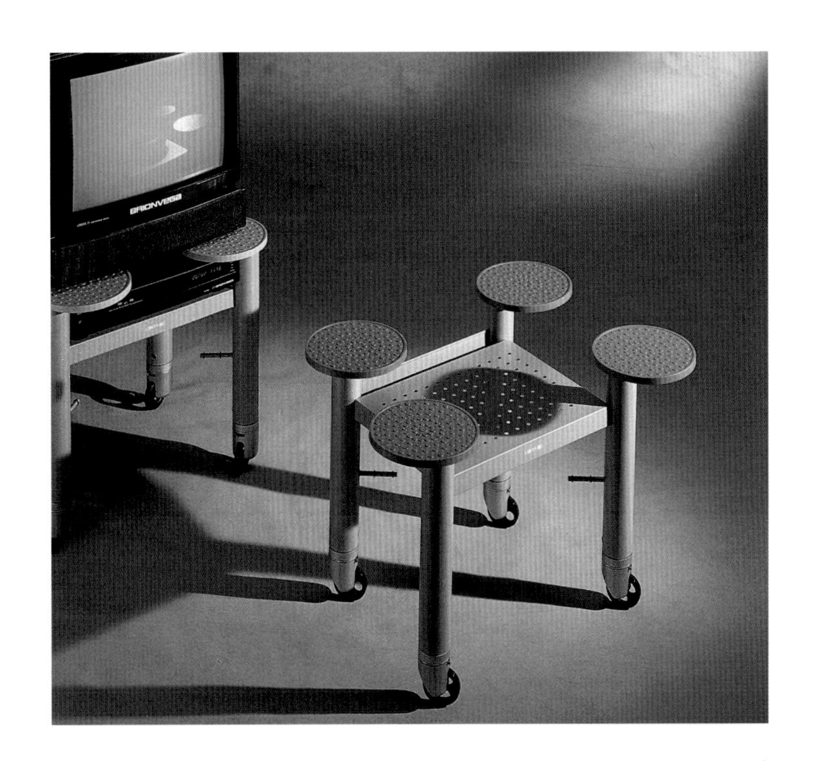

101 Henk Stallinga
design Set Seat
materials Steel
dimensions h 80cm L 240cm d 150cm
h 31½in L 94½in d 59in
manufacturer Droog Design, The Netherlands

102 Aldo Rossi
design Cabinet La Cabina dell'Elba
materials Cherrywood
dimensions h 217cm w 83cm d 60cm
h 85⅜in w 32¾in d 23½in
manufacturer Bruno Longoni, Italy
(re-edition)

103 Hans Hollein
design Bench Onda
materials Wood, metal
dimensions h 90cm, 47cm L 250cm d 70cm, 40cm
h 35½in, 18½in L 98⅜in d 27½in, 15¾in
manufacturer ITA, Italy
(Prototype)

The theme of the Billboard chair is heroic empowerment: quite simply, the clear acrylic facing of the seat and back unclips, so that the user can insert a poster or photograph - the size is calculated to match standard poster images. 'The idea of sitting down on the image of one's hero is certainly original', Nouvel remarked when selecting the chair; his choice of suitable images is unfortunately not for publication! But as a promotional device, for example, the chair could find a keen market. Maurizio Favetta, who previously worked with Matteo Thun, launched this year his own furniture group, King Size, with Antonio Pio Giovanditto.

104 Maurizio Favetta
design Chair Billboard
materials Aluminium, transparent acrylic, choice of poster
dimensions h 85cm w 37cm d 47cm
h 33½in w 14½in d 18½in
manufacturer Lisar SpA, Italy

105 Sarah Murrey
design Rocking stool
materials Plastic moulding, laminated plywood
dimensions h 35cm
h 13¾in
manufacturer Royal College of Art, UK
(Prototype)

106 Toshiyuki Kita
design Table Dopp
materials Laminated chipboard, steel pipe
dimensions h 35cm-76cm w 110cm d 75cm
h 13¾in-30in w 43⅜in d 29½in
manufacturer Altana Arte, Italy

107 William Sawaya
design Chaise longue Tanita
materials Leather
dimensions h 79cm w 153cm d 64cm
h 31in w 60¼in d 25⅛in
manufacturer Sawaya & Moroni SpA, Italy
(Limited batch production)

108 William Sawaya
design Table Sottosopra
materials Multi-layered mahogany or cherrywood veneer
dimensions h 46cm w 124cm d 122cm
h 18⅛in w 48⅜in d 48in
manufacturer Sawaya & Moroni SpA, Italy
(Limited batch production)

109	Pascal Mourgue
design	Chair
materials	Resin, lacquered metal, removable cotton cover
dimensions	h 82cm w 45cm d 37cm
	h 32¼in w 17¾in d 14½in
manufacturer	Ligne Roset SA, France

110	Pascal Mourgue
design	Trolley
materials	Veneered beech, lacquered melamine
dimensions	h 99cm, 62cm di 54.5cm
	h 39in, 24⅜in di 21½in
manufacturer	Ligne Roset SA, France

111	Pascal Mourgue
design	Trolley
materials	Veneered beech, lacquered melamine
dimensions	h 34cm di 100cm
	h 13⅜in di 39½in
manufacturer	Ligne Roset SA, France

112	Pascal Mourgue
design	Fireside chair Kalin
materials	Steel tube, elastic webbing, removable cotton cover
dimensions	h 82cm w 125cm d 103cm
	h 32¼in w 49⅛in d 40½in
manufacturer	Ligne Roset SA, France

113	Borek Sipek
design	Chair
materials	Beechwood, fabric
dimensions	h 88cm w 60cm d 44cm
	h 34⅝in w 23½in d 17¼in
manufacturer	Scarabas/Cumin Luigia, Italy

114 Lawrence Laske
design Table Toothpick from Cactus Collection
materials Maple wood, aluminium, slater
dimensions h 50.8cm di 122cm
h 20in di 48in
manufacturer The Knoll Group, USA

115 Kuno Prey
design Table Astro
materials Sheet metal, stainless steel
dimensions h 72cm di 60cm, 70cm, 100cm
h 28⅜in, di 23½in, 27½in, 29½in
manufacturer Zanotta, SpA, Italy

116 Maurizio Favetta & Antonio Pio Giovanditto for King Size
design Table Blow-up
materials Beechwood, lacquered wood, enamel green frame
dimensions h 90cm di 68cm
h 35½in di 26¾in
manufacturer King Size, Italy

117	Marc Newson
design	Sofa Gluon
materials	Metal, polyurethane foam, cotton
dimensions	h 86.5cm L 133cm d 86cm
	h 34in L 52⅜in d 33⅞in
manufacturer	Moroso SpA, Italy

117a Marc Newson
design Table Mini Event Horizon
materials Polyurethane, varnished metal
dimensions h 80cm w 40cm d 50cm
h 23½in w 15¾in d 19⅝in
manufacturer Cappellini SpA, Italy

118 Tom Dixon
design Chair Loop
materials Bent metal, panno fabric
dimensions h 93cm w 68cm d 92cm
h 36⅝in w 26¾cm d 36⅛in
manufacturer Cappellini SpA, Italy

119 Delo Lindo
design Modular chair Pierpoljac
materials Wood, polyester foam
dimensions (module) h 110cm L52cm d 80cm
(module) h 43⅜in L 20½in d 31½in
manufacturer Soca Line, France

120 Hans Zaugg
design Bed Kwad
materials Aluminium, wood, latex foam
dimensions w 90cm L 200cm
w 35⅜in L 78¾in
manufacturer Sapsa Bedding, Italy

121 Riccardo Dalisi
design Chair Capote
materials Fir wood, poplar plywood, metal, foam rubber, fabric
dimensions h 150cm w 85cm d 110cm
h 59in w 33½in d 43⅜in
manufacturer Playline by SCEP, Italy

122 Ehlen Johansson
design Table Hatten
materials Plastic, metal
dimensions h 58cm di 40cm
h 22⅞in di 15¾in
manufacturer IKEA, Sweden

The IKEA company of Sweden has relaunched the direct and unadorned qualities of Scandinavian design on to a world market, selling both by mail order and from out-of-town superstores. They are punctilious about naming the designers used, and the overall level of products is good. They, and the giant European mail-order companies such as Trois Suisses (Marc Newson's flat-pack plastic table Gello, for Trois Suisses, is at the end of this section) have continued the furniture marketing revolution pioneered by Habitat in Britain in the 1960s, offering well-made, well-designed goods. Trois Suisses has also just announced the ultimate mail-order product, a complete house designed by Philippe Starck: the purchaser receives a set of plans, an instructional video, and supporting documents on planning permission, construction and fitting out.

123	Françoise Chèrif
design	Sofa Inari from the Hommage à Aalto range
materials	Oak wood
dimensions	h 100cm w 84cm L 170cm
	h 39½in w 33in L 66⅞in
manufacturer	Galerie V.I.A, France
	(Limited batch production)

124	Feldmann + Schultchen
design	Armchair Homo
materials	Steel, wood, upholstery
dimensions	h 90cm w 65cm d 55cm
	h 35½in w 25⅝in d 21¾in
manufacturer	Seidel GmbH, Germany
	(Limited batch production)

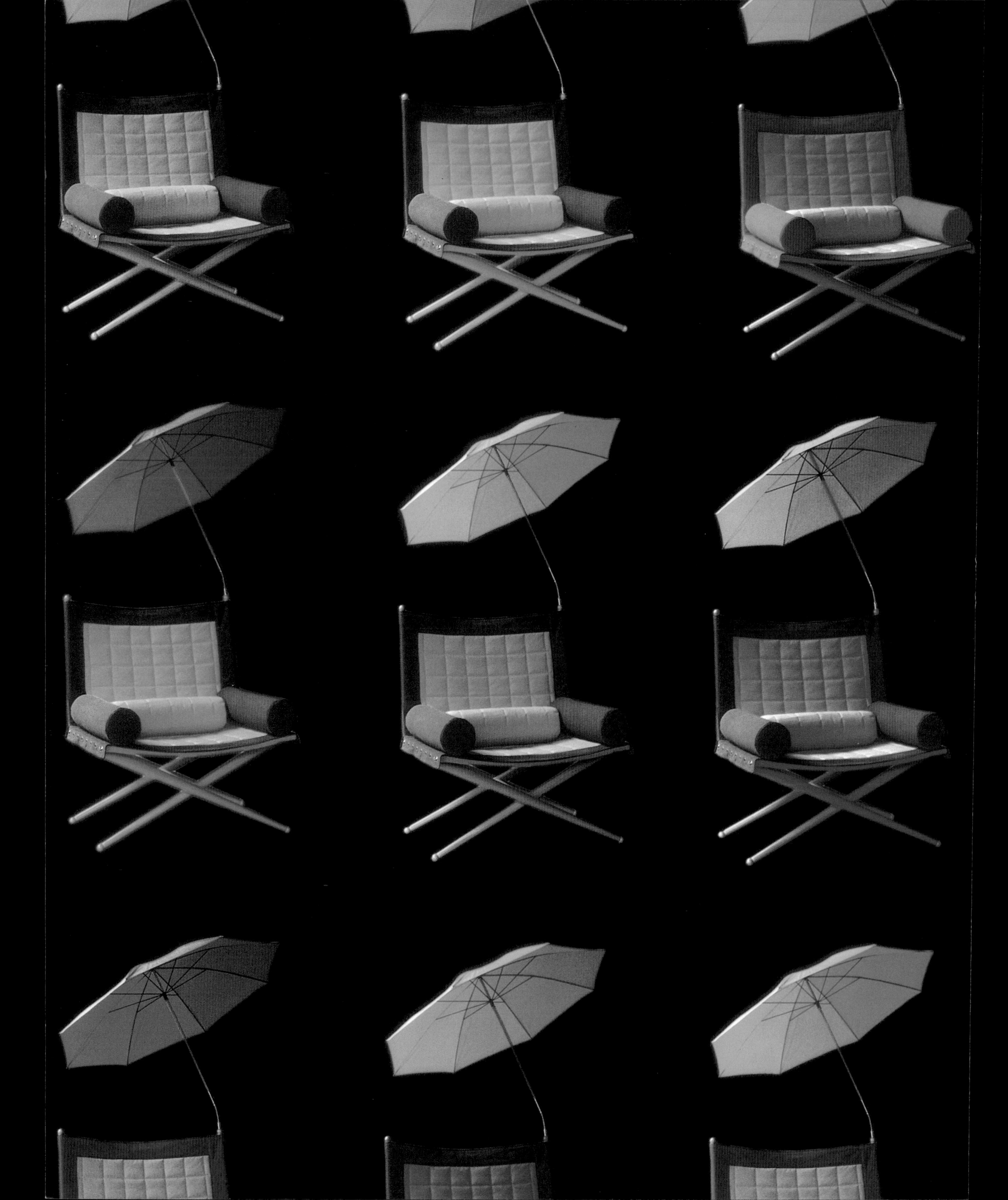

126 Mattias Ljunggren
design Shelf Konstant
materials Ash wood
dimensions h 156cm w 14cm d 15cm
h 61⅜in w 5½in d 6in
manufacturer Källemo AB, Sweden

far left **125** Christian Clerc
design Chair Ami Ami
materials Beechwood, cotton
dimensions h 98cm w 65cm d 55cm
h 38⅝in w 25⅝in d 21¾in
manufacturer Atmosphère, France

127 Mattias Ljunggren
design Shelf Singel
materials Birchwood
dimensions h 185cm w 50cm d 28cm
h 72⅞in w 19⅝in d 11in
manufacturer Källemo AB, Sweden

129 Ayala Sperling-Serfaty
design Seating Purple Joy
materials Metal, wood, hand-painted velvet, polyurethane
dimensions h 80cm L 170cm d 100cm
h 31½in L 66⅞in d 39½in
manufacturer Limited batch production

128 Marc Newson
design Table Gello
materials Plastic sheet
dimensions h 50cm di 100cm
h 19⅝in di 39½in
manufacturer Trois Suisses, France

right **130** Ayala Sperling-Serfaty
design Seating Fresh
materials Hand painted velvet, wood, polyurethane, synthetic quilt
dimensions h 43cm di 90cm
h 16⅞in di 35½in
manufacturer Limited batch production

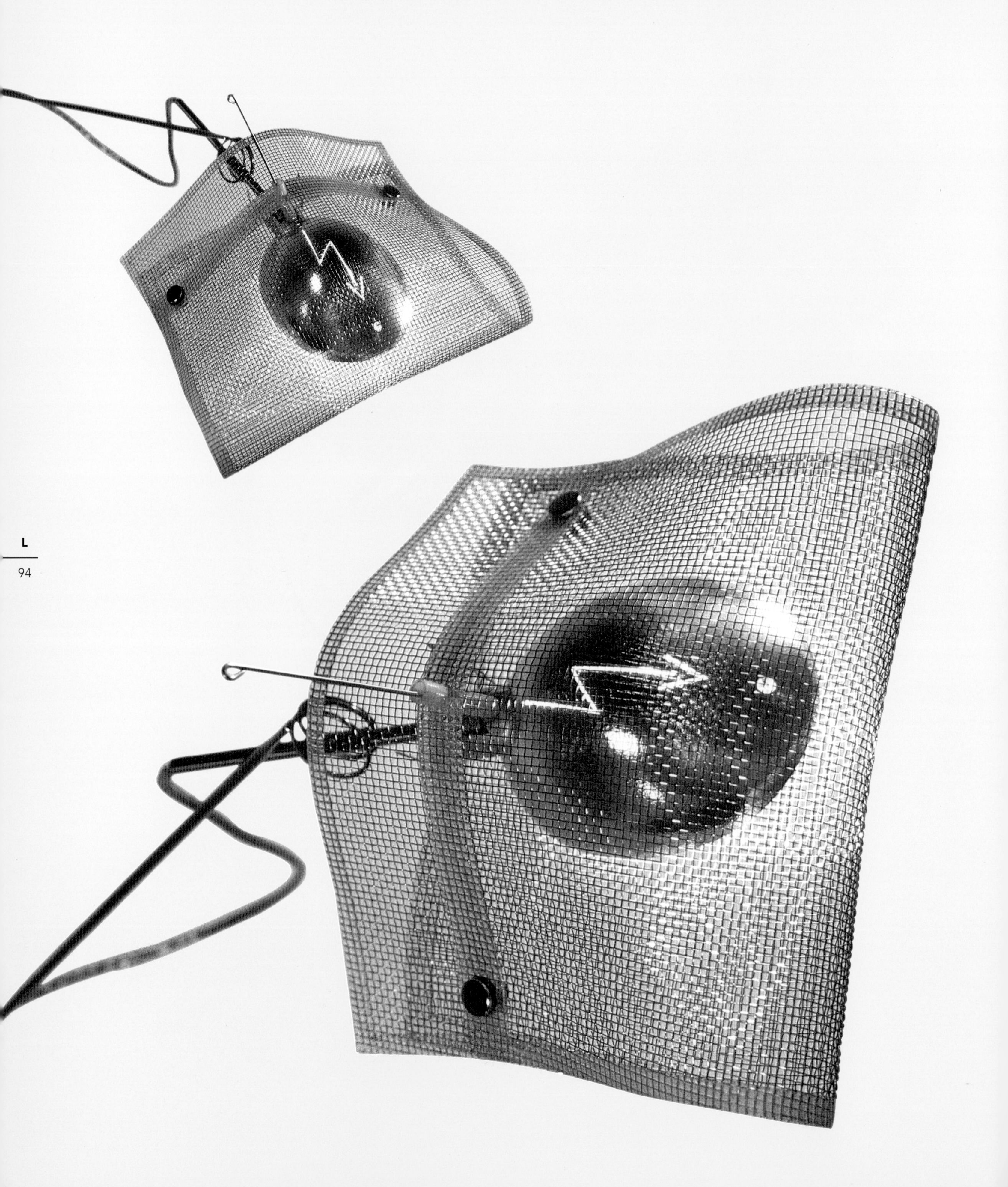

lighting

'What we ask today from our environment is that is keeps us warm or cool, it protects us from the sun, it provides us with the necessary intensity of light at every moment, but, please, without our having to put up with the object that provides it! We must move towards a formal simplification of the object, towards a formal unexpressivity in respect of function.'

Jean Nouvel's comments in a recent *El Croquis* interview can stand as the central theme of his selection of lighting. This does not mean lighting is unimportant to him: in fact he supervises personally and closely the lighting in his own buildings. When we met at the opening of the Fondation Cartier I remarked on the quality of the lighting in the exhibition area, which uses downlighting floods from the double-height ceiling, regularly disposed in the ceiling coffering. He told me that he had selected that solution to balance the nocturnal lighting with the natural daylighting through the glazed walls, but that it had also been important to balance the overall light at night so that, from the exterior, the building was not too sharply defined against the garden behind, and so that successive layers of glazing, from the streetside screen through the building itself, would each play a visible role, while rendering the building itself almost invisible. In the Mediapark project in Cologne, the external glazing also functions as a screen on which images can be projected or displayed at night, also dematerializing the building, though in a different way.

So the selection of lighting here is very much an architect's one. Lighting systems, as opposed to designer objects, are to the fore, comprising an armoury of functional objects, downlighters, spots and uplighters, tracks and linear units. Here the technological aspect of lighting becomes important: Bettonica and Melocchi's Tenso system, for example, is a wire-tension system using high-voltage, while Cimini's Zed wall-lamp is fitted with a fibre-optic supplementary light. Marc Sadler's Drop 2 series of fittings for Arteluce were chosen because of their waterproof material, and Christian Maier's Turn system for Planlicht for its versatility.

Even in the case of individual luminaires it was always the intellectual quality of the design that appealed to Nouvel, particularly in the highly expressive work of Ingo Maurer and the new, simple series of lamps designed by Sottsass Associati. Philippe Starck's Rosy Angelis is a witty restatement of a design by Castiglioni from 1953, now re-edited. Gwen Bertheau-Suzuki's Hanger Light and Masufumi Katsukawa's floor and table lamps show equally free spirits at work.

But the central theme is that light is more important than lighting. So fixtures should be economical - both visually and in energy terms - and versatile. Many of the luminaires chosen will accept a range of different lamps, and can be adapted for different tasks. Some, such as Henk Stallinga's Watt or Meinert's downlighter for Basis Design, make a virtue of their simplicity. This selection is about empowering the user, creating choice rather than imposing form, using the best of current technology to do so.

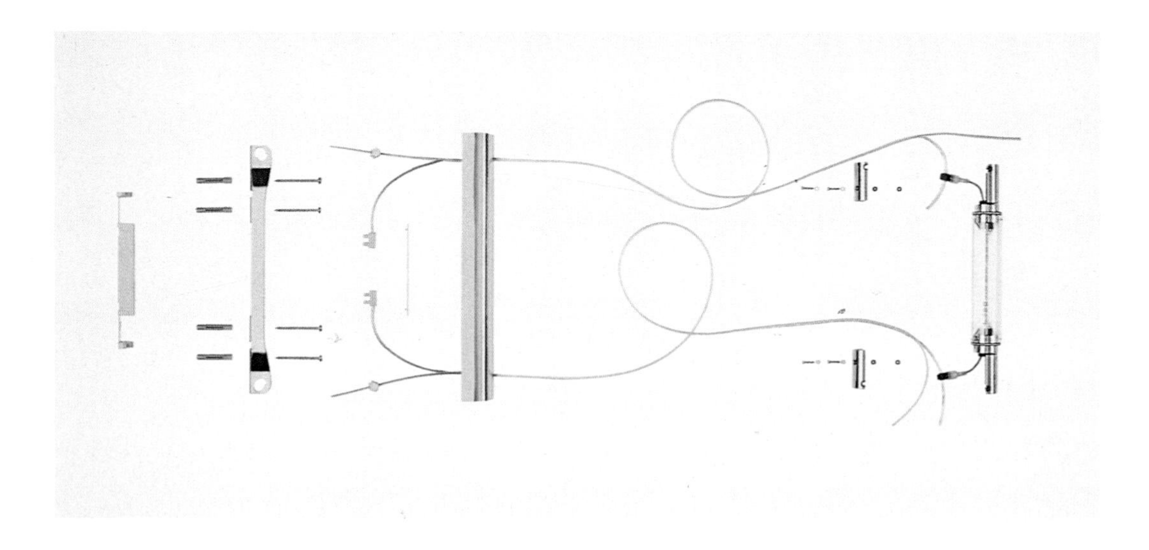

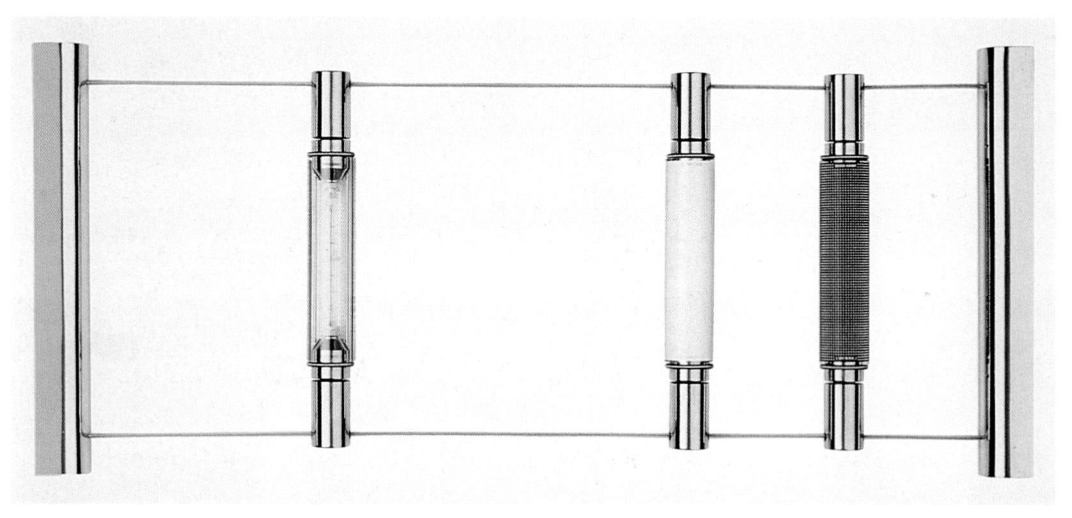

The Tenso lighting system is a high-voltage cable system with a standard 3 metre span. The twin cables supplying the power also support the lamps. It therefore extends into the high voltage area the advantages gained with low-voltage cable systems, and Jean Nouvel admired its simple, functional design, as well as the technical innovation involved. Cimini's Zed lamp is also innovative, using fibre-optic technology to provide a mobile light source in addition to the main light. Fibre-optics offer low-energy, cool light that can be run from remote sources. While the decorative effects of single strand fibre-optics have been used for some time, there is a growing development to use fibre-optics more widely in general lighting.

1	Franco Bettonica, Mario Melocchi
design	Lighting system Tenso 2500W
materials	Steel cable, max 150w bulb
dimensions	L 300cm
	L 118½in
manufacturer	Cini & Nils, Italy

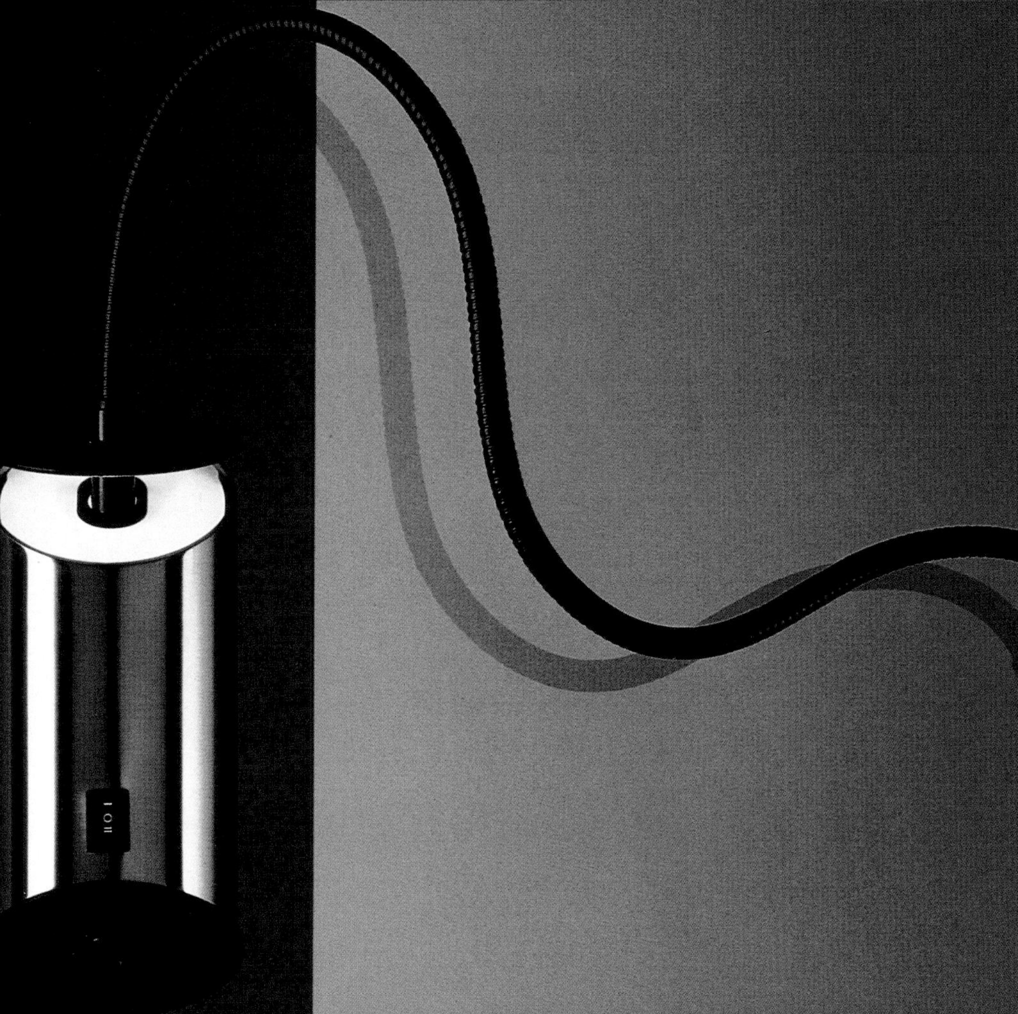

3 R. Lanciani, W. Posern
design Lighting system Plus
materials Extruded aluminium, steel
Max 58w fluorescent tubes
dimensions main unit: h 18cm w 30cm
main unit: h 7in w 11¾in
manufacturer Luxo Italiana SpA, Italy

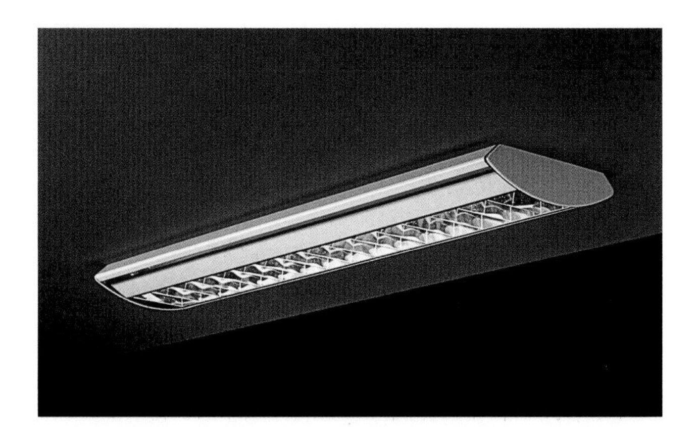

4 R. Lanciani, W. Posern
design Wall lighting system Multipla
materials Aluminium
Max 58w fluorescent tubes
or max 50w downlighters
dimensions main unit: h 10.3cm w 11cm
main unit: h 4in w 4⅜in
manufacturer Luxo Italiana SpA, Italy

5 Paul Newman
design Suspension lamps
materials Matt silver, anodized spun aluminium
Standard screw in bulb
dimensions h 33cm, 23cm, 17cm h 13in, 9in, 6⅝in
di 25cm, 33cm, 43cm di 9⅞in, 13in, 16⅞in
manufacturer Aero Ltd., UK
(Limited batch production)

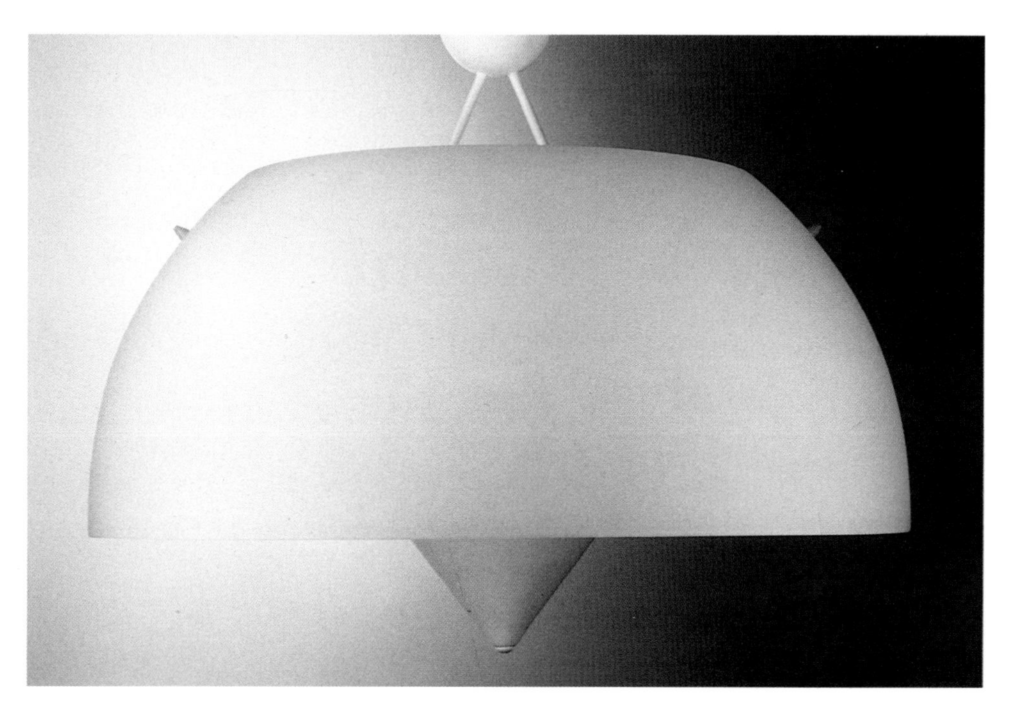

6 Vico Magistretti
design Suspension lamp Kalaari 440
materials Opaline glass
150w bulb
dimensions h 30cm di 50cm
h 11⅞in di 19⅝in
manufacturer Oluce, Italy

7 Piero Lissoni
design Suspension lamp Cap
materials Sanded glass, brass
110w incandescent bulb
dimensions Max h 200cm di 40cm
Max h 78¾in di 15¾in
manufacturer Foscarini Murano, Italy

8 Achille and P.G. Castiglioni
design Floor lamp Luminator
materials Stove enamel steel
Max 300w bulb
dimensions h 185cm di 51cm
h 72⅞in di 20⅛in
manufacturer Flos SpA, Italy

9 Philippe Starck
design Floor Lamp Rosy Angelis
materials Carbon fibre, light weight fabric, technopolymer
150w bulb
dimensions h 185cm di 50cm
h 72⅞in di 19⅝in
manufacturer Flos SpA, Italy

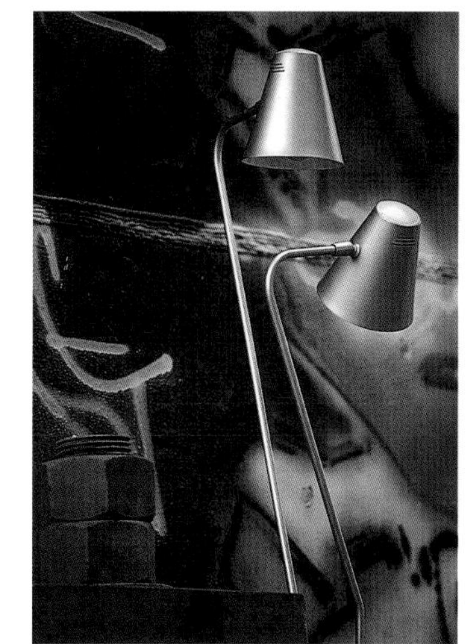

10 Francesco Armato
design Floor lamp Eccomi 94
materials Lacquered metal
2 max 40w bulbs
dimensions h 157.5cm w 25cm d 20cm
h 62in w 9⅞in d 7⅞in
manufacturer Cerva, Italy

To commemorate the Luminator floor lamp designed by Achille and Pier Giacomo Castiglioni in 1955, and reissued this year, Flos invited Philippe Starck to reinterpret the design. The original design had short tripod legs fitted into an aluminium tube and topped by a half-silvered floodlamp. Starck chose to take the thin tripod legs right up to the top of the lamp, and crown it with a diffusing fabric shade. The design is, for all the surface similarities, a radical contrast to its predecessor. Castiglioni sought to express elegant functionality, through contemporary technology. Starck turns aside from technology to make a statement that is both witty and ambiguous, the spiky legs terminating in a rather casual top.

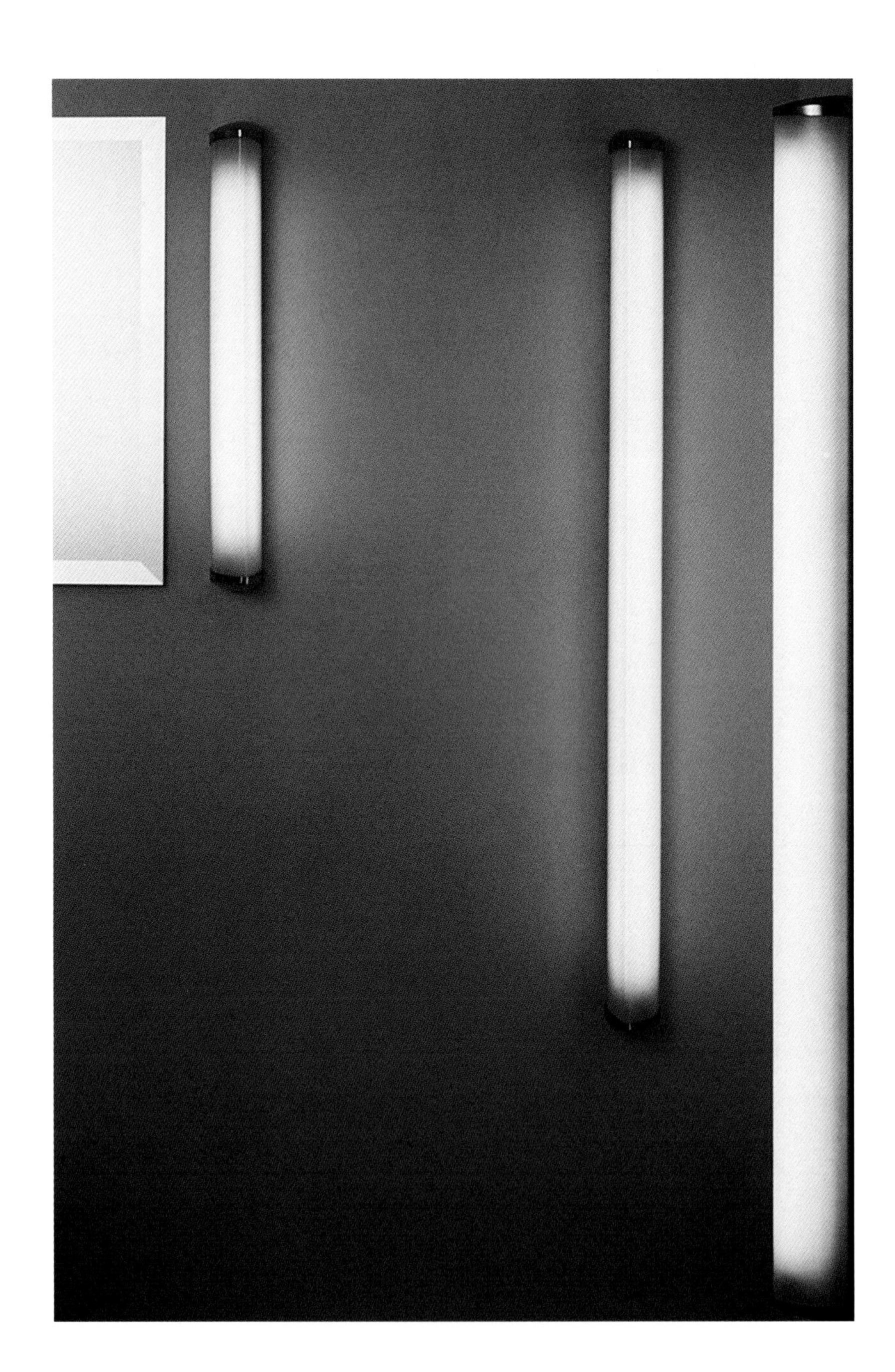

11	Örni Halloween
design	Wall lamp Telefo 70, 120, 170
materials	Thermoplastic resin, metal
	18w, 36w, 58w fluorescent bulb
dimensions	h 8cm w 10cm L 69cm, L 130cm, L 160cm
	h 3⅛in w 4in L 27⅛in, L 51⅛in, L 63in
manufacturer	Artemide, Italy

12 Piero Lissoni
design Revolving floor lamp Filoti
materials Painted metal, polished aluminium
400w halogen bulb
dimensions h 180cm w 27cm di 30cm
h 70⅝in w 10½in di 11⅞in
manufacturer Artemide, Italy

13 Marc Newson
design Floor lamp Helice
materials Aluminium, coloured glass filter, protective glass
300w linear halogen bulb
dimensions h 190cm di 36cm
h 74⅞in di 14⅛in
manufacturer Flos SpA, Italy

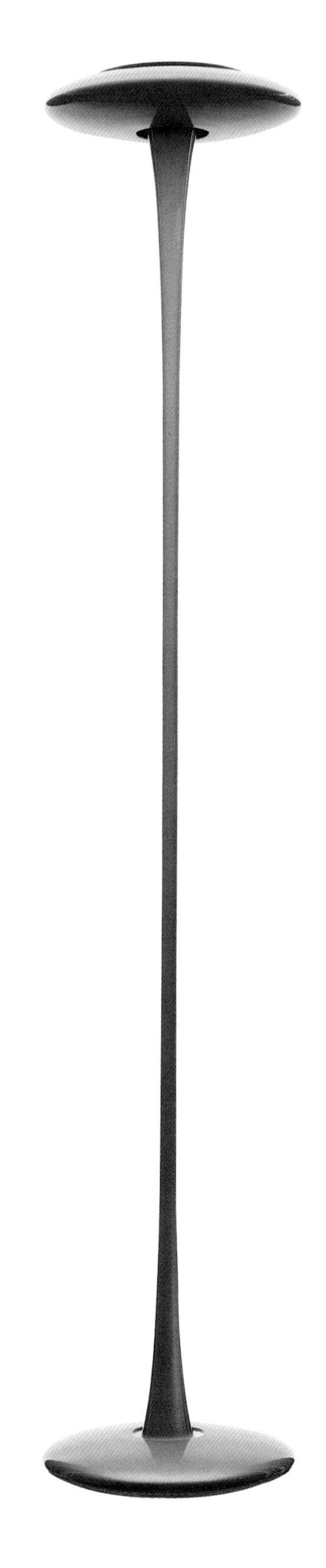

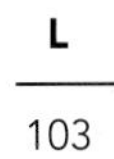

17 Sigeaki Asahara
design Desk light Z-999
materials Metal, plastic
27w neon bulb
dimensions h 43cm w 47cm L 56cm
h 16⅞in w 18½in L 22in
manufacturer Yamada Shomei Lighting Co. Ltd., Japan

14 Gaspar Glusberg
design Table lamp X135
materials Enamelled metal
50w di-chroic bulb
dimensions h 28cm di 16cm
h 11⅞in di 6in
manufacturer Modulor SA, Argentina

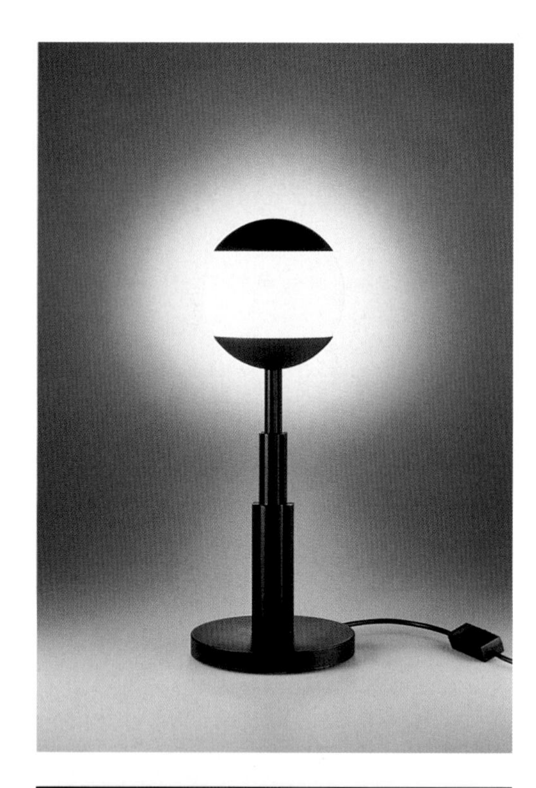

15 Aldo Rossi
design Table lamp
materials Aluminium, glass
Standard bulb
dimensions h 47cm d 15cm
h 18½in d 6in
manufacturer Alessi SpA, Italy

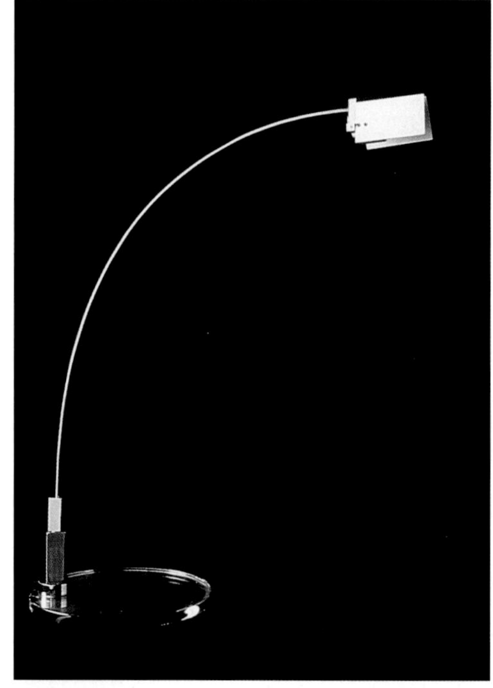

16 Alvaro Siza Viera
design Revolving table lamp Falena Tavolo
materials Crystal, aluminium, brass
50w halogen bulb
dimensions h 52cm di 19.5cm
h 20½in di 7¾in
manufacturer Fontana Arte, Italy

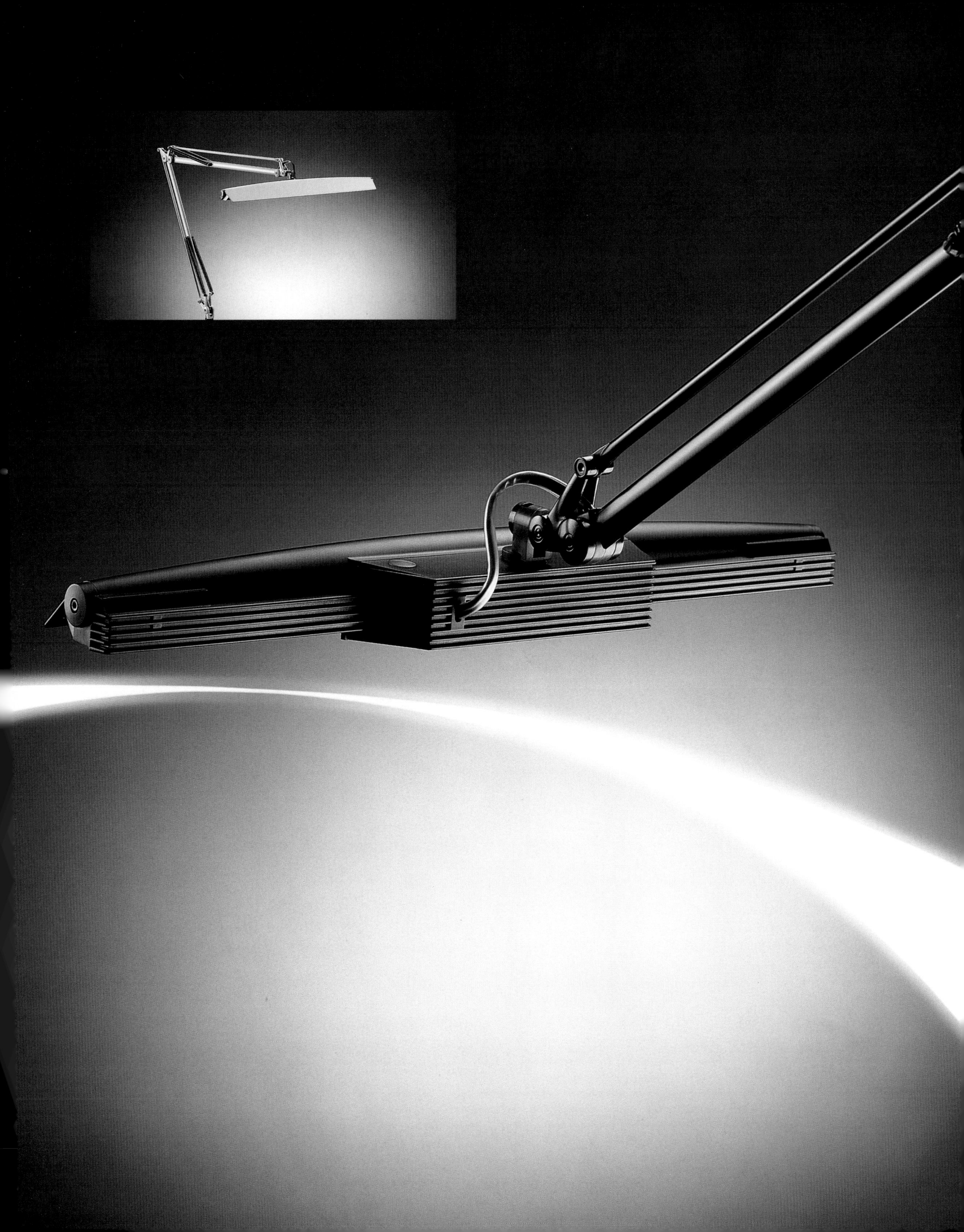

18 Henk Stallinga
design Floor lamp Watt
materials Electric Wire
25w bulb
dimensions h 60cm
h 23½in
manufacturer Droog Design, The Netherlands

19 Bernhard Dessecker
design Suspension light Lampeduso
materials Glass, stainless steel, plastic
11w bulb
dimensions h 22cm L 20cm
h 8⅝in L 7⅞in
manufacturer Ingo Maurer GmbH, Germany
(Limited batch production)

20 Masafumi Katsukawa
design Table lamps Yuri e Sara
materials Copper-plated metal
20w bulb
dimensions h 30cm w 20cm d 8cm
h 11⅞in w 7⅞in d 3⅛in
manufacturer Prototype

21 Masafumi Katsukawa
design Floor lamp Papa e Mama
materials Copper-plated metal
50w bulb
dimensions h 110cm w 40cm d 16cm
h 43⅜in w 15¾in d 6½in
manufacturer Prototype

22	Paul Atkinson
design	Floor lamp Hazel Duct
materials	Alloy cylinders, enamel, steel sheet, aluminium
	150w bulb
dimensions	h 275cm base di 70cm reflector di 120cm
	h 108⅜in base di 27½in reflector di 47¼in
manufacturer	Concord Lighting Ltd., UK

Concord Lighting, part of the SLI Group, are not only manufacturers of light fittings but designers also. A large part of their business, as with many specialist lighting companies, is concerned with 'specials,' one-off designs for specific projects or locations. The Hazel Duct, designed by Paul Atkinson, is one such. It is 'an uplighter with its own ceiling' according to Janet Turner, design director of Concord, 'the lamp is located in the main tube, and the arms, moulded from hazel twigs in the prototype, support a concave reflector. The luminaire is intended for spaces such as atria or exhibition stands where there is no ceiling at the correct level for a standard supported uplighter. A further design executed by Concord is the Marseille lighting wing, designed by Russell Bagley of Box Design for William Alsopp's new Hôtel des Bouches du Rhône in Marseille, where the reversed aerofoil shape of the fitting reflects the curved frames of the building itself.

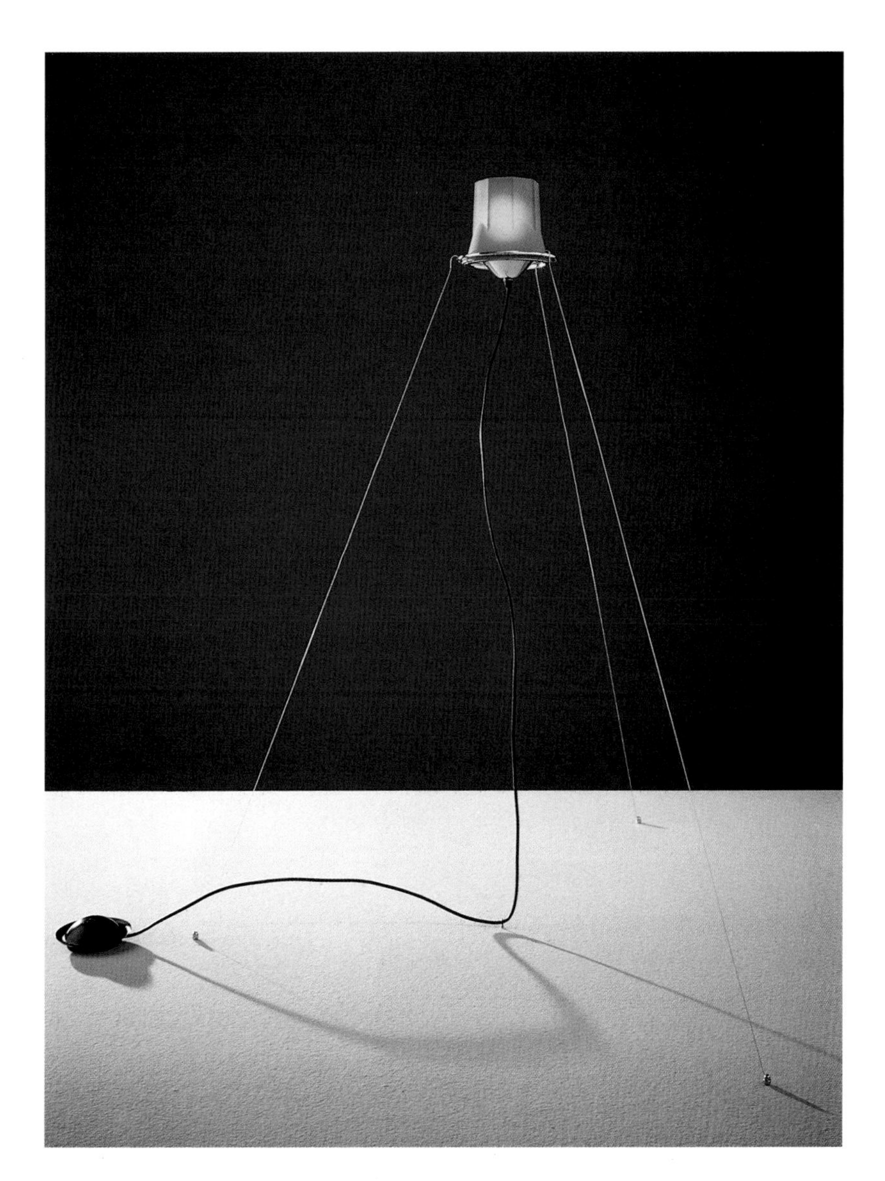

23 Lluis Clotet
design Table lamp Polux
materials Sanded glass, brass
100w bulb
dimensions h 17.5cm di 15cm
h 6⅞in di 6in
manufacturer Bd Ediciones de Diseño, Spain

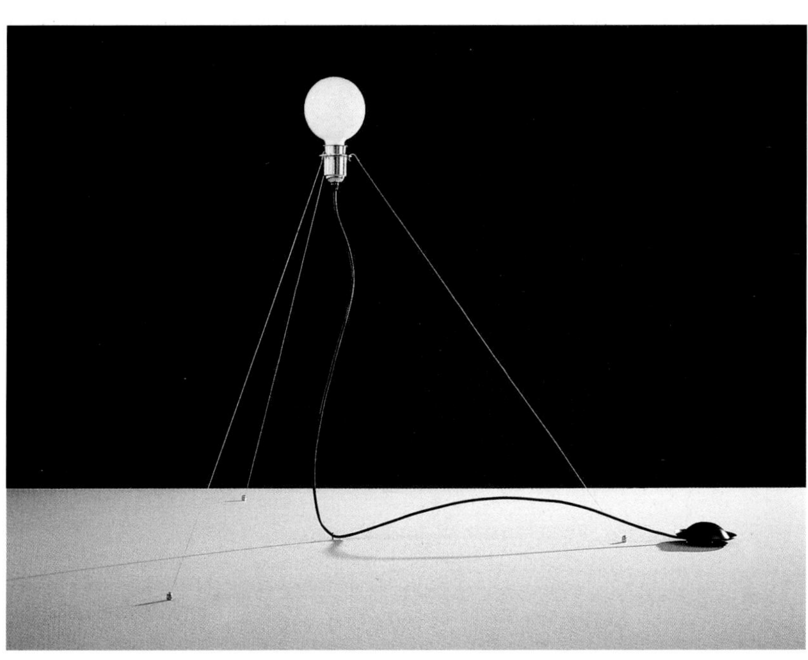

24 Lluis Clotet
design Table lamp Ebro
materials Sanded glass, brass
100/125w 220v bulb
dimensions h 17.5cm di 12.5cm
h 6⅞in di 5in
manufacturer Bd Ediciones de Diseño, Spain

left **25** Ingo Maurer
design Chandelier Think Positive (alias Zabriskie Point)
materials Metal, porcelain
60w 230v bulb
dimensions h max 100cm di max 100cm
h max 39½in di max 39½in
manufacturer One off

26 Ingo Maurer
design Floor to ceiling lamp Hot Achille
materials Aluminium, stainless steel
50w bulb
dimensions h adjustable by up to 100cm
h adjustable by up to 39½in
manufacturer Ingo Maurer GmbH, Germany
(Limited batch production)

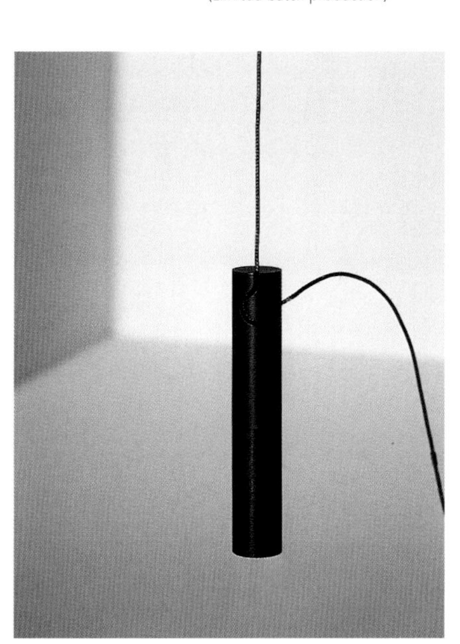

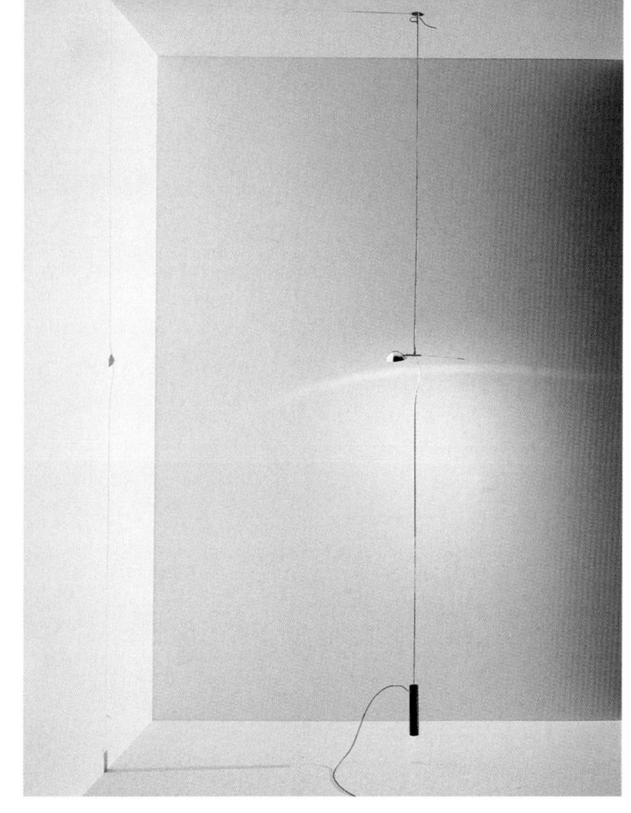

Ingo Maurer's astonishing explosion of broken crockery, Think Positive, dominated his exhibition with Rod Arad at the 1994 Milan Salon. It is the second version of a piece first made as a commission, and the original title, Zabriskie Point, recalls the rolling, sensuous, slow-motion explosion of a house in Death Valley that concludes Antonioni's dark 1969 film of that name. The rest of Maurer's 1994 collection has also a more sober tone than his winged lightbulbs of last year: he himself describes his intention as not only starting from Zabriskie Point (the place in Arizona and the film) but also wanting to make a statement against the drift to the right in politics. 'I wanted to shake up people's ideas, to make them think, and to give them fresh energy to create change: dynamite for aesthetics.' One for the Recession, a red metal heart, fixed to the wall by a magnet to allow rotation, is part Valentine, part Venus fly-trap, while Hot Achille, a floor to ceiling lamp, carries a warning thunderbolt, for all that it is a homage to Achille Castiglioni, especially his Parentesi lamp.

The particular qualities of Maurer's work, which made it the central element in Jean Nouvel's selection, are the absolute mastery of form and material, and the restraint and rigour with which the visual ideas are worked through. As he himself says 'the effort and the result, whether it's a question of the idea or of the technological solution, must have a balanced relationship with each other.'

27	Ingo Maurer
design	Table or wall lamp Los Minimalos
materials	Aluminium, steel
	50w bulb
dimensions	h 45cm w 8cm d 5.5cm
	h 17¾in w 3⅛in d 2⅛in
manufacturer	Ingo Maurer GmbH, Germany
	(Limited batch production)

28	Ingo Maurer
design	One for the Recession
materials	Lacquered steel
	60 w halogen bulb
dimensions	w 21cm L 41cm d 15cm
	w 8¼in L 16⅛in d 6in
manufacturer	Ingo Maurer GmbH, Germany
	(Limited batch production)

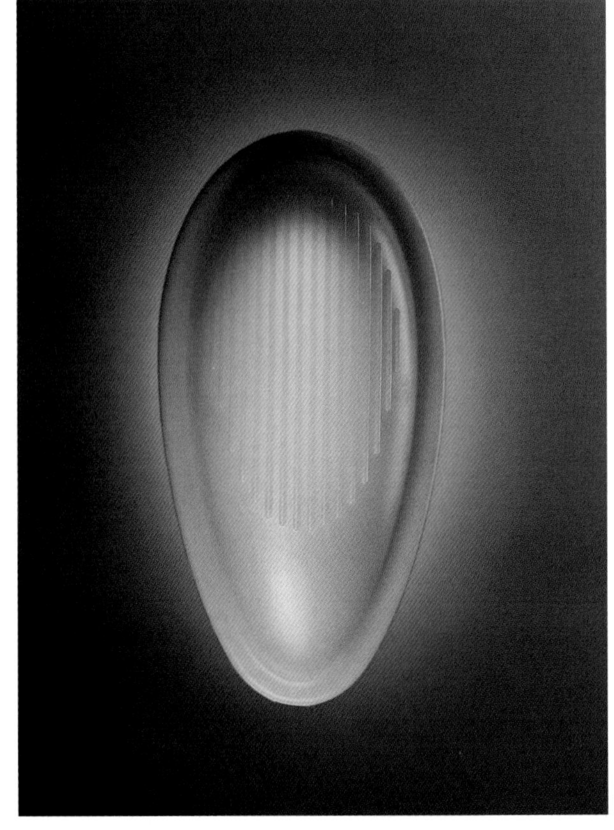

29 Marc Sadler
design Wall or ceiling lamp Drop 2
materials Opalescent silicone elastomer, coloured engineering polymer
2 x 9w fluorescent bulbs
dimensions h 9.9cm w 18.4cm L 25.3cm
h 4in w 7¼in L 10in
manufacturer Arteluce Div. Flos SpA, Italy

30 Marc Sadler
design Wall or ceiling lamp Drop 1
materials Opalescent silicone elastomer, coloured engineering polymer
9w fluorescent bulb
dimensions h 8.5cm w 12.7cm L 24.6cm
h 3⅜in w 5in L 9⅝in
manufacturer Arteluce Div. Flos SpA, Italy

32 Enrico Franzolini
design Flight Boxes
materials Lacquered MDF
50w halogen lamp
dimensions h 180cm w 45cm d 45cm
h 70⅝in w 17⅜in d 17⅜in
manufacturer Cappellini SpA, Italy

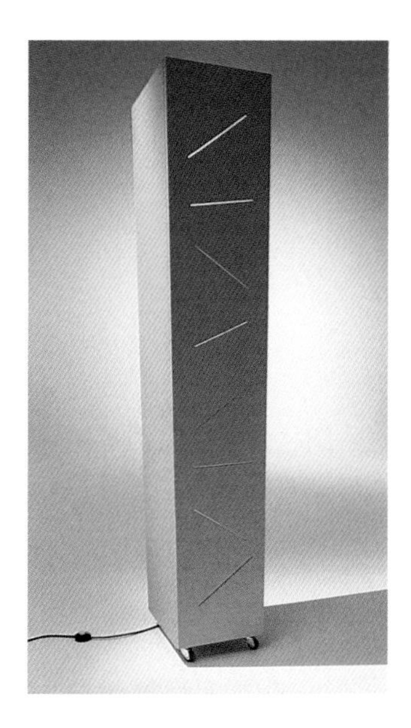

31 Peter Purwin
design Floor lamp Tube 450
materials Coloured metal, coloured neon tube
dimensions h 210cm d 10cm di 6cm
h 82⅝in d 4in di 2¾in
manufacturer DDM, Germany

33 Philippe Starck
design Wall lamp Wall. A Wall. A
materials Coloured thermopolymer plastic, opaline plastic, coloured filters
9w compact fluorescent bulb
dimensions h 37cm w 30cm d 10cm
h 14½in w 11⅞in d 4in
manufacturer Flos SpA, Italy

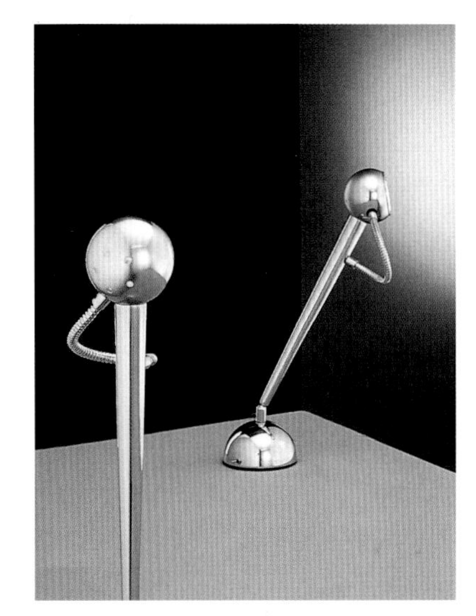

34	Masafumi Katsukawa
design	Table lamp Sub
materials	Chrome or lacquered epoxy
	50w dichroic bulb
dimensions	h 46cm di 12cm
	h 18⅛in di 4¾in
manufacturer	Lumen Center, Italy

35	Christian Maier
design	Lighting system Turn
materials	Aluminium, steel, 24ct gold plate, chrome plate,
	Saturn spot max 35w bulb, Pentax spot max 50w dichroic bulb
	Luna spot max 50w bulb, Itoc spot max 50w dichroic bulb,
	Lucifer spot max 50w bulb, Mars suspension lamp max 50w dichroic or
	halostar bulb
dimensions	Straight track 200cm (78¾in)/400cm (157½in), circular track 50cm
	(19⅝in))/100cm (39½in)
manufacturer	Planlicht, Austria

36	Ernesto Gismondi, Giancarlo Fassina
design	Wall lamp Arcadia
materials	Painted and chromed metal, sanded glass
	100w incandescent or opaline bulb
dimensions	d 16.5cm di 36cm
	d 6½in di 14⅛in
manufacturer	Artemide, Italy

37	Michele de Lucchi
design	Wall lamp Libera
materials	Painted metal, thermoplastic resin, coloured
	moulded-sanded-glass
	100w bulb
dimensions	h 38.5cm di 15cm
	h 15⅛in di 6in
manufacturer	Artemide, Italy

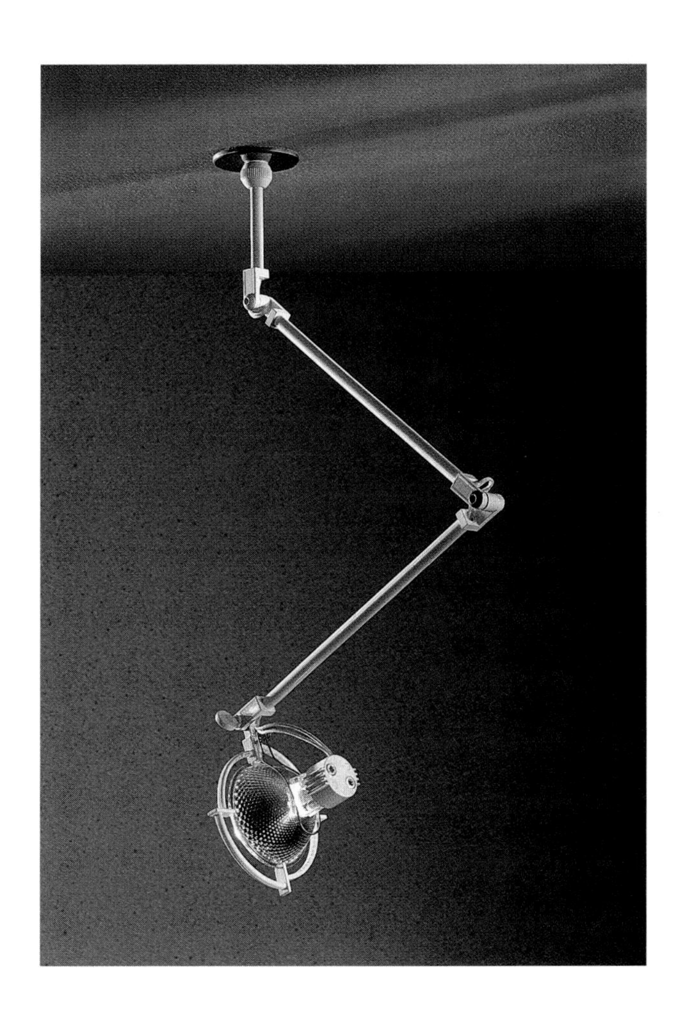

38	Barry Cook
design	Lighting system Option-Lv
materials	20-50w dichroic bulb
dimensions	h 280cm di 7.5cm
	h 110¼in di 3in
manufacturer	Basis Design Ltd., UK

39 Karin Pesau
design Downlighter FZ
materials Polycarbonate
2 x max 58w bulb
dimensions h 11cm w 12cm L 127cm
h 4⅜in w 4¾in L 50in
manufacturer Zumtobel Licht GmbH, Germany

40 Barry Cook
design Spotlight Option spot
materials 20-50w dichroic bulb
dimensions h 22cm
h 8⅝in
manufacturer Basis Design Ltd., UK

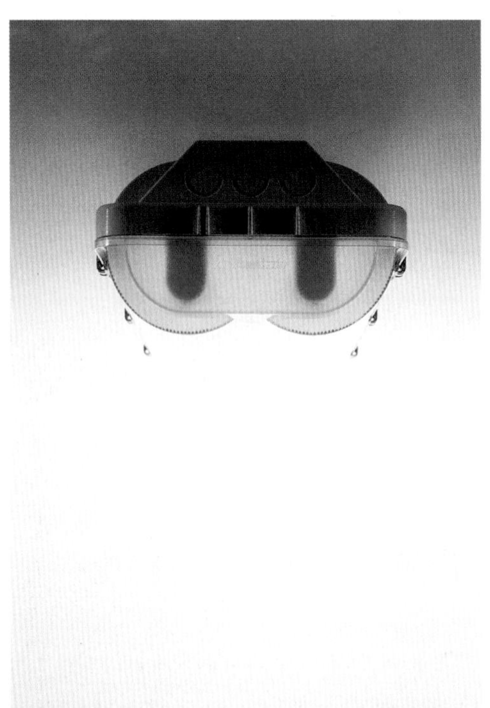

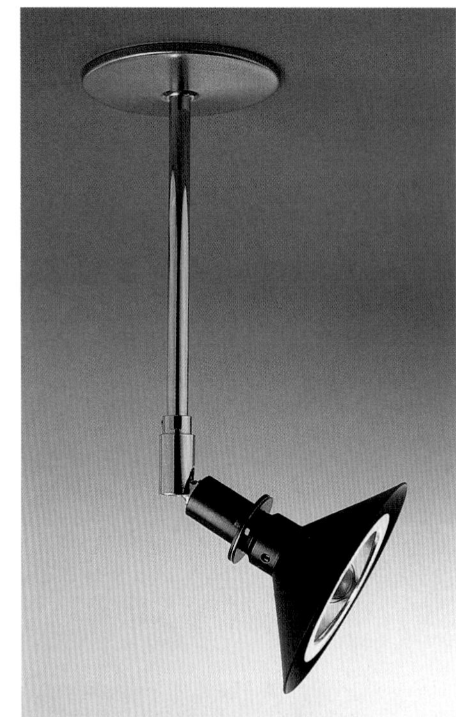

41 Basis Design
design Fluorescent downlighter
materials Ballast box, glass diffuser
2 x max 18w fluorescent downlighter
dimensions di 27cm
di 10½in
manufacturer Basis Design, UK

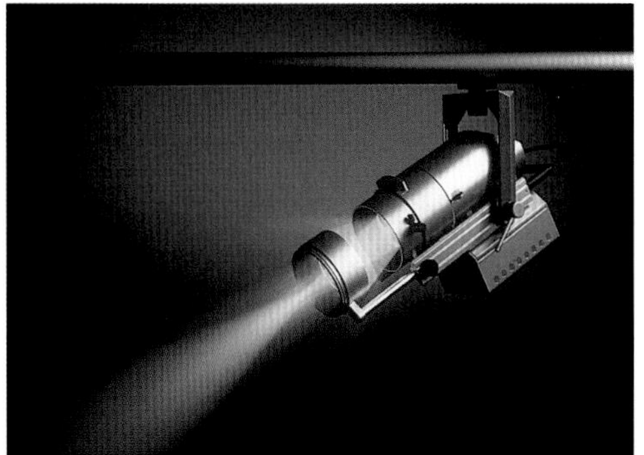

42 Franco Clivio
design Projector Stella
materials Cast aluminium, plastic, safety glass
11w halogen bulb or 70w & 150w metal halide bulb
dimensions h 32.7cm w 18.3cm d max 49.2cm, h 12⅞in w 7⅛in d max 19⅝in
h 31.1cm w 14.8cm d max 43.5cm, h 12¼in w 5¾in d max 17⅛in
manufacturer Erco Leuchten GmbH, Germany

43 Maurizio Ferrari
design Spotlight Jago
materials Chrome, brass, blown glass
50w dichroic bulb
dimensions h 17cm, 37cm, 77cm, 117cm di 7cm
h 6⅝in, 14½in, 30⅜in, 46in di 2¾in
manufacturer Solzi Luce srl

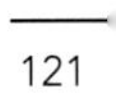

44 Sigeaki Asahara, Akira Yamamoto

design Lighting system Kri

materials Aluminium

20w, 30w, 35w dichroic bulb

dimensions h 11cm - 52.5cm w 7.7cm L 7cm

h 4⅜in - 20⅝in w 3⅛in L 2¾in

manufacturer Lucitala SpA, Italy

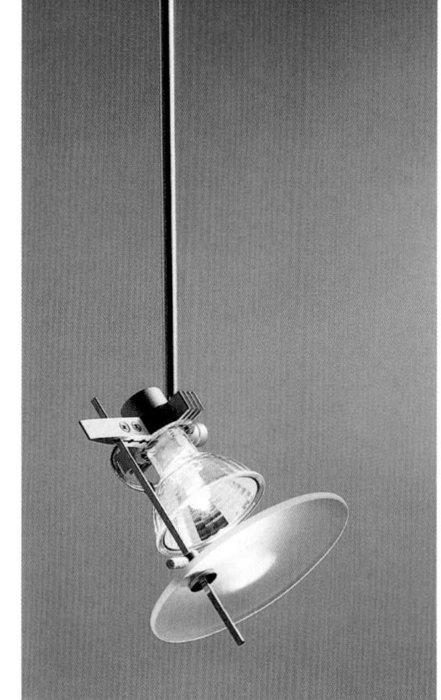

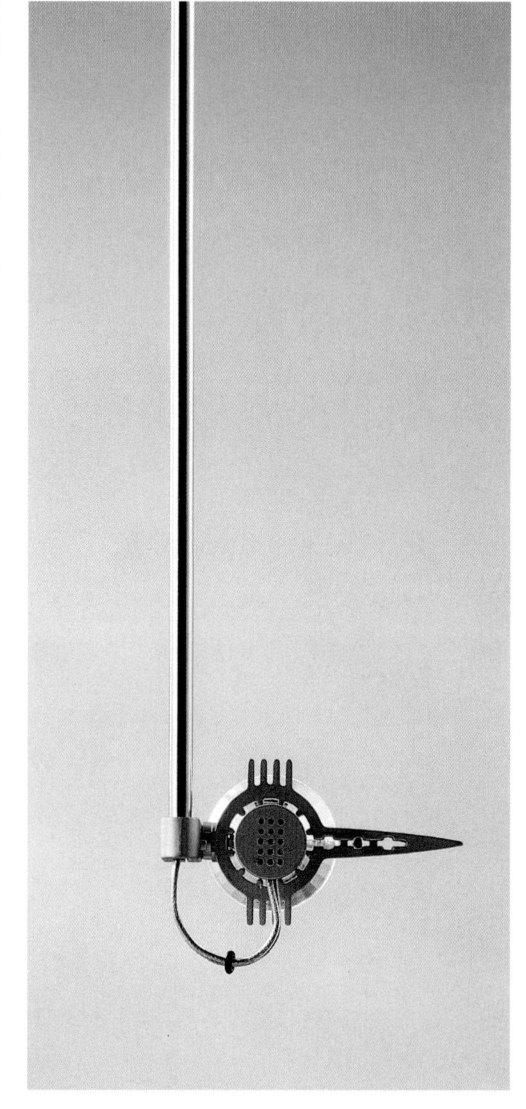

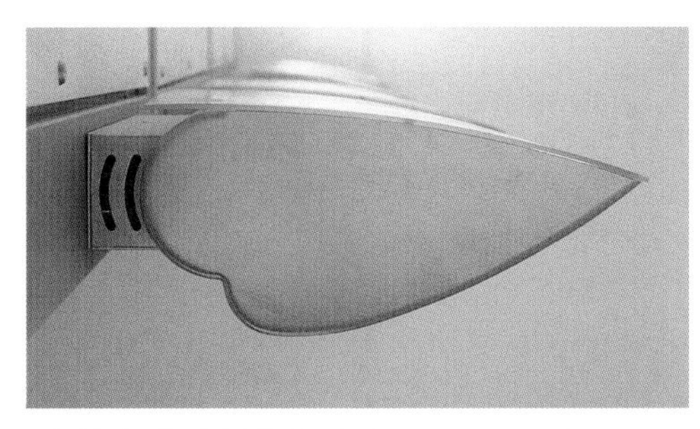

45 Russell Bagley
design Wall mounted uplighter Marseille
materials Mild steel
55w compact fluorescent bulb
dimensions h 135cm L 330cm
h 53⅛in L 120in
manufacturer Concord Lighting Ltd., UK

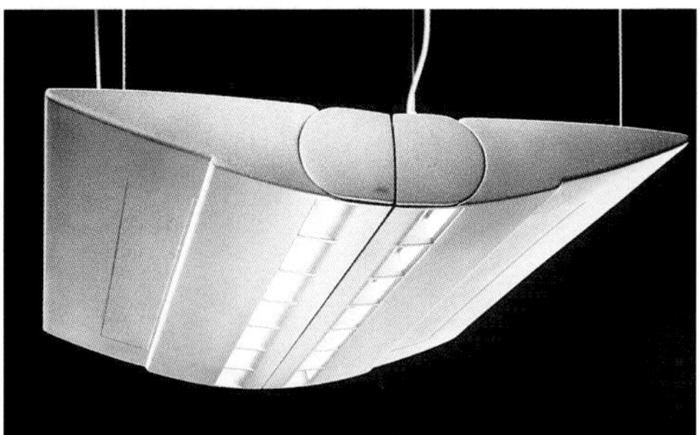

46 Luigi Trenti
design Lighting system Arianne
materials Polyurethane
55w compact fluorescent bulb
dimensions h 9.1cm L 62.5cm d 31.2cm
h 3½in L 24½in d 12in
manufacturer Targetti Sankey SpA, Italy

47 Alain Brux, Philippe Gourdon
design Downlighter Canal
materials Matt anodized aluminium
dimensions main unit h 5.2cm w 13.4cm
main unit h 2in w 5½in
manufacturer Optelma AG, Switzerland

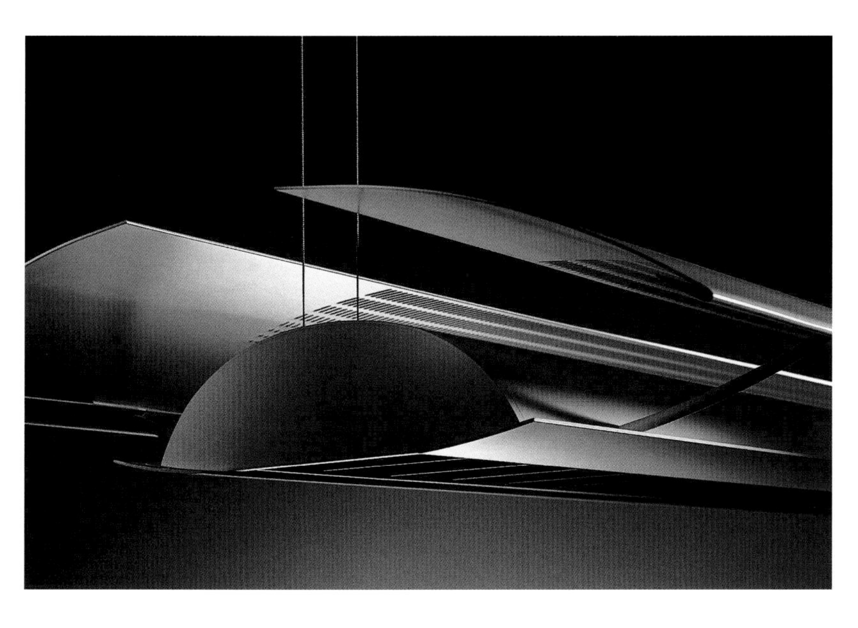

48 Andreas Gössel
design Suspension lamp Astron
materials Perforated sheet metal
36w fluorescent bulb and 2 x 36w bulbs or
58w fluorescent bulb and 2 x 58w bulbs
dimensions h 140cm L 149cm, 179cm
h 55⅛in L 58⅝in, 70⅝in
manufacturer Trilux-Lenze GmbH, Germany

49 Josep Aregall
design Floor lamp Hong Kong
materials Nickel, PVC
3 max 60w bulbs
dimensions h 111cm di 41cm
h 43¾in di 16⅛in
manufacturer Metalarte SA, Spain

50 Shiu-Kay Kan
design Table lamp Tricycle
materials Metal, paper
Max 40w bulb
dimensions h 25cm di 13cm
h 9⅞in di 5⅛in
manufacturer SKK, UK

51 Florian Borkenhagen
design Floor lamp Teodolite
materials Wood, steel, aluminium
150w bulb
dimensions h 200cm di 50cm
h 78¾in di 19⅝in
manufacturer Limited batch production

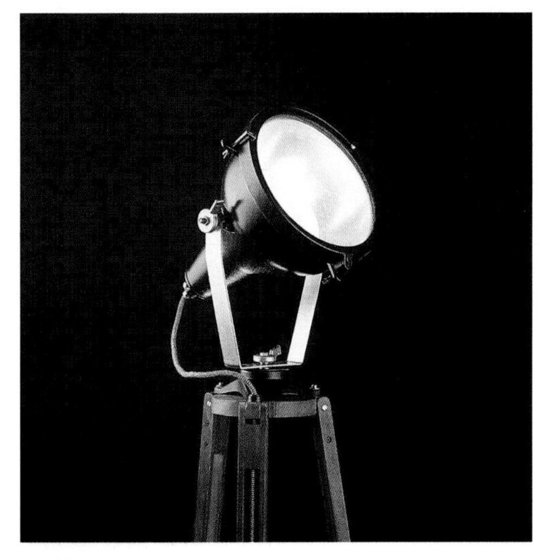

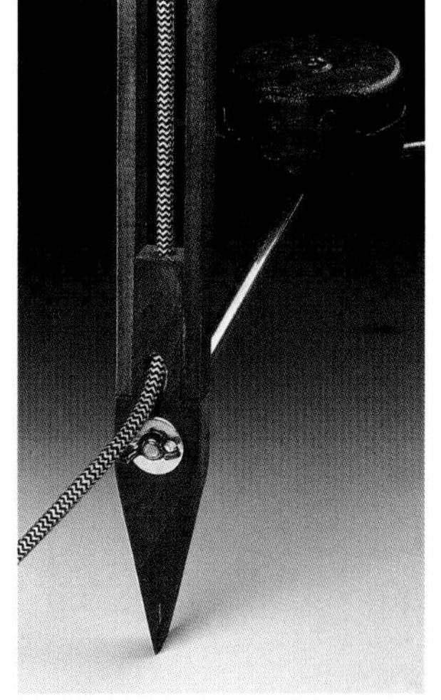

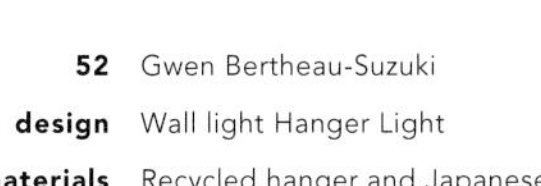

52 Gwen Bertheau-Suzuki
design Wall light Hanger Light
materials Recycled hanger and Japanese paper
110v bulb
dimensions h 78cm w 59cm d 30cm
h 30¾in w 23in d 11⅞in
manufacturer G.B.S. Ltd, Japan
(Prototype)

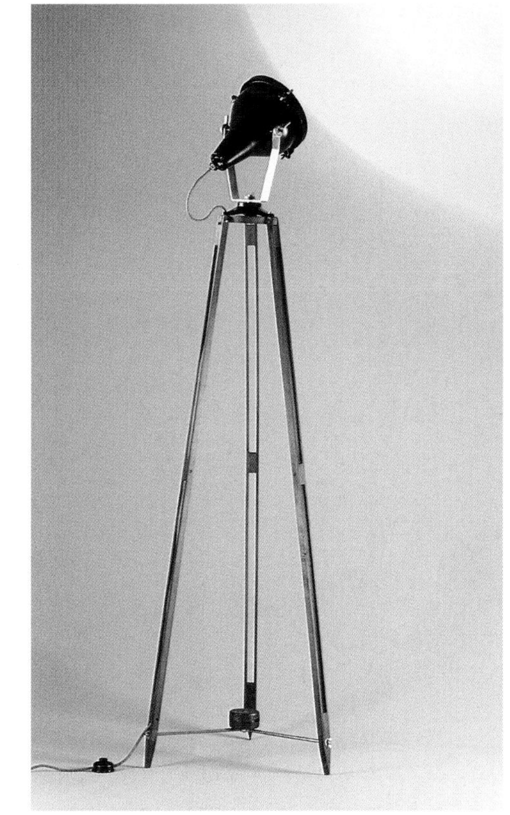

53 Renato Toso, Noti Massari
design Wall lamp Golf
materials Blown glass, gold/chrome plate, cut glass
60w bulb
dimensions h 50cm di 42cm
h 19⅝in di 16½in
manufacturer Leucos srl, Italy

54 Roberto Pamio
design Table lamp Grillo T
materials Satin-finished blown glass, chrome plate or copper 60w bulb
dimensions h 41cm di 20cm
h 16⅛in di 7⅞in
manufacturer Leucos srl, Italy

55 Alessandro Mendini
design Table lamp Idalino Luminoso
materials Opaline glass, chrome metal
dimensions 60w bulb: h 24cm di 11cm, h 9⅜in di 4⅜in
150w bulb: h 45cm di 15cm, h 17¾in di 6in
manufacturer Venini, Italy

56 Sottsass Associati
design Downlight Optos (Saturn)
materials Hand-blown glass
13w, 18w, 26w Compact fluorescent,
metal halide or tungsten halogen bulbs
dimensions h 6cm di 22cm - 28cm
h 2⅜in di 8⅝in - 11in
manufacturer Zumtobel Licht GmbH, Germany

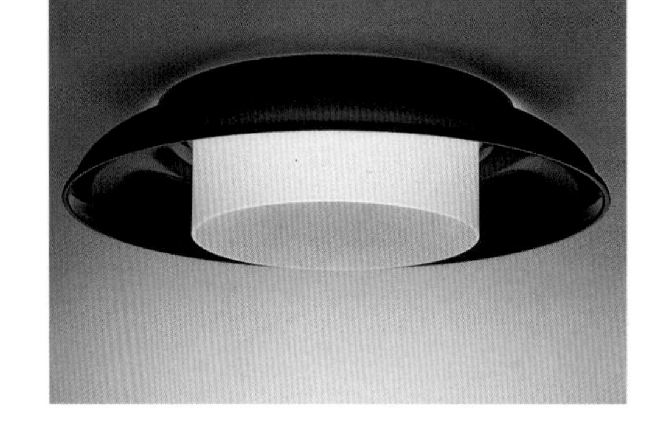

57 Sottsass Associati
design Downlight Auriga
materials Hand-blown glass
13w, 18w, 26w Compact fluorescent, metal
halide or tungsten halogen bulbs
dimensions h 10cm di 25cm - 30cm
h 4in di 9 ⅞in - 11 ⅞in
manufacturer Zumtobel Licht GmbH, Germany

58 Sottsass Associati
design Downlighter Mizar
materials Hand-blown glass
13w, 18w, 26w compact fluorescent,
metal halide or tungsten halogen bulbs
dimensions h 10cm di 25cm - 30cm
h 4in di 9⅞in - 11⅞in
manufacturer Zumtobel Licht GmbH, Germany

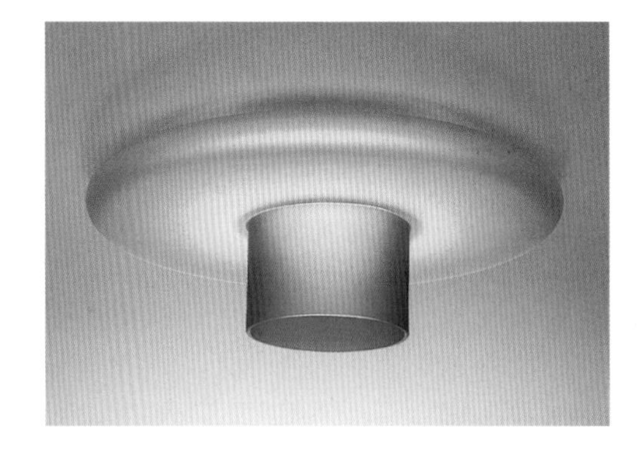

'I very much enjoyed Sottsass's Pompidou exhibition,' Nouvel told me during the selection meeting,'he still has this wonderful childlike facility for finding forms and making objects, whatever his age.' The Aero series of hanging lamps are a splendid example of this - simple globes marked with a single line of colour almost like a brush-stroke, moving and diffusing into the opal glass.

59 Sottsass Associati
design Suspension lamps Aero
materials Murano glass
dimensions 150w lamp: h 58cm - 83cm
150w lamp: h 22⅞in - 32¾in
manufacturer Venini, Italy

tableware

In discussing his own buildings on France-Culture recently Jean Nouvel talked about their being placed in a 'hypothesis of contextualism and modification, both in terms of history and risk'; by this he referred to the responsibility he sees the architect as having both to the present and the future, as well as to the past. For him, past forms in architecture and in design can be respected if they continue to have validity to the present - in his introduction he cites the case of the traditional Bordeaux glass, suggesting it is a design that is beyond improvement.

The choice of work for the tableware section was made with this precept very much in mind, and so it is not surprising that the majority of pieces selected are simple in form and plain in colour. Dieter Sieger's flatware, and his Milk Glass series, are typical of the work that met with his approval. Yet Nouvel also realizes that tableware design, like other areas of design, offers special opportunities for developing new ideas. Not only are the objects involved relatively small, so holding down the cost of design, but on the one hand there is an established vocabulary of objects to reflect on, and on the other a growing range of new materials and applications to study. From an economic point of view, the consumers' replacement rates for items such as kitchen equipment are much faster than for furniture, and in flatware and glassware there is an additional professional market to restaurants and hotels. In this respect, the success of Alessi in promoting small scale design by internationally known designers is perhaps the contemporary epitome of tableware design, and so was chosen to round off this section.

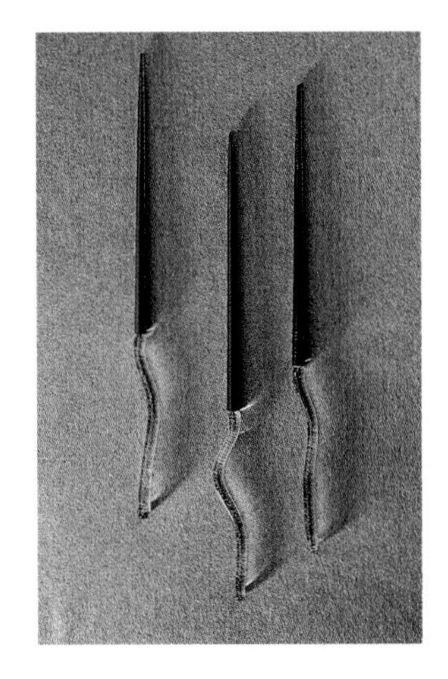

1 Julia Cheng
design Chopsticks Ondine
materials Lacquered wood, Murano glass
dimensions L 25cm di 0.3cm - 0.7cm
L 9⅞in di ⅛in - ¼in
manufacturer Ondine Industries, France
(Prototype)

2 Dominic Habsburg
design Flower Vase
materials Lead-free crystal
dimensions h 41cm di 24cm
h 16in di 9½in
manufacturer Sugahara Glassworks Inc., Japan

3 Massimo Vignelli
design Glassware Whirlwind
materials Hand blown glass
dimensions serving platter di 29cm di 11½in
cylinder carafe h 19cm h 7½in
round carafe h 19cm h 7½in
manufacturer Steuben Glass, USA

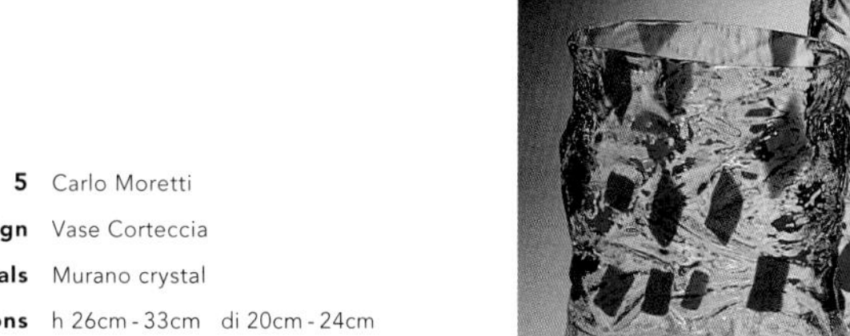

5 Carlo Moretti
design Vase Corteccia
materials Murano crystal
dimensions h 26cm - 33cm di 20cm - 24cm
h 10¼in - 13in di 7⅞in - 9½in
manufacturer Carlo Moretti s.r.l, Italy
(Limited batch production)

4 Philip Baldwin & Monica Guggisberg
design Vase Nikki
materials Lead-free glass
dimensions h 39cm di 20cm
h 15⅜in di 7⅞in
manufacturer Verrerie de Nonfoux, Switzerland

6 Aldo Rossi
design Coffee pot
materials Porcelain, crystal
dimensions h 29.5cm di 12cm
h 11⅝in di 4¾in
manufacturer Rosenthal, Germany

above **7** Makoto Komatsu
design Pitcher and tumbler set Fine Line
materials Glass
dimensions h 17cm, 11cm, 7cm di 8cm, 7cm, 5cm
h 6⅝in, 4⅜in, 2¾in di 3⅛in, 2¾in, 2in
manufacturer Kimura Glass, Japan

above **8** Maria Grazia Fiocco
design Cutlery, condiment set and tray Soft
materials Stainless steel, ABS, glass
dimensions rectangular tray L 42cm w 27cm
rectangular tray L 16½in w 10⅝in
fork L 19.7cm
fork L 7¾in
manufacturer Mori Produzione Inox SpA, Italy

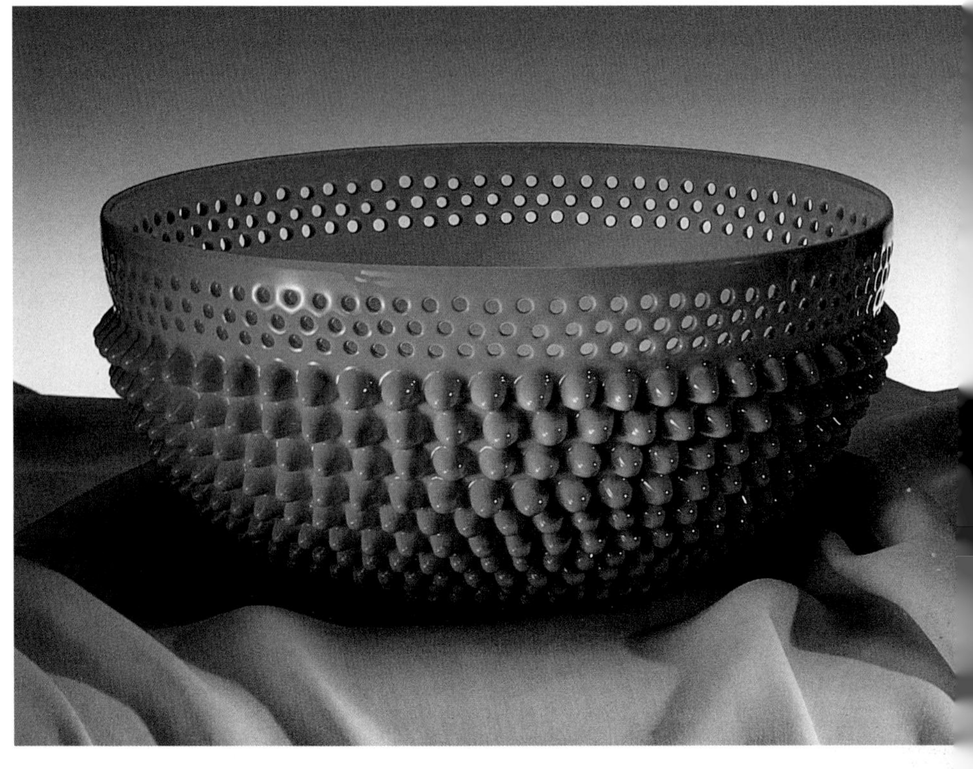

9 Borek Sipek
design Bowl Vendome
materials Porcelain
dimensions h 13cm di 28cm
h 5⅛in di 11in
manufacturer Driade SpA, Italy

10 Lino Sabattini
design Champagne bucket, ice bucket, shaker, bottle-holder and box for snacks
Cartoccio
materials Silver-plated brass alloy
dimensions Champagne bucket: h 21cm 8¼in
Snack box: h 7.5cm 3in
manufacturer Sabattini Argenteria SpA, Italy
(Limited batch production)

top **11** Nigel Coates
design Perfume bottles, A bottles
materials Lead crystal
dimensions h 20.3cm and 30.5cm
h 8in and 12in
manufacturer Hand blown by Simon Moore
(Limited batch production)

12 Minora Sugahara
design Tumblers
materials Soda glass
dimensions h 11.5cm,14cm di 5.5cm, 6.5cm
h 4½in, 5½in di 2⅛in, 2⅝in
manufacturer Sugahara Glassworks Inc., Japan

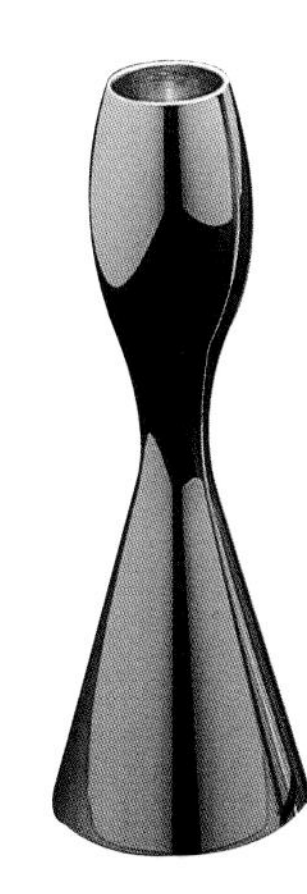

right **13** Karim Rashid
design Candlestick Shimmer
materials Mixed metal alloy
dimensions h 29.3cm, 20.3cm, 14cm di 4.5cm
h 11½in, 8in, 5½in di 1¾in
manufacturer Nambe Mills Inc., USA

14 Thomas Ericksson
design Vase Progetto 9407
materials Polished pewter
dimensions h 40cm di 12cm
h 15¾in di 4¾in
manufacturer Progetto Oggetto/Cappellini, Italy

15	Ron Arad
design	Vase Jive
materials	Ceramic
dimensions	h 25cm di 17cm
	h 9⅞in di 6⅝in
manufacturer	Cor Unum, The Netherlands

The title of Hans Hollein's new collection of tableware and furniture is Simplexity. Plain shapes with simple linear patterns of decoration, the vases, candlesticks, goblets and jugs were intended to create a family of basic forms, though interpreted with subtlety of design and richness of material. The cool silvered and bronze shapes, exhibited in the white classical spaces of Design Gallery Milan, had an almost Etruscan quality of remoteness, suggesting, in D.H.Lawrence's words, that 'we can know the living world only symbolically'.

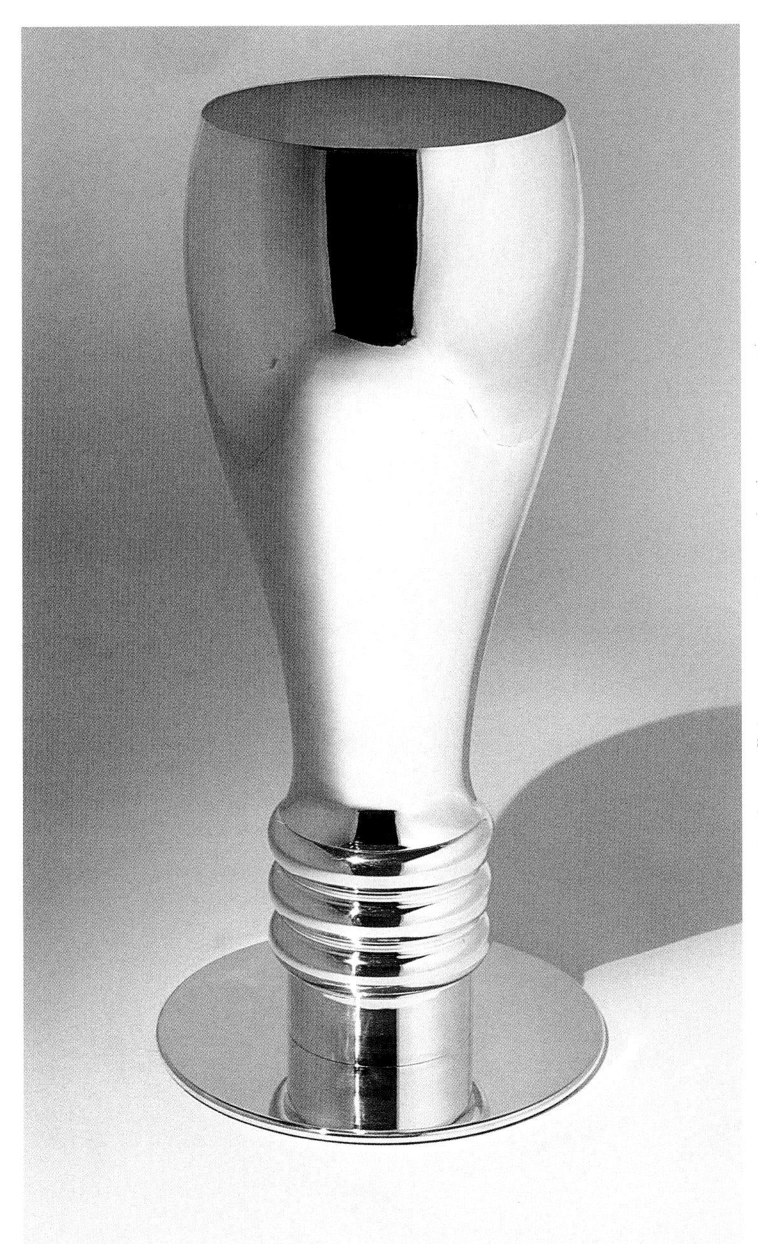

16	Hans Hollein
design	Vase Sinex
materials	Silver-plated turned brass
dimensions	h 55cm di 24cm
	h 21¾in di 9½in
manufacturer	Design Gallery Milan, Italy
	(Limited batch production)

17	Hans Hollein
design	Vase Silo
materials	Silver-plated turned brass
dimensions	h 55cm di 24cm
	h 21¾in di 9½in
manufacturer	Design Gallery Milan, Italy
	(Limited batch production)

The idea behind Dieter Sieger's Milk Glass collection is delightfully simple. Take an ordinary clear half-pint milk glass, ask a well-known designer or artist to design a silk-screen decoration for it, then fill it with milk. The result provides a cross-comparison of contemporary graphic styles, from George Sowden's glass-within-a-glass homage to Picasso's dove to Hannes Wettstein's white on black Guinness parody. Both of these - and many of the others - can only be read when the glass is full, and full of milk at that. The series is a nice illustration of the value of constraints in decorative design.

18 Olivier Védrine
design Table service Noctiluca
materials Blown pyrex glass
Prototype
dimensions Glass: h 8.3cm di 6cm, h 3¼in di 2½in
Small plate: h 4.5cm di 13.2cm, h 1¾in di 5⅛in
Medium plate: h 2.9cm di 20.4cm, h 1⅛in di 8⅛in
Large plate: h 3.9cm di 22cm, h 1½in di 8⅝in
manufacturer Le C.I.R.V.A, France

19 Dieter Sieger

design Milk Glass

1993 collection from left to right (top) Ron Arad Associates, Riccardo Dalisi, Louise Gibb, Kunstflug, Heinz te Laake, (bottom) Nathalie du Pasquier, Werner Pawlok, George Sowden, Oscar Tusquets Blanca, Hannes Wettstein.

materials Glass, screen-printed colours

dimensions h 15cm di 6.8cm

h 6in di 2⅝in

manufacturer Marsberger Glaswerke, Germany

20	Dieter Sieger
design	Cult
materials	Porcelain
dimensions	round plates di 31cm-18cm
	round plates di 12⅛in-7in
manufacturer	Porzellanfabrik Arzberg, Germany

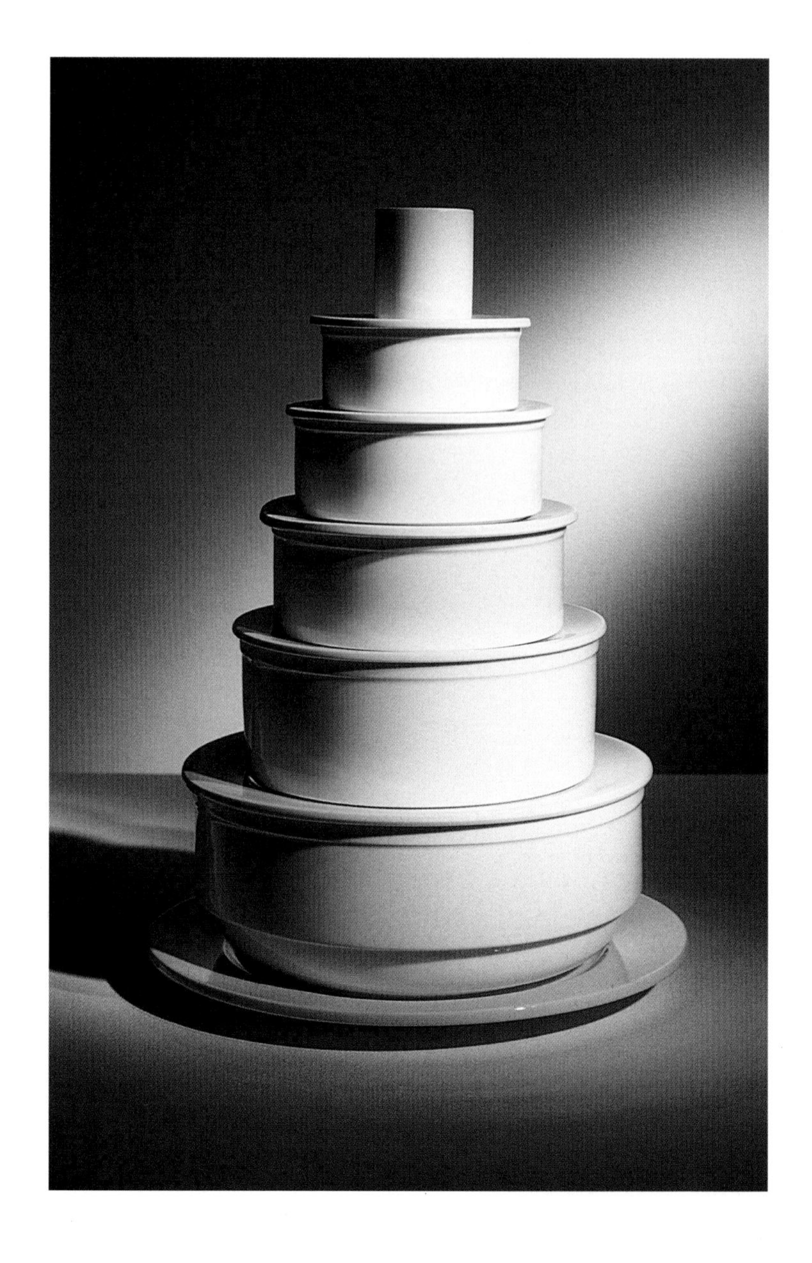

21	Maria Grazia Fiocco
design	Pans
materials	Enamelled steel
dimensions	casserole w 94cm di 61cm
	casserole w 37in di 24in
manufacturer	TVS SpA, Italy

22 Kati Tuominen-Niittyl
design Jugs Storybirds Ollie and Olga
materials Stoneware
dimensions h 15cm di 10.7cm, h 23.5cm di 13cm
h 6in di 4½in, h 9¼in di 5⅛in
manufacturer Arabia, Finland

23 Masatoshi Sakaegi
design Japanese teapots
materials Porcelain
dimensions h 6.5cm di 6.7cm
h 2⅝in di 2⅞in
manufacturer Sakaegi Design Studio, Japan

24 Marc Newson
design Vase S.F.
materials Ceramic
dimensions h 34cm di 31cm
h 13in di 12¼in
manufacturer Cor Unum, The Netherlands

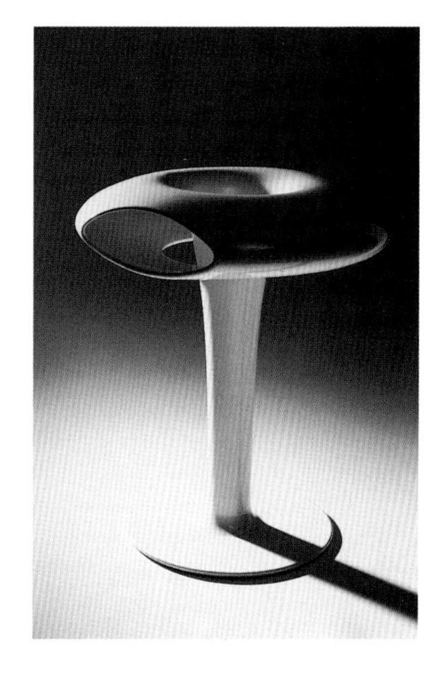

It has sometimes been suggested that Marc Newson worked with Ron Arad. He did not, but it is an understandable mistake. Both are interested in fluid metal forms, and in pushing the formal limits of design outwards. Newson's current work explores interior surfaces and hidden forms, whether in the Helice floor lamp in the Lighting section or here in the S.F. vase, modelled on his Mini Event Horizon table, in the Furniture section.

25 Jasper Morrison
design Vase
materials Ceramic
dimensions h 32cm w 24cm
h 12½in w 9½in
manufacturer Cor Unum, The Netherlands

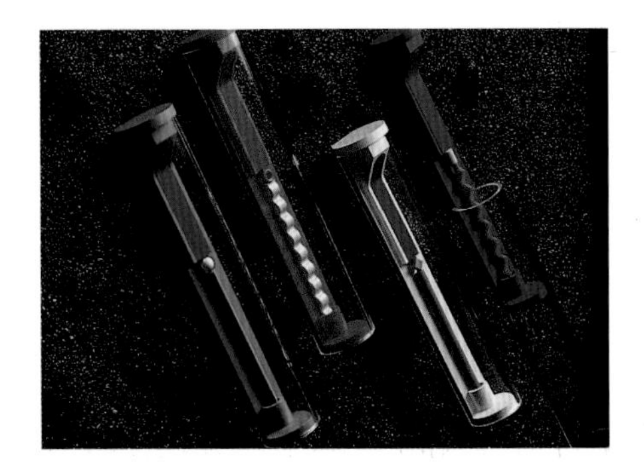

26 Kazuo Kawasaki
design Tea ceremony ladle Riki.i.ki.Totsu
materials ABS
dimensions L 18cm w 2cm
L 7⅛in w ¾in
manufacturer Sabie, Japan

27 Arnout Visser
design Sugar and Milk set
materials Pyrex glass
dimensions h 10cm di 5cm
h 4in di 2in
manufacturer DMD Development Manufacturing
Distribution, The Netherlands

28 Henk Stallinga
design Sponge vase
materials Pure sponge
dimensions h 4cm w 15cm d 10cm
h 1½in w 6in d 4in
manufacturer Droog Design, The Netherlands

29 Massimo Morozzi
design Bottle opener Stappo
materials PC, stainless steel
dimensions L 20cm w 7cm
L 8in w 2¾in
manufacturer Alessi, Italy

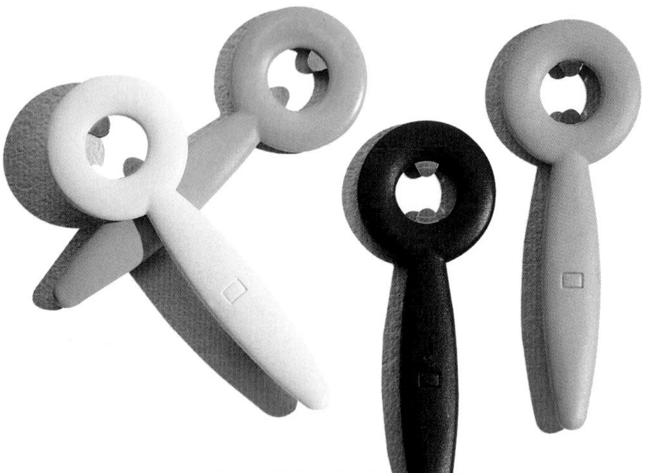

above **30** Alejandro Ruiz
design Parmesan cheese grater Parmenide
materials Stainless steel, plastic
dimensions h 6.7cm w 15.3cm d 7.5cm
h 2¾in w 6⅛in d 3in
manufacturer Alessi, Italy

31 King Kong
design Espresso coffee maker with jug and bowl Mix Italia
materials Stainless steel, polyamide
dimensions 6 cups: h 17.2cm di 11cm, h 6¾in di 4½in
3 cups: h 15cm di 8.8cm, h 6in di 3½in
manufacturer Alessi, Italy

Michael Graves's Bird and Mickey kettles for Alessi have been taken either as the *ne plus ultra* of post-Modernism, or proof of its logical dead-end, depending on your point of view. But if Alessi designs then hall-marked the 1980s, its current design policy is broader and maturer, with the emphasis moving to younger designers, to themed designs as well as narrative ones. Alberto Alessi attributes the success of his commissions in design to the ability of designers to create 'transitional objects', which enable the user to translate experiences and emotions from one context to another. Design, for him, 'is a global creative discipline with a strictly artistic and poetic matrix.'

32 Joanna Lyle
design Centre piece bowl Chimu
materials Stainless steel, wood, aluminium
dimensions h 13.5cm di 26cm
h 5in di 10¼in
manufacturer Alessi, Italy

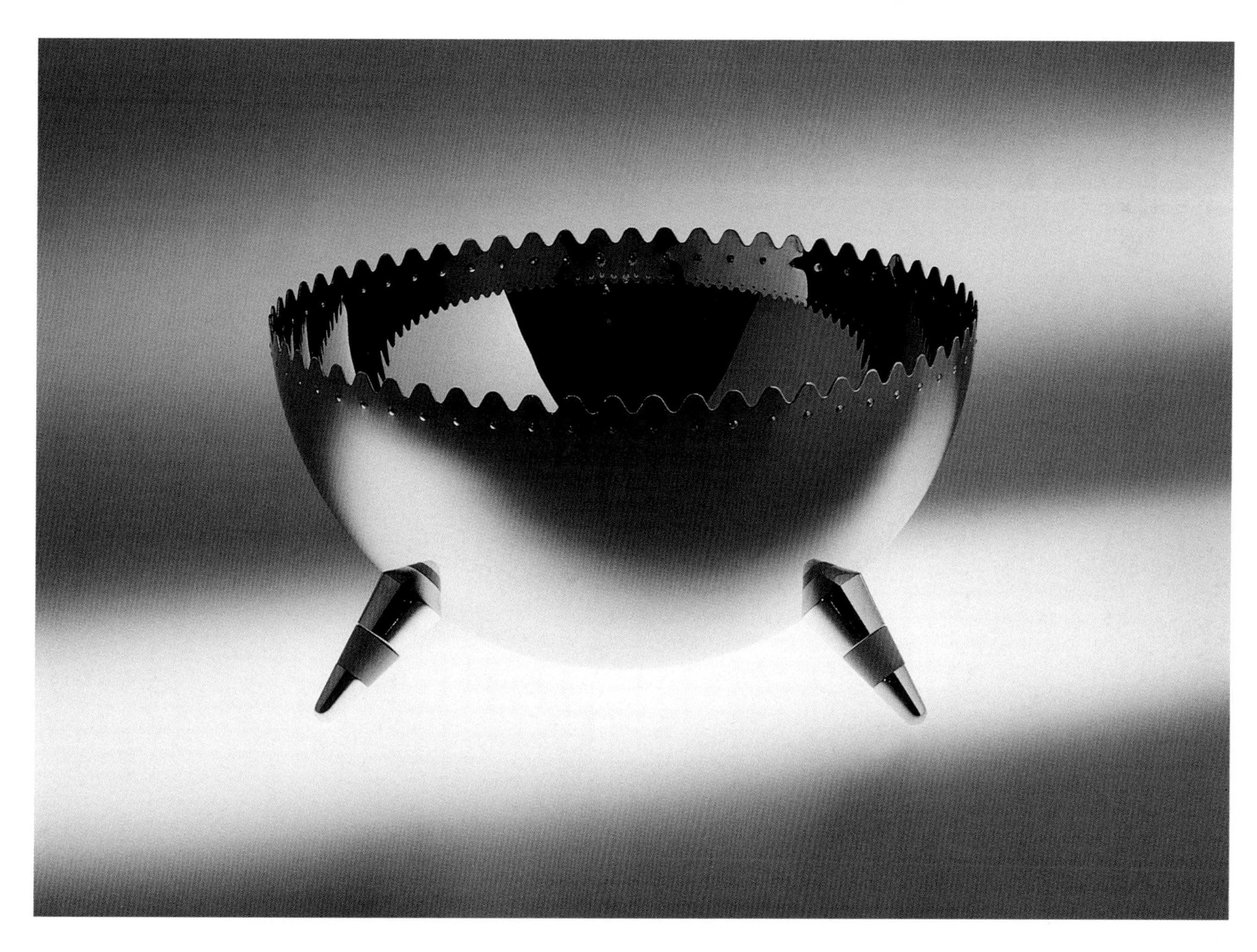

textiles

The textile section comprises groups of works by seven designers, all Japanese, and two individual pieces by designers working in Europe. This very exacting choice by Nouvel stems from an immediate appreciation of the quality of the Japanese work in particular, but also from a definition of design that in effect excluded many of the other designs submitted.

Just as Nouvel has a horror of self-indulgence in architecture, so he felt that a lot of the textile work should not even be considered because it was a work of art passed off as a design. In some cases what Nouvel was objecting to was a decorative style or effect that was too pictorial, too overtly working in an artistic frame of reference rather than a design one. In other cases it was the choice of materials that he felt had not been sufficiently thought through. As, in fact, the designs chosen all have what can only be called a strong personal style, Nouvel was not arguing only against subjectivity in design. Rather, he was making, as often before, an argument for understanding the true nature and purpose of the design in hand, and relating it to its context. This, he felt, could be applied to textile design in the same way that it can be applied to furniture or lighting, and to architecture. While the work chosen is mainly by Japanese designers, and can be seen as part of an on-going Japanese tradition, it should be stressed that Japanese designers now draw their inspiration from a broad international base. Typical of this is the work of the Maki sisters, who trained in the USA as well as in Japan, and who have studied textiles in Central and South America and today work closely with fellow weavers in India.

In one sense, the designs here can been seen as a rich and subtle parcel of shadows. The phrase comes from a book we discussed during the selection meetings and which Nouvel admires, Junichiro Tanizaki's *In'Ei Raisan*. This essay, published in 1933, is both a nostalgic homage to the role of shadow in Japanese dress, interiors and architecture, and a defence - though not at all a nationalistic one - of the traditional values of Japanese life. Tanizaki argues that the true beauty of rich materials such as lacquer and gold silks only appears when glimpsed in shadow, and he speaks of the beauty of shadows themselves. Writing of dress under the previous regime he points out that 'women generally wore clothes in incredibly dark colours: their costume, in a word, was nothing more than a parcel of shadows, a transition between background and face.'

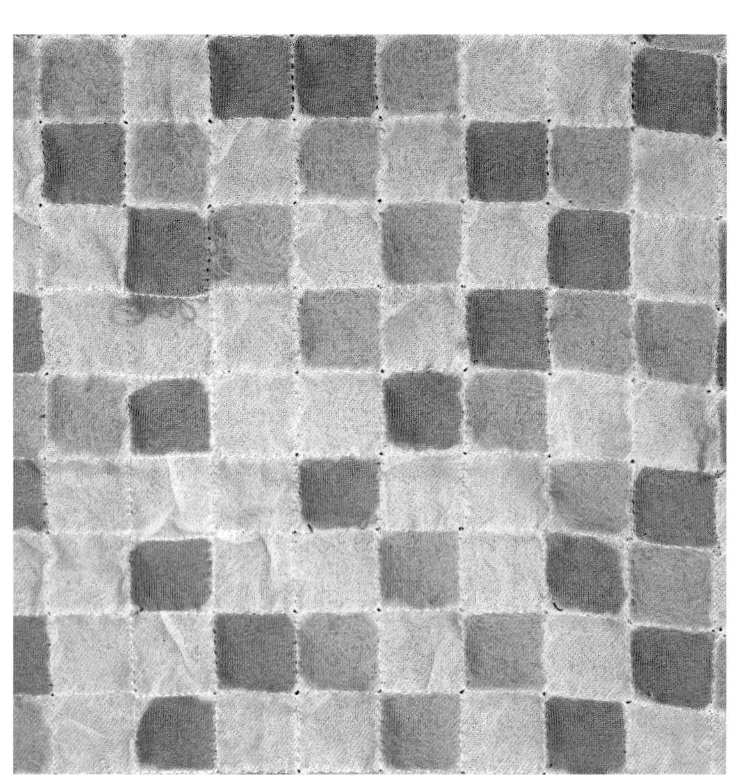

1 Koji Hamai
design Cocoon
materials Acrylic fibre, cotton
dimensions w 100cm L 100cm repeat 50cm
w 39½in L 39½in repeat 19⅝in
manufacturer Prototype

2 Koji Hamai
design Gradation
materials Acrylic fibre
dimensions L 100cm repeat 50cm
L 39½in repeat 19⅝in
manufacturer Protoype

3 Koji Hamai
design Mica
materials Polyester
dimensions w 100cm L 100cm repeat 50cm
w 39½in L 39½in repeat 19⅝in
manufacturer Protoype

4 Koji Hamai
design Ray stripes
materials Polyester
dimensions w 100cm L 150cm repeat 30cm
w 39½in L 59in repeat 11⅞in
manufacturer Prototype

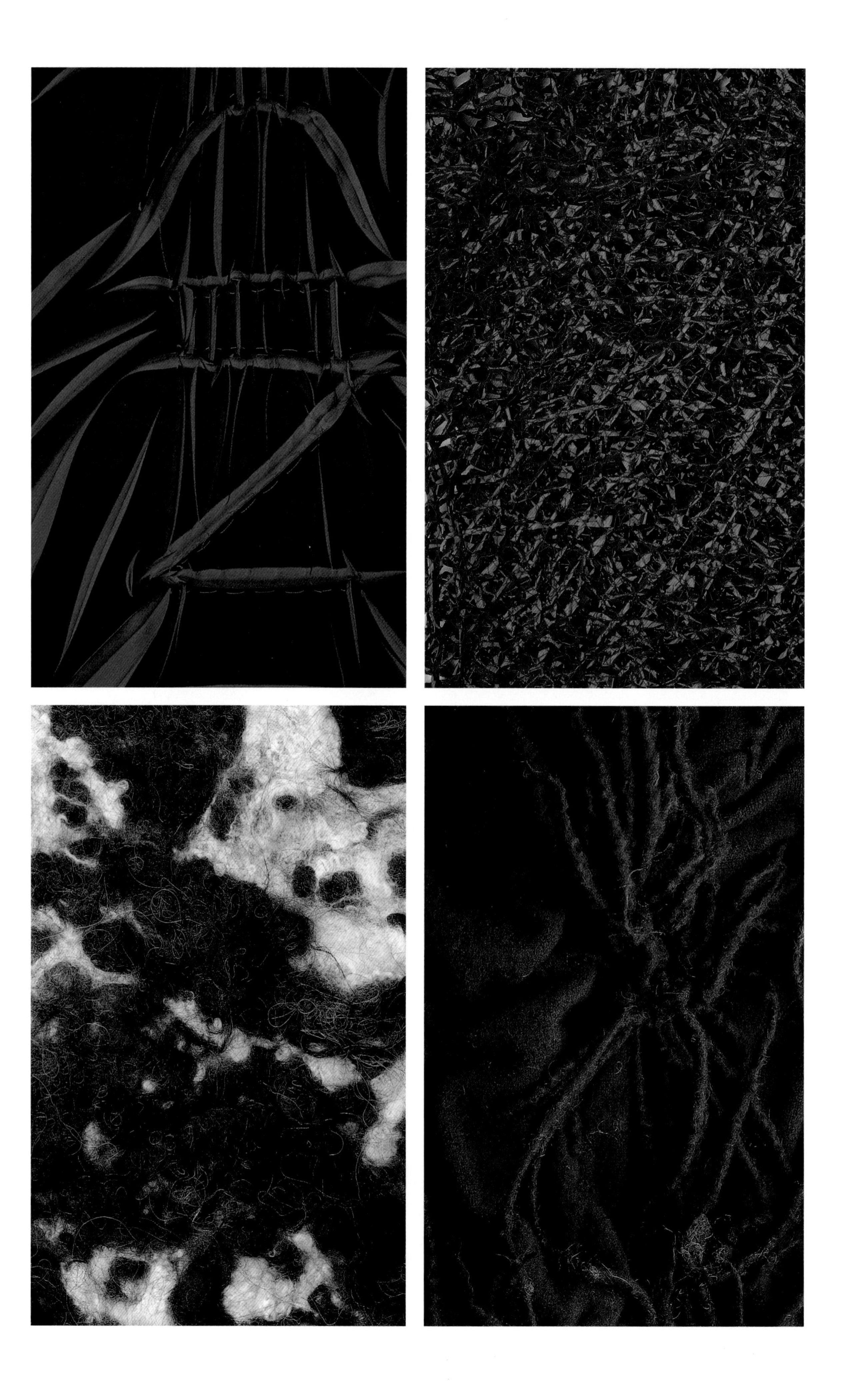

5-9 Yoshiki Hishinuma
design Fabric designs
materials / dimensions Yoshiki Hishinuma uses these fabrics for fashion design, and so information on materials and measurements is not relevant or available
manufacturer Hishinuma Institute Co. Ltd., Japan.

10	Djoke de Jong
design	Curtain
materials	Cotton
dimensions	w 150cm
	w 59in
manufacturer	Droog Design, The Netherlands

This design is called Curtain, but that is only half of its story. On the cotton material a pattern is printed, and as the designer Djoke de Jong says 'when you decide to change the curtain, you can use the printed image as a pattern for a jacket.' Jean Nouvel was delighted with the directness and simplicity of the design: 'how can any architect resist selecting a design with a plan on it!' was his comment. Once again one of the designers from Droog Design has given the supposedly straightforward a slight but witty twist.

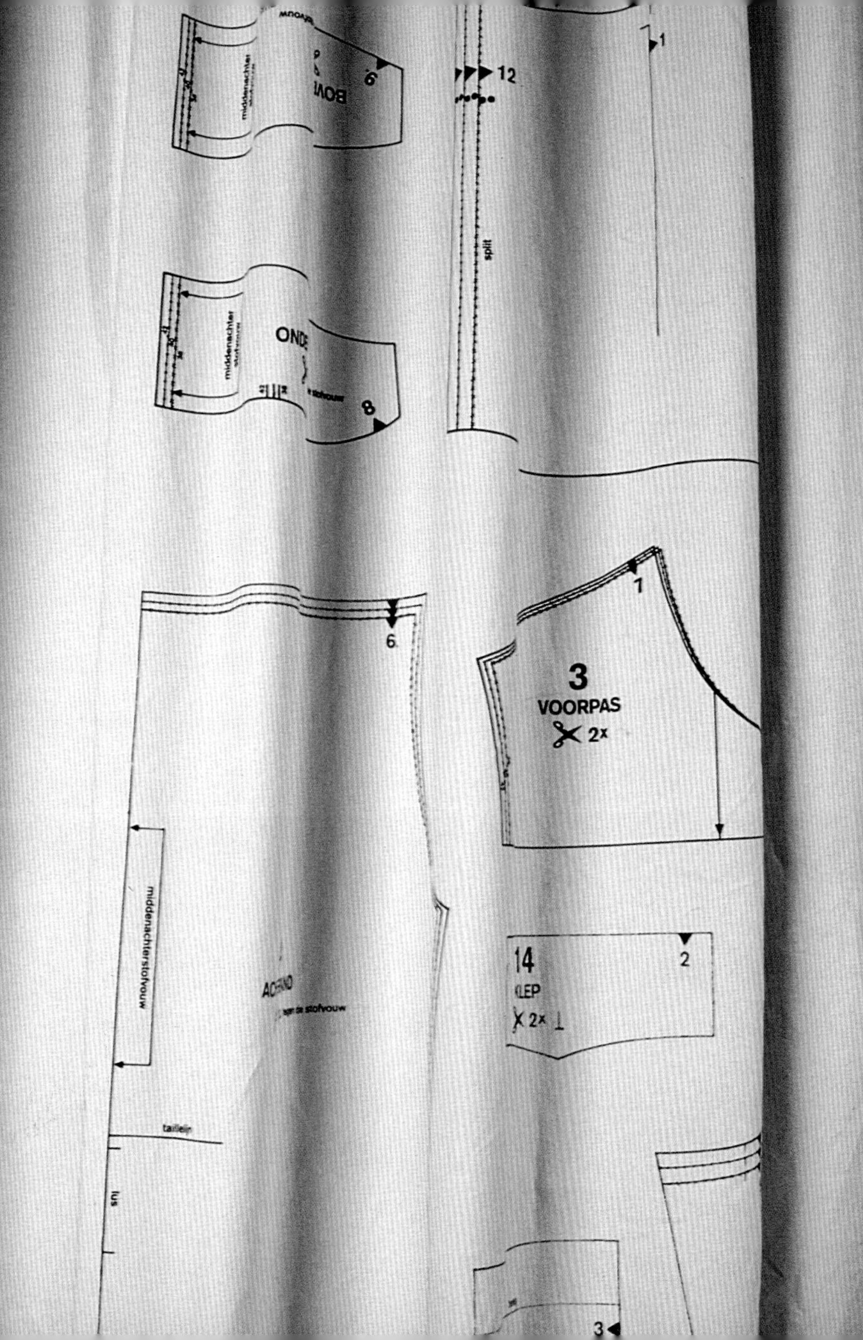

12
1
split
ONDE
8
middenachter
3
VOORPAS
2x
1
6
middenachterstofvouw
tailleljn
lus
14
KLEP
2x
2
3

12 Chiaki Maki
design Design 2
materials Silk, Japanese mulberry silk, tassar silk
dimensions w 35cm L 120cm
w 13¾in L 47¼in
manufacturer Maki Textile Studio, Japan
(One-off)

11 Kaori Maki
design Design 7
materials Natural wool, linen, handspun tassar silk
dimensions w 60cm L 200cm
w 23½in L 78¾in
manufacturer Maki Textile Studio, Japan
(Limited batch production)

The work of the Maki sisters, Chiaki and Kaori, can be seen as in the forefront of the new movement in Japanese textile design, but it is useful to record that the sisters trained at Rhode Island College of Design in the USA, and that the inspiration for their designs comes not only from a Japanese tradition, but also from visits to Central America. Though the studio was started by Chiaki Maki, the design work is now shared between the sisters. Today much of their work is developed and produced with a workshop in India run by Neeru Kumar, herself a textile designer. This choice of working location is not primarily economic, but relates to the sisters' aim 'to create new textiles that fit modern Japanese and Western lifestyles using the best of Asian materials and handwork.'

14 Reiko Sudo
design Feather Flurries
materials Silk, feather organdy
dimensions w 115cm repeat 37cm
w 45¼in repeat 14½in
manufacturer Nuno Corporation, Japan

15 Reiko Sudo
design Squeezee Wipe
materials Silk
dimensions w 100cm
w 39½in
manufacturer Nuno Corporation, Japan

13 Chiaki Maki
design Design 5
materials Linen, spun silk, tassar silk
dimensions w 150cm L 150cm
w 59in L 59in
manufacturer Maki Textile Studio, Japan
(Prototype)

right **17** Junichi Arai
design No. B
materials Polyester, wool, nylon
dimensions w 110cm L 400cm
w 43⅜in L 157½in
manufacturer Kay Tay Co., Japan
(Handmade one-off)

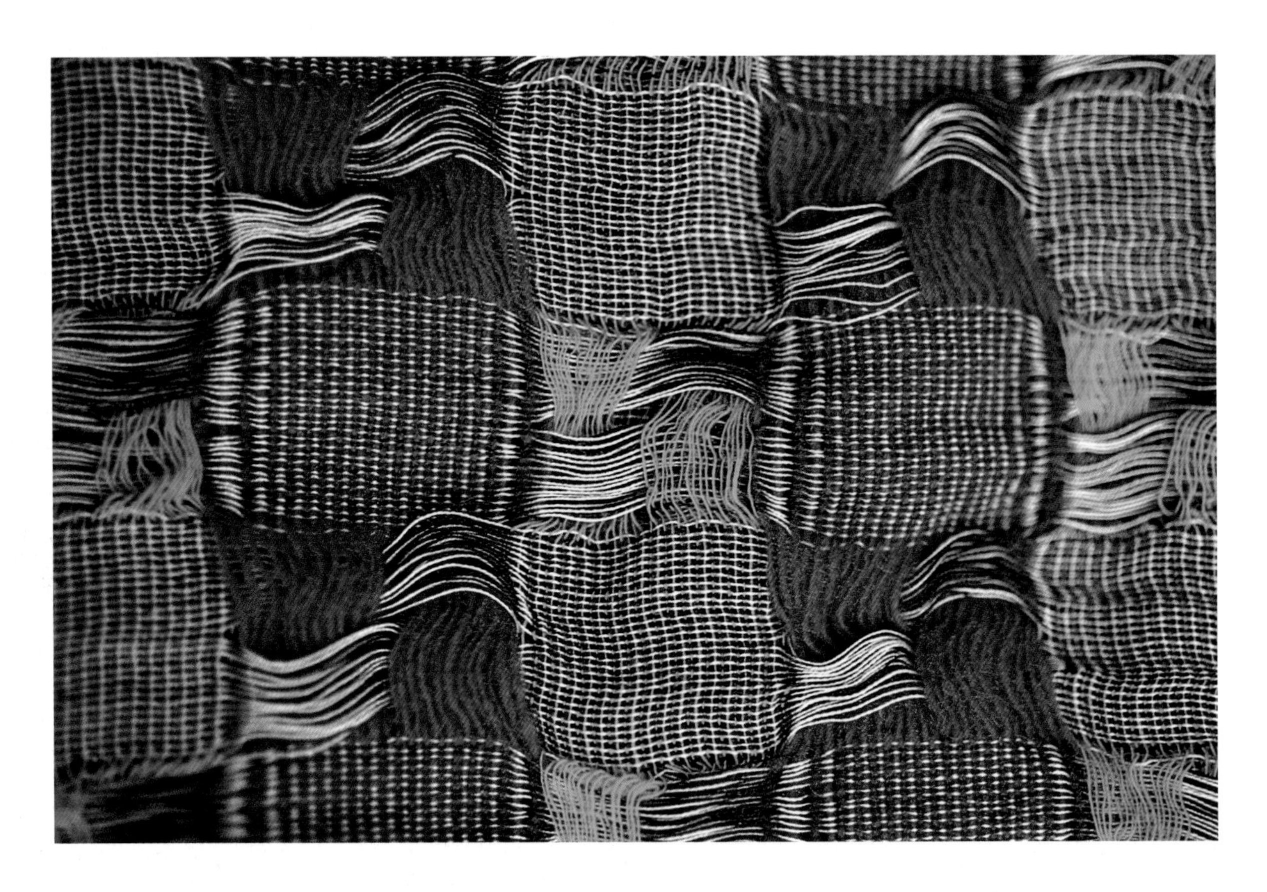

16 Eiji Miyamoto
design 4D
materials Silk, cotton
dimensions w 120cm L 200cm
w 47¼in L 78¾in
manufacturer Myashin Co. Ltd., Japan
(Limited batch production)

18 Junichi Arai
design No. F
materials Polyester
dimensions w 80cm L 400cm
w 31½in L 157½in
manufacturer Kay Tay Co., Japan
(Handmade one-off)

19 Junichi Arai
design No. G
materials Polyester
dimensions w 75cm L 250cm
w 29½in L 98 in
manufacturer Kay Tay Co., Japan
(Handmade one-off)

20 Junichi Arai
design No. E
materials Polyester
dimensions w 100cm L 400cm
w 39½in L 157½in
manufacturer Kay Tay Co., Japan
(Handmade one-off)

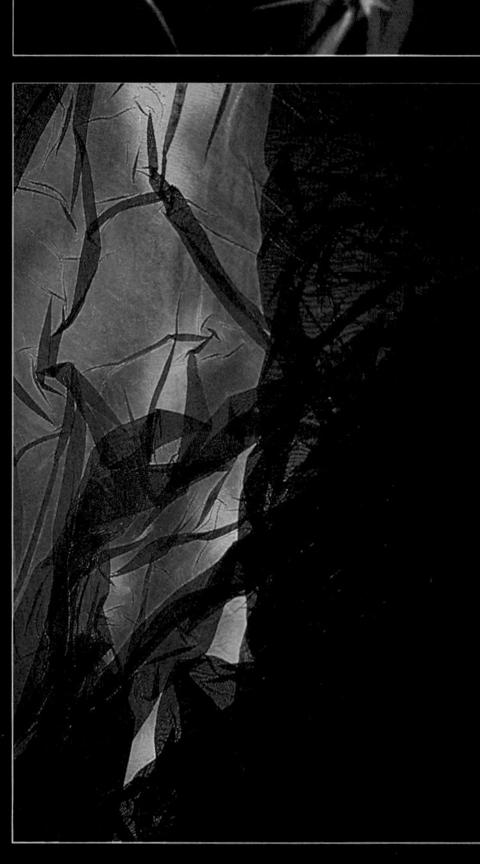

21 Junichi Arai
design No. C
materials Polyester, wool nylon
dimensions w 90cm L 400cm
w 35½in L 157½in
manufacturer Kay Tay Co., Japan
(Handmade one-off)

22 Junichi Arai
design No A
materials Nylon Silk
dimensions w 100cm L 400cm
w 39½in L 157½in
manufacturer Kay Tay Co., Japan
(Handmade one-off)

23 Junichi Arai
design No. D
materials Polyester
dimensions w 65cm L 200cm d 0.1cm
w 25⅝in L 78¾in d ⅛in
manufacturer Kay Tay Co., Japan
(Handmade one-off)

24 Junichi Arai
design No.O
materials Polyester, nylon
dimensions w 100cm L 700cm di 100cm
w 39½in L 276½in di 39½in
manufacturer Itozen Co., Japan
(Limited batch production)

25 Junichi Arai
design No. N
materials Wool, acrylic
dimensions w 90cm L 2,500cm
w 35½in L 987½in
manufacturer Jovian Christie Inc., Japan

26 Junichi Arai
design No. H
materials Polyester
dimensions w 85cm L 90cm
w 33½in L 35½in
manufacturer Kay Tay Co., Japan
(Handmade one-off)

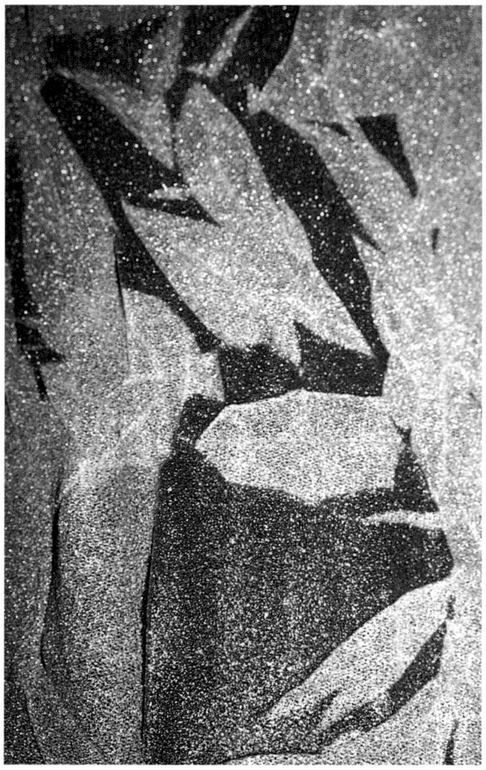

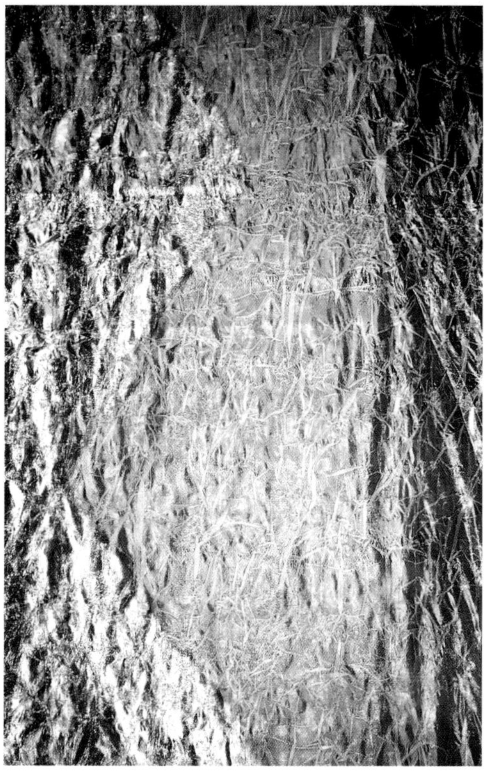

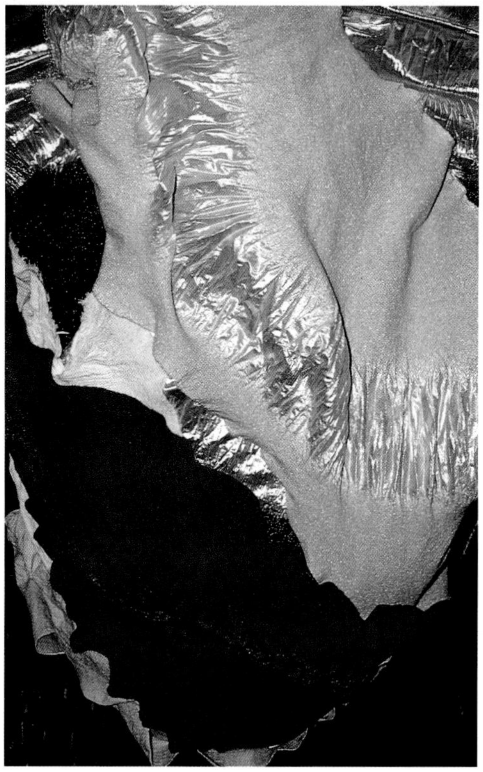

27 Junichi Arai
design No. J
materials Polyester
dimensions w 100cm L 400cm
w 39½in L 157½in
manufacturer Kay Tay Co., Japan
(Handmade limited batch production)

28 Junichi Arai
design No. I
materials Polyester
dimensions w 85cm L 90cm
w 33½in L 35½in
manufacturer Kay Tay Co., Japan
(Handmade one-off)

29 Junichi Arai
design No. L
materials Nylon, wool with aluminium
dimensions w 80cm L 300cm
w 31½in L 119⅛in
manufacturer Kay Tay Co., Japan
(Handmade limited batch production)

31	Junichi Arai
design	No. K
materials	Nylon wool with aluminium
dimensions	w 100cm L 500cm
	w 39½in L 197in
manufacturer	Kay Tay Co., Japan
	(Handmade limited batch production)

above **30**	Junichi Arai
design	No. M
materials	Polyester
dimensions	w 100cm L 2,500cm
	w 39½in L 987½in
manufacturer	Limited batch production

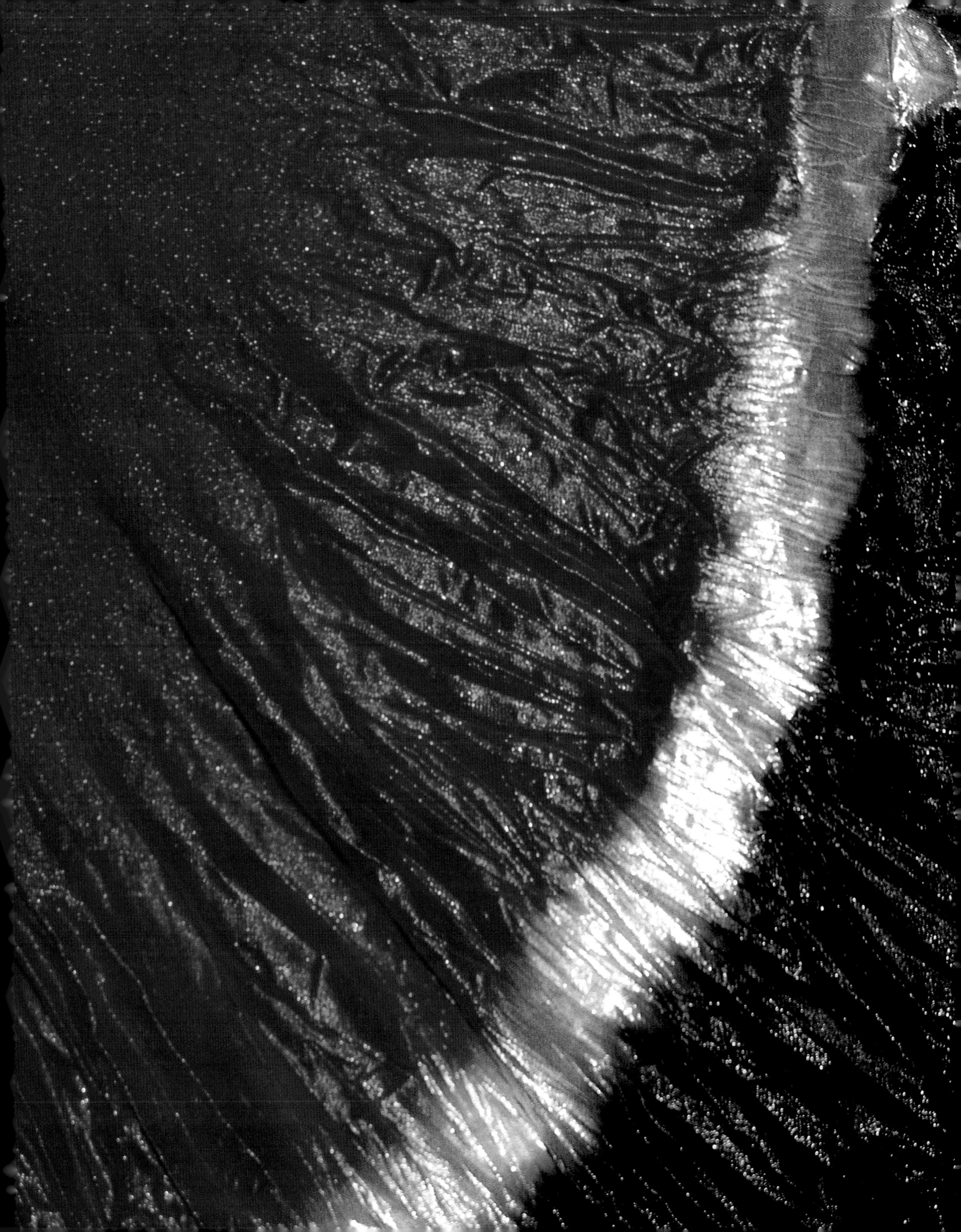

33 Hiroshi Awatsuji
design Michi
materials Cotton
dimensions w 135cm repeat 180cm
w 53⅛in repeat 70⅝in
manufacturer Design House AWA, Japan

34 Hiroshi Awatsuji
design Yuu
materials Cotton
dimensions w 135cm repeat 110cm
w 53⅛in repeat 43⅜in
manufacturer Design House AWA, Japan

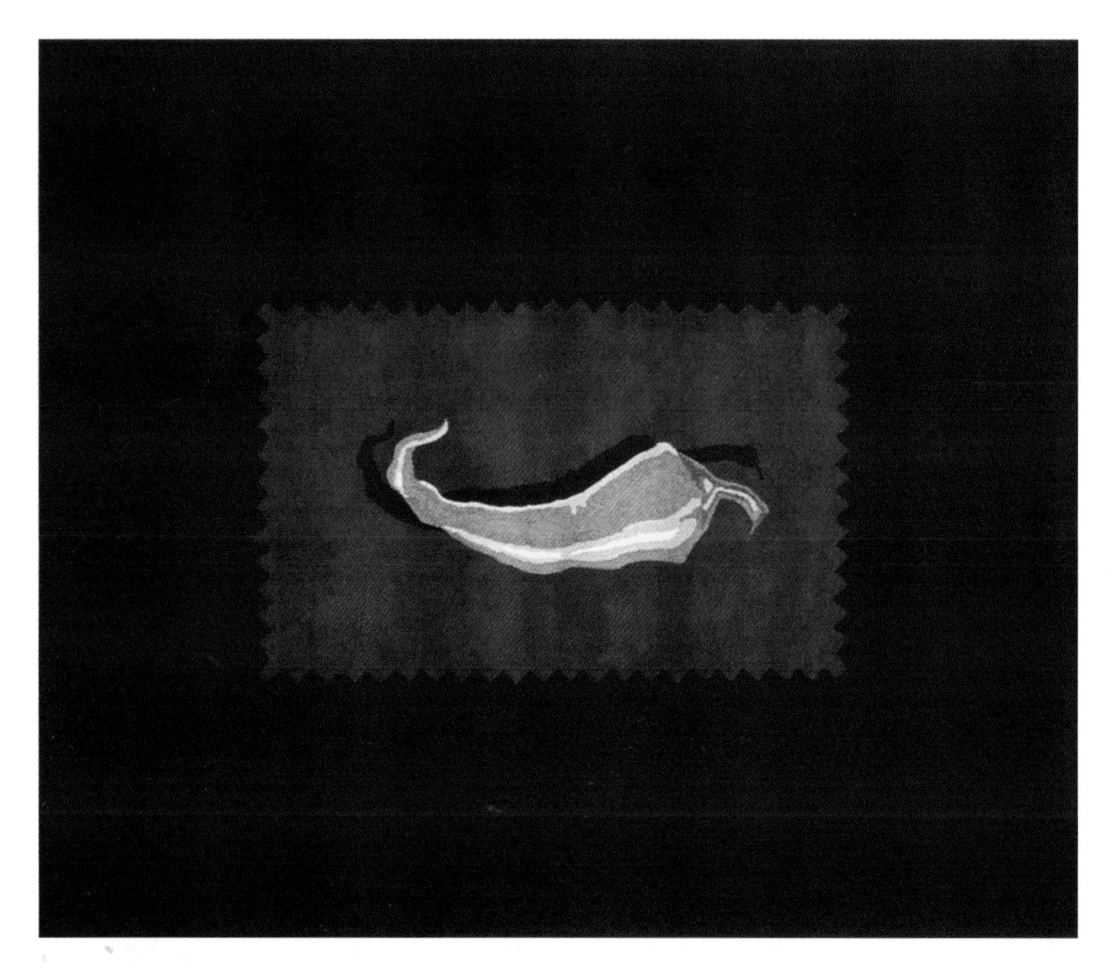

32 Hilton McConnico
design Carpet Pimento
materials Wool
dimensions w 140cm L 200cm
w 78¾in L 98¾in
manufacturer Toulemonde Bochart, France

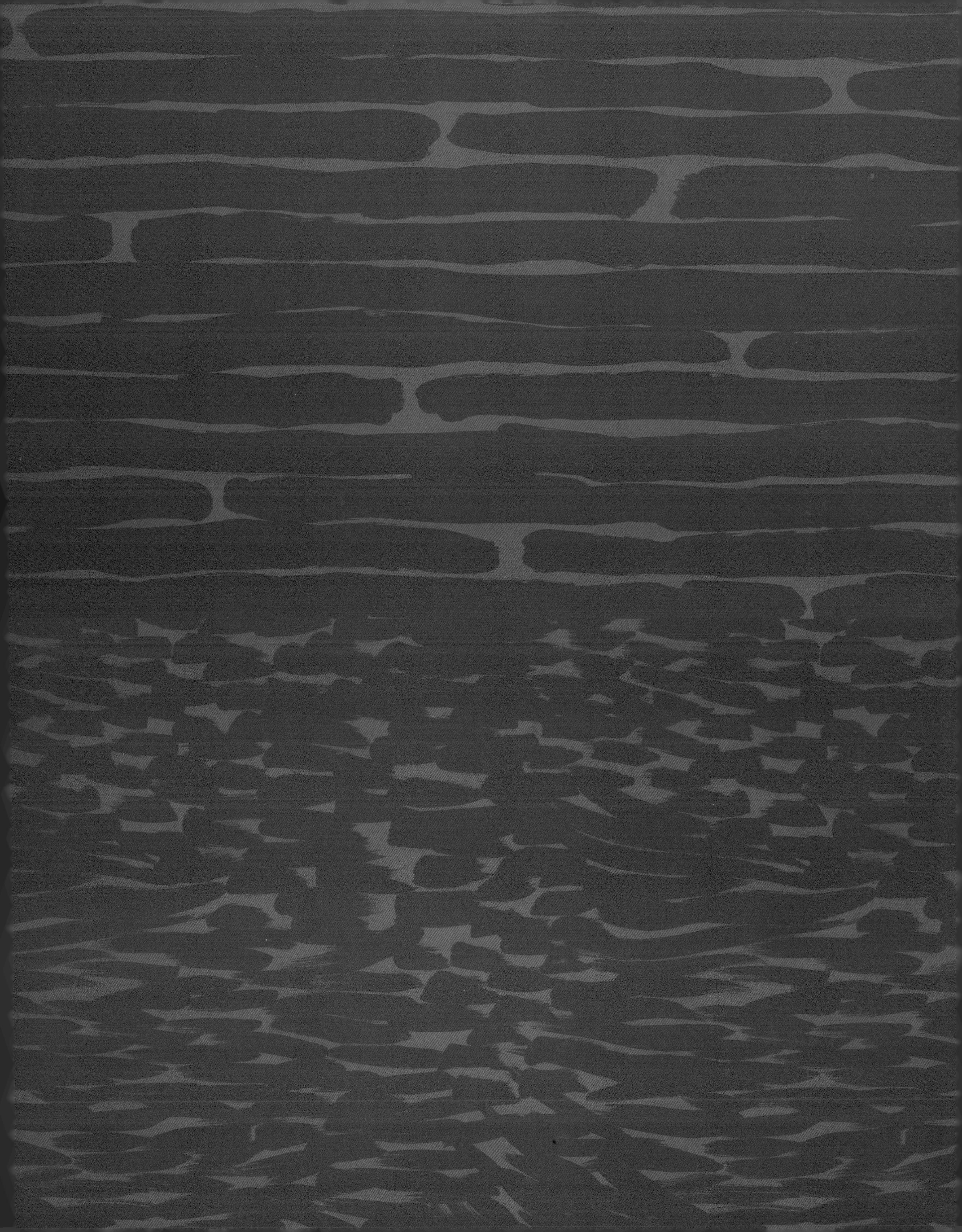

Architraf

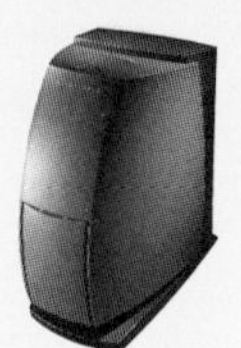

products

The first decade of the International Design Yearbook has shown designers manipulating new design vocabularies such as post-Modernism and deconstructivism, and surviving the white-water race of boom and recession. Much of what came out of the last decade, according to Jean Nouvel, can be left there. It was irrelevant and superficial to the point of meretricious. But also over the last decade designers have been providing their insights and inspirations for a whole new range of product designs - portable telephones, camcorders, laptop and palmtop computers, to mention just a few examples. That many of these new developments have been in the field of electronics is hardly surprising: the electronics industry has been the development boundary of product design for the last decade as well.

In selecting work for this year's Yearbook Nouvel has insisted on technological advance and design quality as his two lodestars. His definition of design quality, as we have already seen, is based on directness of approach, and simplicity of form and function. Scale, weight and colour also play an important role here: decorative values have little or no place, unless as an expression of technological value, as in Michele de Lucchi's experimental projects for Philips and Olivetti. Technological importance also lay behind the selection of products as diverse as the Apple Newton, Arcom's Barryvox rescue system, Virtual Vision's VR Vision glasses or Matsushita's flat vision monitor. Other such products are a new portable Mini-Disc recorder/ player from Panasonic, and Canon's new lightweight cameras. Miniaturization was thus another important theme. Because size is a key value in such products, part of the design brief for this book was to reproduce a certain number of objects (or details) full-size, and to respect relative proportions in sizing related groups of objects.

Well-stated traditional products, particularly those using new materials, were also welcome: Kawasaki's Cano pencil sharpener, for example, Scheuer's simple Paper bin, or Sottsass's new collection of wrist-watches. 'It doesn't matter', Nouvel pointed out during the selection, 'whether an object is familiar, even banal. What we are including are examples of products that form a statement about the aesthetics of our time, and the real nature of contemporary industrial design.'

What became very clear in the process was the contemporary disappearance of the formal barriers between living and work space. In looking at furniture it became apparent how the 'new modesty', the idea of living space as temporary and impermanent, influenced some areas of design, with simple, portable items. The interpenetration of work and living has also widened the range of product designs to consider. For example, Hauser Associates Architstrat, which handles the flow of information to and from computers with the Internet and other information highways, cannot be defined as only for the office, since the highway carries not only work data but entertainment, social and leisure information. Driving to work will soon mean setting off down the infobahn.

So products such as computers, faxes, copiers, phones have a double importance. Not only are they along the current front line of technological development, they are also evidence of the fundamental changes at work in the home, just as the emphasis on portability, target markets and multiplicity of use also highlights different emerging social patterns. In many cities, singles now match or exceed families as a proportion of occupants: as well as creating new markets, this and similar changes (the rise of single parents with children, the increase in the active elderly, the phenomenon of working couples without children) lead to new challenges and opportunities for designers. As Michele de Lucchi has suggested 'design for the home has a meaning not when it isolates the theme of the home, but when it makes it interact with a whole series of other issues, making it a point of intersection in a cultural debate.' Product design, along with furniture and lighting, has an important place in suggesting new scenarios for the home, new pointers to the ways we can live.

right **3** Apple Computers
design Hand computer Newton
materials Plastic, glass
dimensions h 20.2cm w 10.6cm d 3.1cm
h 8in w 4in d 1⅛in
manufacturer Apple Comptuters, UK

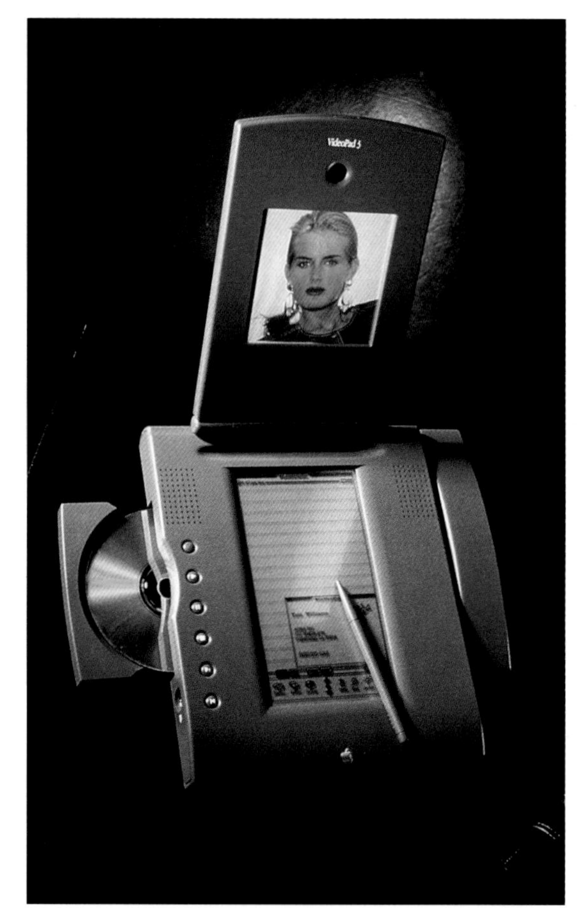

1 David Laituri of Lunar Design, Bob Brunner of
right **3** Apple Computers
design Newton Message Pad
materials Plastic, glass
dimensions h 20.2cm w 10.6cm d 3.1cm
h 8in w 4in d 1⅛in
manufacturer Apple Computers, UK

below **2** David Laituri of Lunar Design, Ray Riley of Apple
design Child's personal assistant Kids' Newton
materials ABS
dimensions h 3cm w 17.5cm L 26cm
h 1⅛in w 6⅞in L 10¼in
manufacturer Apple Computers, USA
(Prototype)

The Apple Newton is one of a new generation of computers to break away from the keyboard as a main input device. It is designed to read handwritten messages and convert them into computable data, for transfer to a PC, to a printer or for transmission by fax. As such, it opens up new possibilities and new markets - indeed it is ahead of some of its markets. For example, it has potential as a computer accessible by children, an application studied here by Apple and Lunar Design.

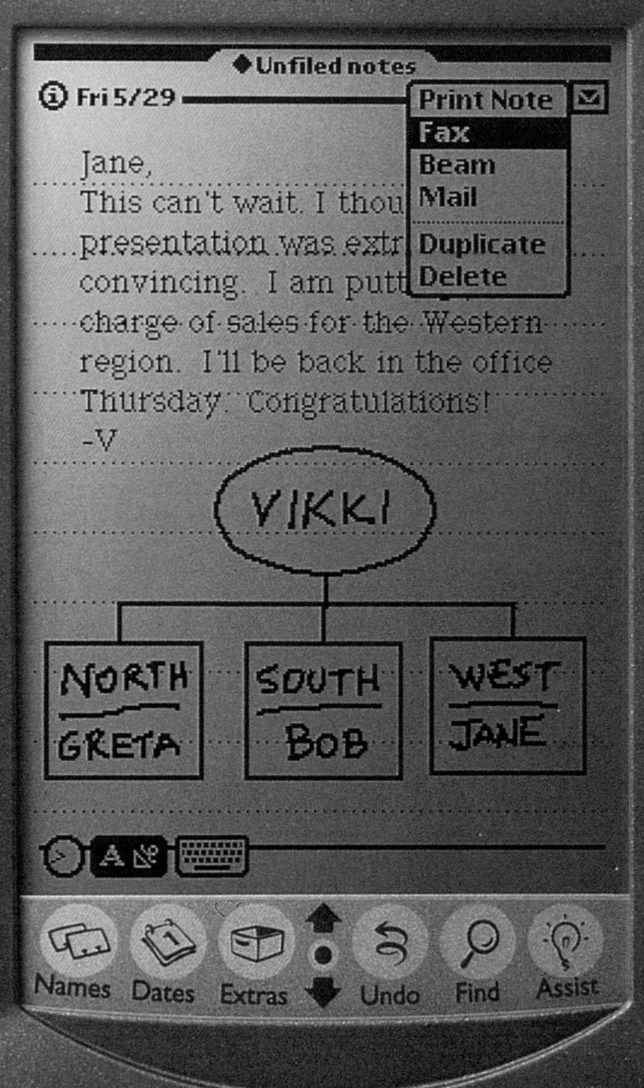
Unfiled notes
Fri 5/29
Print Note
Fax
Beam
Mail
Duplicate
Delete
Jane,
This can't wait. I thou
presentation was extr
convincing. I am putt
charge of sales for the Western
region. I'll be back in the office
Thursday. Congratulations!
-V
VIKKI
NORTH
GRETA
SOUTH
BOB
WEST
JANE
Names
Dates
Extras
Undo
Find
Assist

MessagePad

5 Shinichi Sumikawa
design Multi media information collection device Memo Book
materials Plastic, aluminium
dimensions h 3.6cm w 18cm L 10cm
h 1⅜in w 7⅛in L 4in
manufacturer Fujitsu, Japan
(Prototype)

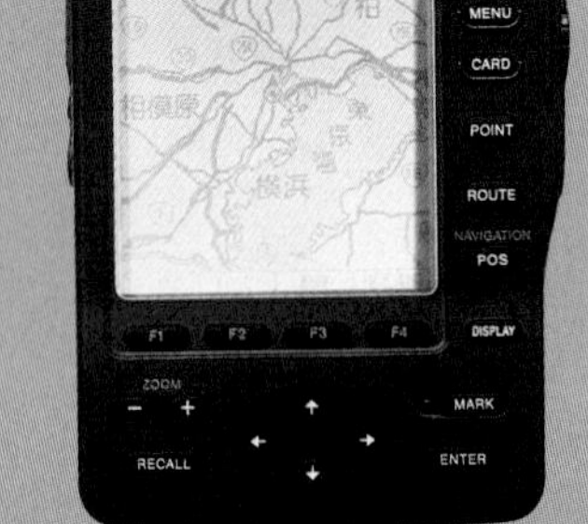

4 Sony Corporation Design Centre
design Handy Map PYXIS IPS-760
materials Plastic
dimensions h 23cm w 11cm d 3.4cm
h 9in w 4¾in d 1⅝in
manufacturer Sony Corporation, Japan

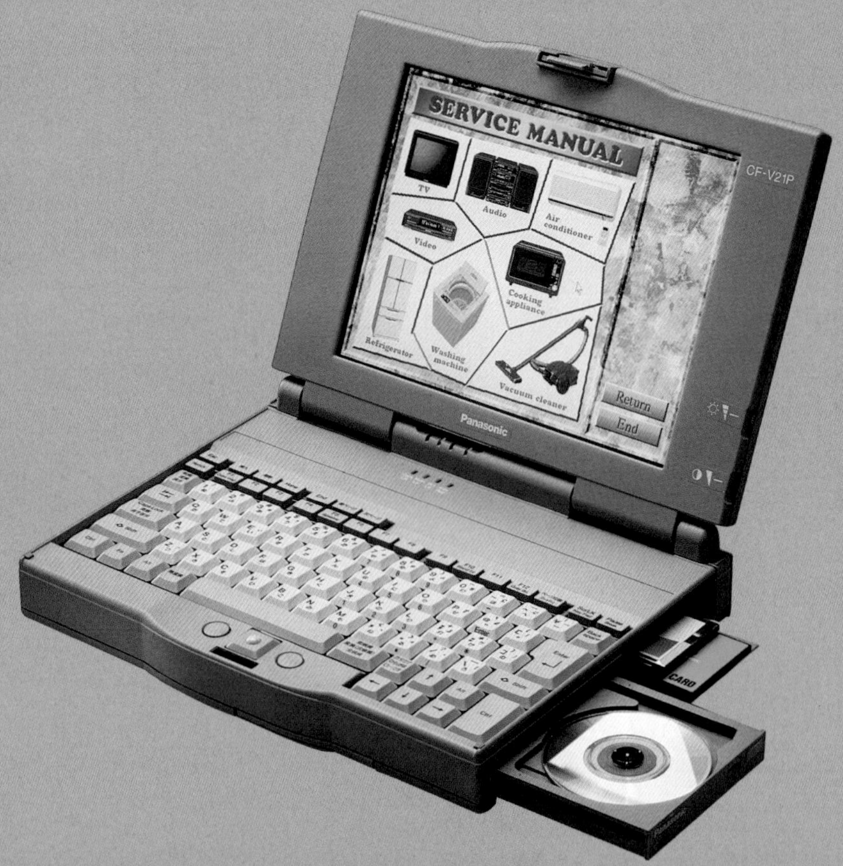

6 Computer Design Department
design Notebook Computer Panasonic CF-V21P
materials ABS
dimensions h 5.4cm w 29.7cm L 22cm
h 2⅛in w 11¾in L 8⅝in
manufacturer Matsushita Electric Industiral Co. Ltd., Japan

7 Sony Corporation Design Centre
design Electronic book Data Discman DD-20
materials Plastic
dimensions h 4cm w 16.6cm d 11.3cm
h 1½in w 6½in d 4½in
manufacturer Sony Corporation, Japan

8	S. G. Hauser Associates Inc.
	(Edward Cruz, Shaun Fynn, Vince Razo, Barry Sween)
design	Information processor The Archistrat & Workstation
materials	Aluminium extrusions and casting, sheet metal, RIM housing
dimensions	h 61cm w 38cm L 55.9cm
	h 24in w 15in L 22in
manufacturer	Archistrat Systems, USA
	(Limited batch production)

9	S. G. Hauser Associates Inc.
	(Edward Hoard, David Cruz, Vince Razo)
design	Computer Modem PC 288 LCD
materials	ABS blend/injection moulded plastic
dimensions	h 18.5cm w 7.5cm L 9.4cm
	h 7¼in w 3in L 3¾in
manufacturer	Practical Peripherals, USA

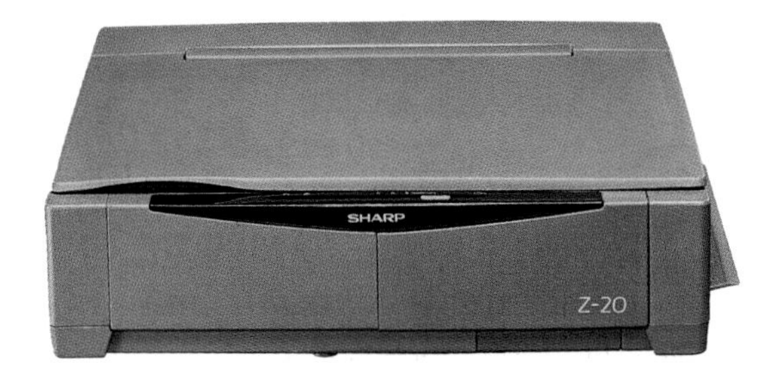

10 Sharp Corporation Printing & Reprographic Systems Design Group
design Plain paper copier Z-20
materials Plastic
dimensions h 10cm w 36.3cm L 35.5cm
h 3⅞in w 14¼in L 14in
manufacturer Sharp Corporation, Japan

11 Yoshihito Saitou
design Optical Time Domain Reflectometer MW9070A
materials Magnesium, ABS, rubber
dimensions h 19.5cm w 25.4cm d 7cm
h 17¾in w 10¾in d 2¾in
manufacturer Anritsu Corporation, Japan

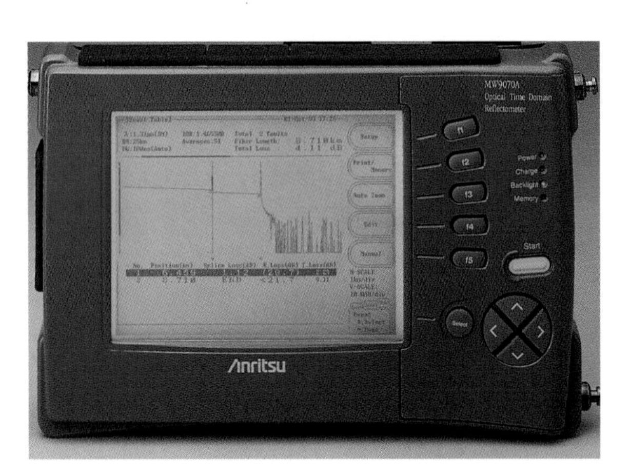

12 S. G. Hauser Associates Inc. (John von Buelow, Kevin Clay, Karel Slovacek)
design Satellite telecommunication terminal Act One
materials ABS moulded plastic, sheet metal
dimensions h 7cm w 43.2cm L 35.5cm
h 2¼in w 17in L 14in
manufacturer Ark Telecom, USA

13 Sharp Corporation Information Systems Design Group

design Computer Japanese word processor

materials ABS plastic

dimensions h 8.6cm w 36.8cm L 38.7cm

h 3⅜in w 14½in L 15¼in

manufacturer Sharp Corporation, Japan

14 Sharp Corporation Electronic Components Design Group
design Computer projection panel QA-350
materials ABS plastic
dimensions h 5.6cm w 36.5cm L 31.6cm
h 2⅛in w 14½in L 12⅜in
manufacturer Sharp Corporation, Japan

15 Max Yoshimoto, Kyle Swen of Lunar Design
design Networking peripheral Ether Wave
materials Cyclopolycarbonate, ABS
dimensions h 9.2cm w 9.2cm d 3.3cm
h 3⅝in w 3⅝in d 1¼in
manufacturer Farallon Computing, USA

16 Matsushita Electric Design Department
design Flat Vision Monitor
materials ABS resin, glass
dimensions h 28.3cm w 36.5cm d 8cm
h 11⅛in w 14⅜in d 3⅛in
manufacturer Matsushita Electric Industrial Co. Ltd., Japan
(Prototype)

Flat vision monitors are a major technical and engineering innovation. They offer new opportunities for television and home entertainment systems, and in the workplace propose different ways of handling information. No longer is the user tied to a vertical screen taking up a cube of desk space, as the monitor can be laid flat among papers or mounted into a drawing-board, beside designs and diagrams. As with other electronic products, the saving in size inherent in flat vision monitors is not only a technological feat, but empowers the user to adapt the working environment to personal taste and preference.

top **17** Sharp Corporation TV & Video Design Group
design Camcorder Viewcam VL-H400U
materials ABS plastic
dimensions h 15.5cm w 20.1cm L 9.1cm
h 6⅛in w 8¼in L 3½in
manufacturer Sharp Corporation, Japan

18 Sony Corporation Design Centre
design Handycam Comixs CCD-SC7
materials ABS plastic
dimensions h 15.3cm w 10.5cm d 8.5cm
h 6½in w 4⅛in d 3⅜in
manufacturer Sony Corporation, Japan

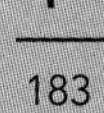

19 Philips Corporate Design
design LCD Projector LCP 5000
materials ABS
dimensions h 14cm w 16.7cm L 7.2cm
h 5½in w 6½in L 2⅞in
manufacturer Marantz Japan Inc. for Philips
The LCD projector coverts video or computer generated images for projection onto a large screen.

20 Mamoru Shiozaki
design Movie camera S85
materials Plastics
dimensions h 11.7cm w 11.2cm L 21.6cm
h 4⅝in w 4½in L 8½in
manufacturer Matsushita Electric Industrial Co. Ltd., Japan

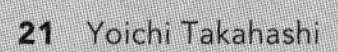

21 Yoichi Takahashi
design Movie Camera MS4/M40
materials Plastic
dimensions h 24.5cm w 13cm L 45.9cm
h 9⅝in w 5⅛in L 18⅛in
manufacturer Matsushita Electric Industrial Co. Ltd., Japan

22 Mamoru Shiozaki
design Movie camera R50
materials Plastics
dimensions h 11.8cm w 7.6cm L 23.5cm
h 4⅝in w 3in L 9¼in
manufacturer Matsushita Electric Industrial Co. Ltd., Japan

23 Matsushita Design Centre
design Camcorder PV-IQ404
materials Plastic, steel
dimensions h 11.7cm w 10.2cm L 17.4cm
h 4½in w 4⅛in L 6⅞in
manufacturer Matsushita-Kotobuki Electronics Industries Ltd., Japan

24 Sony Corporation Design Centre
design Waterproof mini colour TV FDL-KB31
materials ABS plastic
dimensions h 11.9cm w 6.8cm d 8.5cm
h 4⅝in w 2⅝in d 3⅜in
manufacturer Sony Corporation, Japan

25 Matsushita Design Centre
design Audio/Video Multi 14in TV TH-14AVI
materials Plastic, steel
dimensions h 42cm w 41cm d 39.3cm
h 16½in w 16⅛in d 15½in
manufacturer Matsushita-Kotobuki Electronics Industries Ltd., Japan

26 Sharp Corporation TV & Video Systems Design Group
design Wide screen video TV VT-24WS1
materials Plastic
dimensions h 46.2cm w 66.4cm L 45.5cm
h 18¼in w 26½in L 17⅞in
manufacturer Sharp Corporation, Japan

27 Yoshihito Saitou
design Digital radio test bed MS8604A
materials Polycarbonate, steel sheet, rubber
dimensions h 22cm w 42.5cm d 45cm
h 8¾in w 16¾in d 17¾in
manufacturer Anritsu Corporation, Japan

28 Philips Corporate Design
design Television GR 2.3
materials Polystyrene, glass
dimensions h 49cm d 47cm w 68.5cm
h 19¼in d 18½in w 27in
manufacturer Philips Electronique Grand Public, France

29 Philips Corporate Design
design Television Sensuval
materials Polystyrene, glass
dimensions h 60cm L 59cm w 61cm
h 23½in L 23in w 24in
manufacturer Philips SpA, Italy

30 S. G. Hauser Associates Inc.
(Edward Cruz, Ernesto Quinteros, Matias Ocana)
design Handheld voice activated VCR controller
materials ABS polycarbonate, santoprene
dimensions h 5cm w 1.7cm L 19cm
h 2in w ¾in L 7½in
manufacturer Voice Powered Technology, USA

Voice activation and input is already being developed for computer systems, and its wider application will be one of the major innovations of the future. Here the technology is applied to the simpler context of programming and controlling a video cassette recorder: its vocabulary includes the useful command 'zap!' to skip over commercial breaks! The choice of the name Magic Wand (right) is also a neat reminder of the key role sociologists have marked for the remote control unit in inter-family relations: in the future having one's finger on the button may be less important that having the loudest voice!

32 S. G. Hauser Associates Inc.
design Voice activated VCR controller Magic Wand
materials ABS injection moulded plastic
dimensions h 4cm w 2.5cm L 17.8cm
h 1½in w 1in L 7in
manufacturer Voice Powered Technology, USA

below **33** Philips Corporate Design
design Remote control RC 82
materials ABS
dimensions h 15cm w 2.7cm L 6cm
h 6in w 1⅛in L 2⅜in
manufacturer Philips Remote Control Systems, Belgium

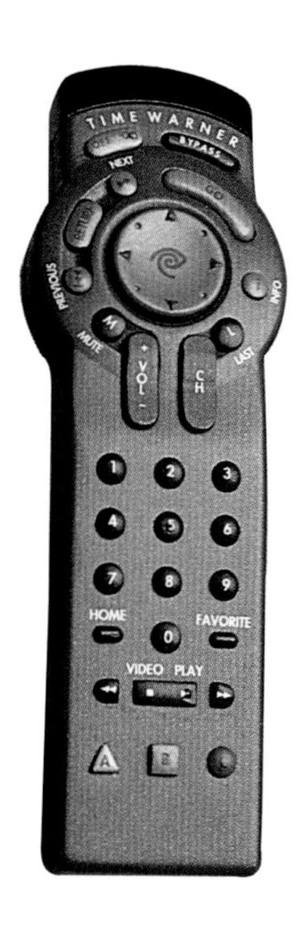

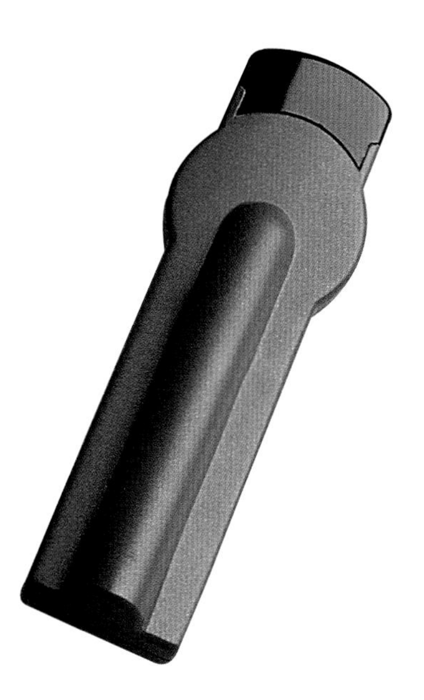

31 Doug Patten, Brandt Thompson for Patton Design
design VCR controller SG1 remote
materials ABS
dimensions h 17.7cm w 4.6cm d 1.6cm
h 7in w 1¾in d ¾in
manufacturer Time-Warner / Silicon Graphics

34 Lamberto Angelini
design TV control protection Bodyguard
materials Polyurethane
dimensions h 2.5cm w 7cm L 15cm
h 1in w 2¾in L 6in
manufacturer Meliconi SpA, Italy

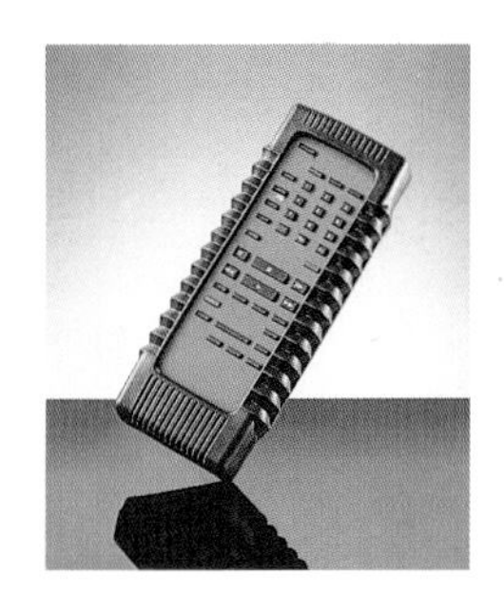

35 Nelson Au
design Virtual Reality headset Sega VR
materials Injection-moulded plastic
dimensions h 15cm w 19cm d 29cm
h 6in w 7½in d 11⅝in
manufacturer Sega of America, Inc., USA

36 Paul Bradley
design Input device Cyberman
materials Recyclable ABS thermoplastic
dimensions h 7.5cm w 17cm d 19cm
h 3in w 6⅝in d 7½in
manufacturer Logitech Inc., USA

This headset solves the problem of whether to go the beach or the ball-game. Externally it resembles a pair of sunglasses with a walkman attached. In fact, on the inside of one lens a miniature television image is projected, the signal fed from an aerial on the walkman. So you can sit on the beach *and* see the ballgame. As a leisure product its success was limited, but it is now being re-developed as an information and training device.

37 Virtual Vision, Inc
design Video headset Virtual Vision
materials Injection moulded polycarbonate, nylon, santaprene, rubberized coating with silk screened graphics
dimensions Eye-wear: h 9cm w 18cm d 17cm
h 3½in w 7⅛in d 6⅝in
Belt-pack: w 4.5cm h 9cm d 12cm
w 1¾in h 3½in d 4¾in
manufacturer Virtual Vision, Inc., USA

38	Canon Design Team
design	Camera Prima Super 115
materials	Plastics, aluminium
dimensions	h 7cm w 13cm L 6cm
	h 2¾in w 5½in L 2⅜in
manufacturer	Canon Inc, Japan

Jean Nouvel picked the Canon Prima as summing up a trend in product design towards compactness, lightness and complexity. It is both a technically superior camera and simple to use. Its clean exterior lines belie the sophisticated engineering beneath, which include auto-focus, zoom, and anti-red-eye flash. The product semantics of the design convey this to the user, and for Nouvel this kind of user-empowerment is a key factor in contemporary design.

40 Canon Design Team
design Water-proof camera Prima As-1
materials Plastics
dimensions h 8.8cm w 13.3cm d 5.6cm
h 3½in w 5½in d 2⅛in
manufacturer Canon Inc, Japan

39 John Betts
design Single lens reflex camera Polaroid Vision Date
materials Injection moulded plastic
dimensions h 5.8cm w 9.6cm L 22.3cm
h 2⅜in w 3¾in L 8¾in
manufacturer Polaroid Corporation, USA

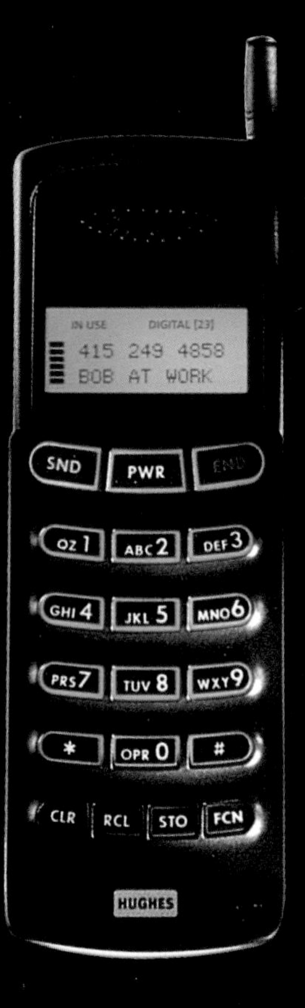

41 Marlan Polhemus
design Cellphone Cellular portable phone USA 777
materials Polycarbonate and silicone plastics
dimensions h 15cm w 5.8cm d 2.5cm
h 6in w 2¼in d 1in
manufacturer Omni Cellular Ltd., USA
(Prototype)

42 Mark Biasotti
design Cellphone Hughes Digital Cellular Phone
materials Recyclable ABS blend-injected moulded plastic, silicon rubber key technology
dimensions h 17cm w 5.9cm d 2.1cm
h 6⅝in w 2⅜in d ⅞in
manufacturer Hughes Network Systems, USA

43 Steve McGugan, Harry Haun, Sally Beardsley for Steve McGugan Industrial Design
design Pocket telephone Beocom 9500
materials Plastic, magnesium
dimensions w 5cm L 13cm d 2.5cm
w 2in L 5⅛in d 1in
manufacturer Bang & Olufsen Technology A/S, Denmark

44 Marc Tanner, Peter Spreenberg, Alison Black
design Flip phone Mercury One to One M33 Mobile Phone
materials Injection-moulded plastic, rubber keyboard
dimensions w 5.8cm L 14cm d 3.9cm
w 2⅜in L 5⅞in d 1⅛in
manufacturer Mercury Personal Communications, UK

45 Tucker Viemeister, Stuart Harvey Lee, David Hales for Smart Design
design Home Phone
materials Injection-moulded ABS plastic, silicon
dimensions h 8.9cm w 9.4cm L 23cm
h 3½in w 3¾in L 9in
manufacturer Cicena, USA

46 Marc Tanner, Philip Davies, Colin Burns
design Personal emergency response LifeLine 8500
materials ABS
dimensions h 6.3cm L 21.5cm d 21.5cm
h 2½in L 8½in d 8½in
manufacturer LifeLine Systems Inc., USA

47 Matsushita Design Centre
design Home cordless telephone VE-D60J
materials ABS plastic
dimensions h 8.5cm w 18.6cm d 21.1cm
h 3⅜in w 7⅜in d 8¼in
manufacturer Matsushita Communication Industrial Co. Ltd., Japan

48 Ascom Corporate Industrial Design
design Electronic locating device Barryvox
materials Makrolon 8325
dimensions w 7.5cm L 13.5cm d 2.3cm
w 3in L 5¾in d ⅞in
manufacturer Ascom Radiocom AG., Switzerland

The Barryvox is designed for use by skiers, as a rescue device in case of avalanche. Research shows that it is rare for a whole group to be caught by an avalanche, but also that speed of response is essential if lives are to be saved. Finding buried victims quickly is therefore important. Using the Barryvox, each member of a group wears one of the combined receiver/transmitters, set to transmit. In the event of an avalanche, the survivors switch to receive and use the device's direction finding system to locate their companions.

49 Matsushita Design Centre
design Car audio CQ-AV100D
materials ABS
dimensions h 10cm w 17.8cm d 15.5cm
h 4in w 7in d 6⅛in
manufacturer Matsushita Communication Industrial Co., Ltd., Japan

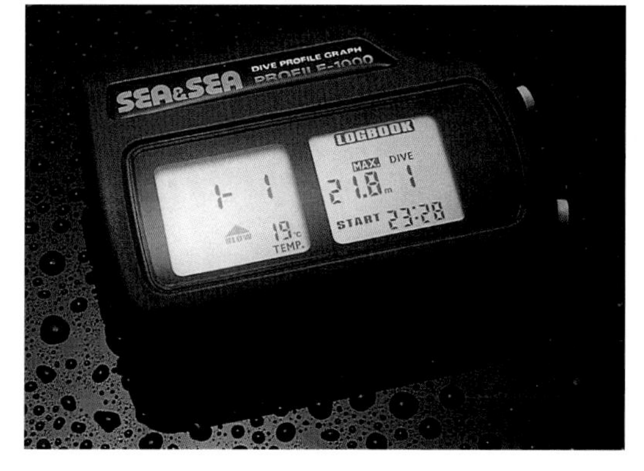

50 Shinichi Sumikawa
design Diving computer Profile-1000
materials Plastic
dimensions h 3cm w 7.2cm L 10.1cm
h 1⅛in w 2⅞in L 4in
manufacturer Sea & Sea, Japan

51 Ken Mori and Doug Patton for Patton Design
design Amplifier Soundstream Crossover
materials Aluminium
dimensions w 17.9cm L 25.5cm
w 7in L 10in
manufacturer Patton Design, USA

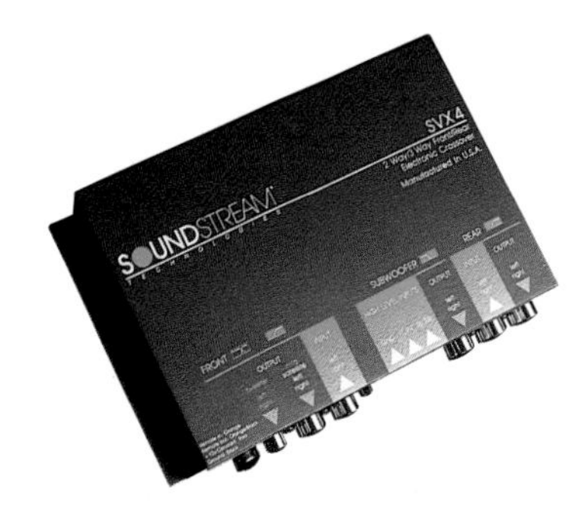

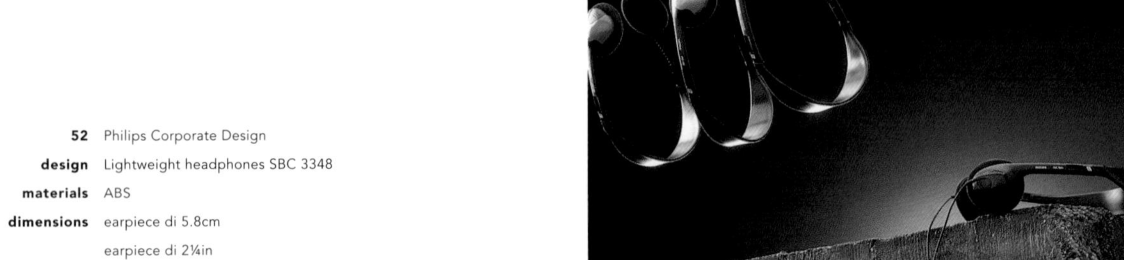

52 Philips Corporate Design
design Lightweight headphones SBC 3348
materials ABS
dimensions earpiece di 5.8cm
earpiece di 2¼in
manufacturer Philips Tapes & Accessories, The Netherlands

53 Ken Mori and Doug Patton for Patton Design
design Soundstream Amplifier
materials Formed sheet metal
dimensions w 16cm L 10cm
w 6¾in L 4in
manufacturer Patton Design, USA

54 Yamaha Product Design Laboratory
design Recording console MTX 8
materials ABS plastic
dimensions w 61cm L 44.5cm
w 24in L 17½in
manufacturer Yamaha Corporation, Japan

Yamaha here extend their well-known craftsmanship in traditional musical instruments to electronic music. The Drum trigger system can be played like a traditional drum kit, with snare, side and bass drums and cymbals, but the sound is handled and output electronically through the control unit on the right.

55 Yamaha Product Design Laboratory
design Drum trigger system TMX. EP75.
materials TMS Output system: Aluminium, steel
dimensions h 4.4cm w 48cm d 26cm
h 3¾in w 18⅞in d 10¼in
materials EP75 (snare drum): Aluminium, rubber
dimensions h 10.5cm di 21cm
h 4⅛in di 8¼in
manufacturer Yamaha Corporation, Japan

56 Sony Corporation Design Centre
design Speaker system SRS-N100
materials ABS plastic
dimensions h 9cm w 11cm d 7.5cm
h 3½in w 4⅜in d 3in
manufacturer Sony Corporation, Japan

57 ninaber/peters/krouwel industrial design
design World radio receiver Yachtboy 500
materials ABS
dimensions h 3.8cm w 11.2cm L 18.5cm
h 1½in w 4½in L 7¼in
manufacturer Grundig AG, Germany

58 Koji Mochizuki
design Compact audio system SC-CH150
materials ABS, BMC
dimensions h 25cm w 51cm d 27.2cm
h 9⅞in w 20⅛in d 10⅝in
manufacturer Matsushita Electric Industrial Co. Ltd., Japan

60 Kondo Osamu
design Stereo radio cassette recorder with CD player RX-DT75
materials Plastic
dimensions h 19.2cm w 68cm d 28.4cm
h 7½in w 26¾in d 11⅛in
manufacturer Matsushita Electric Industrial Co. Ltd., Japan

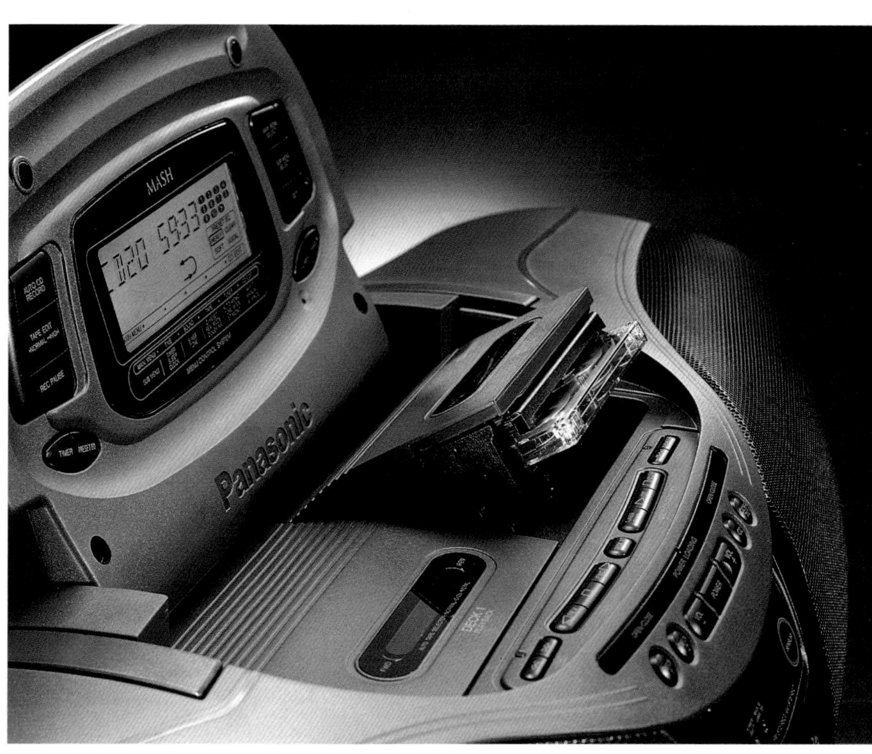

59 Sony Corporation Design Centre
design Radio with telescope X-sight
materials ABS plastic
dimensions h 12.7cm w 11cm d 41.7cm
h 5in w 4⅜in d 16⅜in
manufacturer Sony Corporation, Japan

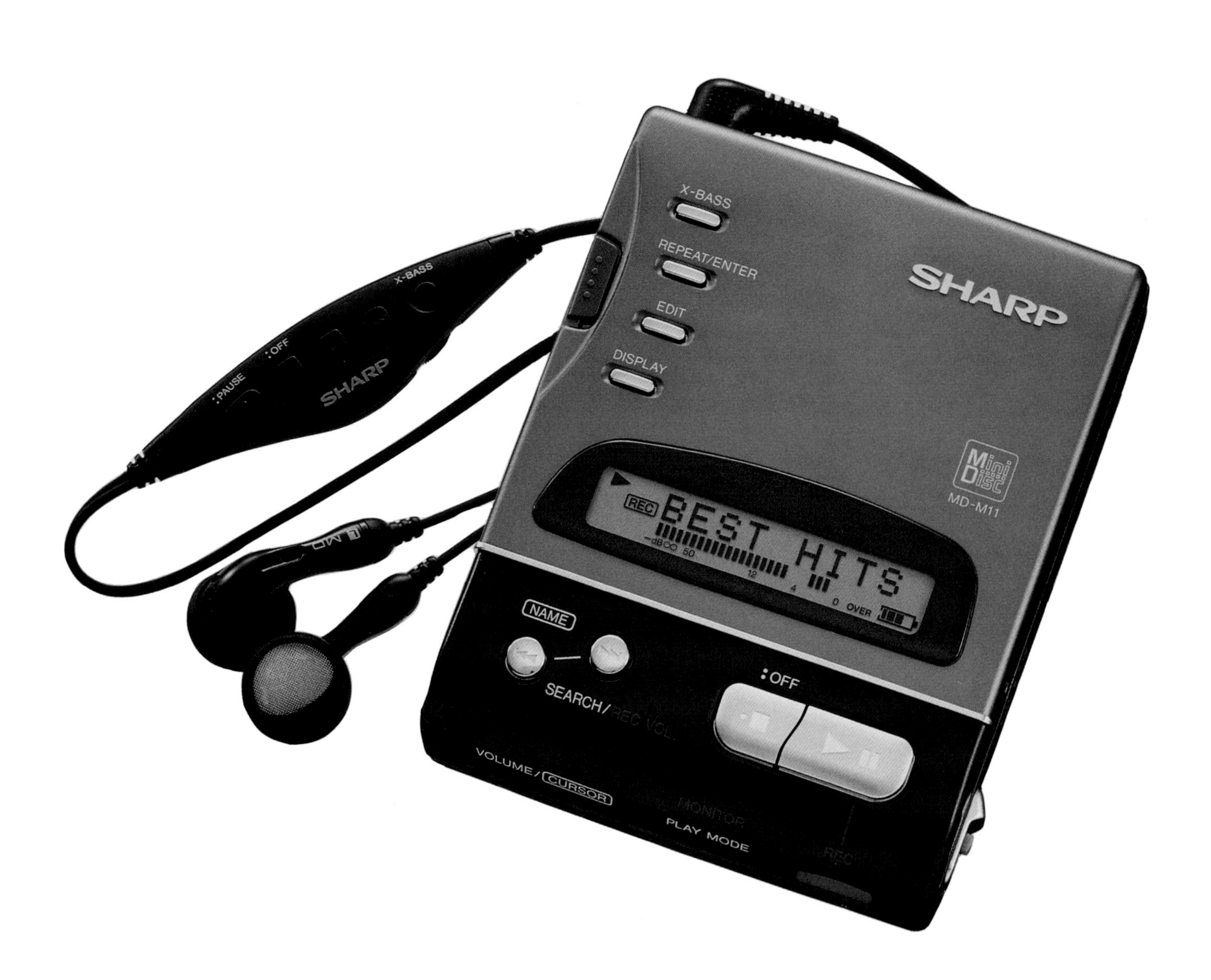

61 Sharp Corporation Communication and Audio Systems Design Group
design MD recorder MD-M11
materials ABS plastic
dimensions h 10.6cm w 8.4cm L 2.9cm
h 4¼in w 3¼in L 1⅛in
manufacturer Sharp Corporation, Japan

62 Sony Corporation Design Centre
design Walkman FX808
materials ABS plastic
dimensions h 7.75cm w 10.9cm d 23.8cm
h 3⅛in w 4¼in d 9⅜in
manufacturer Sony Corporation, Japan

63 Hirose Ryuichiro
design Personal stereo casssette player
with remote control RQ-S95
materials Aluminium, plastic
dimensions h 2.9cm w 10.9cm d 2.6cm
h 1⅛in w 4¼in d 1½in
manufacturer Matsushita Electric Industrial Co. Ltd., Japan

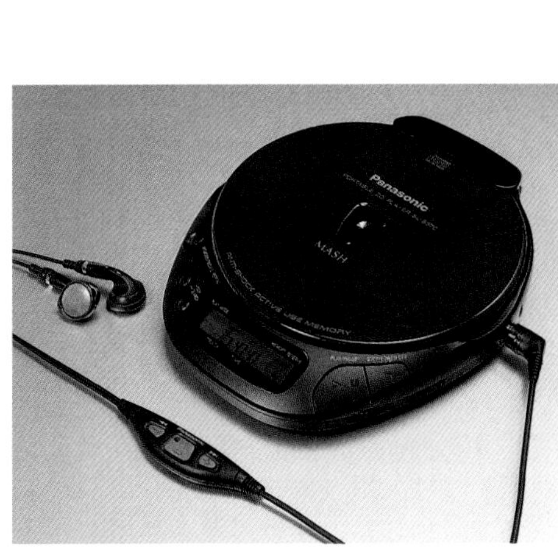

64 Sony Corporation Design Centre
design Disc-man D-223
materials ABS plastic
dimensions h 2.7cm w 10.9cm d 15.1cm
h 1⅛in w 5¼in d 6in
manufacturer Sony Corporation, Japan

65 Kiyoshi Suzuki
design Portable CD player SL-S570/SL-S670
materials Plastic
dimensions h 3cm w 14cm d 17.2cm
h 1⅛in w 5½in d 6¾in
manufacturer Matsushita Electric Industrial Co. Ltd., Japan

66 Sony Corporation Design Centre
design CD players MZ-E2, MZR2
materials ABS plastic
dimensions Max size 10.6 cm
Max size 4¼in
manufacturer Sony Corporation, Japan

67	Michele de Lucchi with Hagai Shvadron
design	Portable computer Echos
materials	Plastic, rubber
dimensions	h 4cm w 21.6cm L 28.6cm
	h 1½in w 8½in L 11¼in
manufacturer	Ing. C.Olivetti & C. SpA, Italy

68 Michele de Lucchi
design Portable computer Philos
materials Plastic
dimensions h 4.1cm w 21.7cm L 29cm
h 1⅝in w 8½in L 11in
manufacturer Ing. C. Olivetti & C. SpA, Italy

69 Michele de Lucchi with James Irvine
design Keyboard Computer Keyboard
materials Plastic
dimensions h 1.8cm w 14.8cm L 45.7cm
h ¾in w 5⅞in L 18in
manufacturer Ing C. Olivetti & C. SpA, Italy

70 Michele de Lucchi with Mario Trimarchi
design Computer tower SNX
materials Plastic, metal
dimensions h 64.3cm w 43.2cm L 19cm
h 25¼in w 17in L 7½in
manufacturer Ing. C. Olivetti & C. SpA, Italy

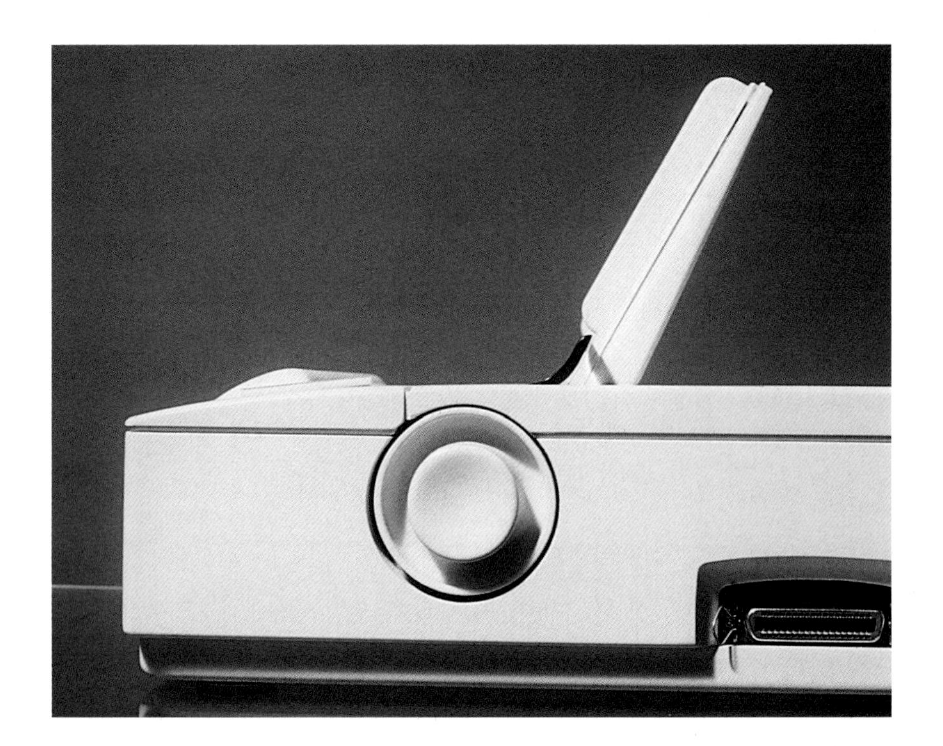

top **71** Michele de Lucchi
design Computer OM 119
materials Plastic
dimensions h 8.1cm w 21cm L 29cm
h 3⅛in w 8⅛in L 11¼in
manufacturer Ing. C.Olivetti & C. SpA, Italy

72 Michele de Lucchi with Mario Trimarchi
design Computer Desk Top Tin M6
materials Plastic, metal
dimensions h 15.9cm w 41.5cm L 37.2cm
h 6¼in w 16⅜in L 14⅝in
manufacturer Ing. C.Olivetti & C. SpA, Italy

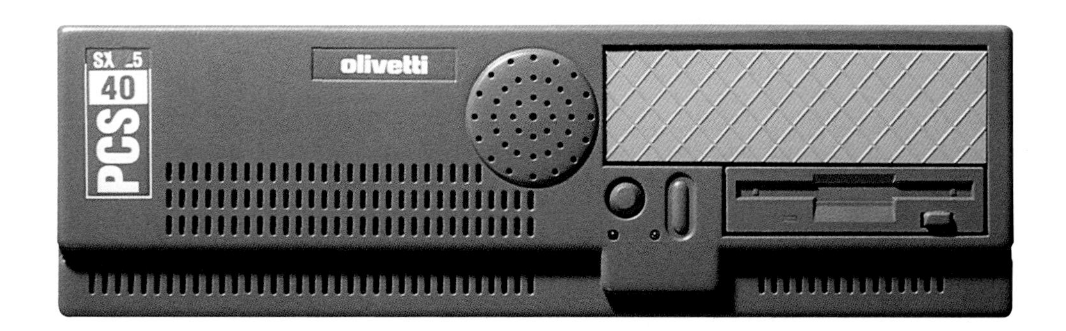

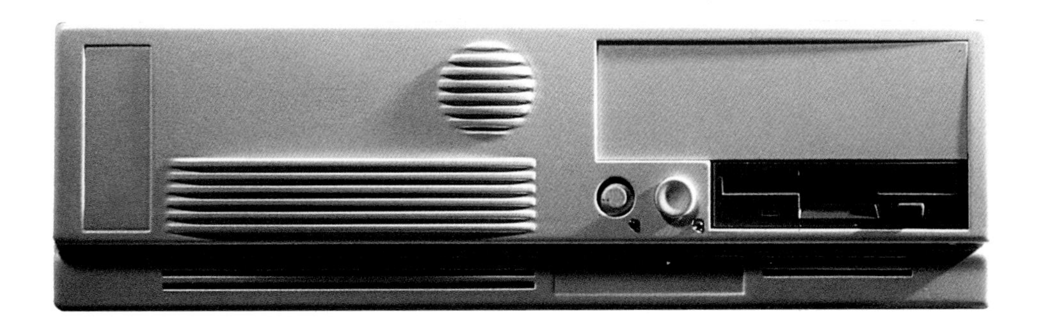

73, 74, 75 Michele de Lucchi with Mario Trimarchi

design Computer Desk Top Tin M4, Tin Slim M4, Tin Slim M6

materials Plastic, metal

dimensions h 11.1cm w 41.5cm L 37.2cm

h 4¾in w 16⅜in L 14½in

manufacturer Ing. C. Olivetti & C. SpA, Italy

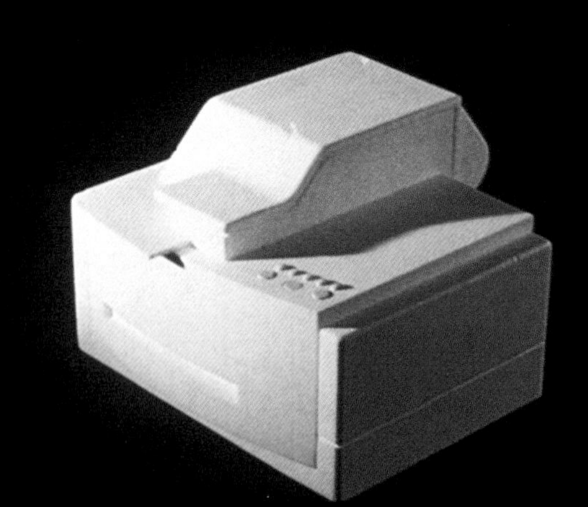

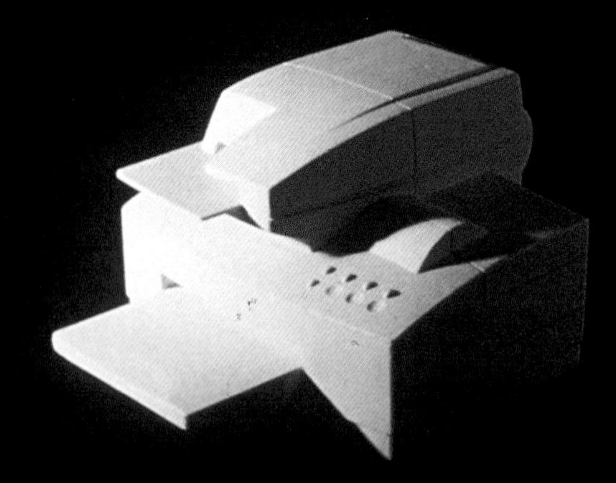

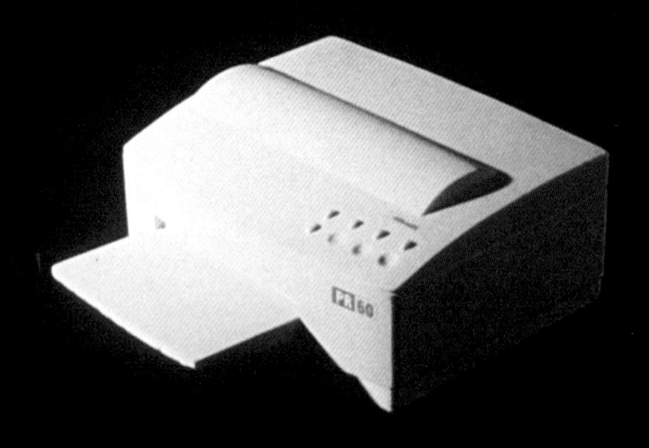

76 Michele de Lucchi with Alessandro Chairato
design Computer printer DPS 6000, DPS 6500
materials ABS plastic, metal
dimensions h 32cm w 45cm L 48cm
h 12½in w 17¾in L 18⅞in
manufacturer Ing. G. Olivetti & C. SpA, Italy

77 Michele de Lucchi with Tony Macchi and Enrico Quell
design Multimedia Kiosks
materials Expanded polyurethane
dimensions h 195.4cm, 145.4cm w 60.9cm L 57cm
h 65⅛in, 57¼in w 24in L 22⅜in
manufacturer Ing. C.Olivetti & C. SpA, Italy

The infotechnology revolution needs public access points. These kiosks are designed to house interactive screen information systems for areas such as airports, shopping malls and tourist centres. In developing the designs Michele de Lucchi drew on his earlier work on user-friendly banking machines: here the hole-in-the-wall comes out into the street, able to listen, ready to talk.

78 Torsten Fritze
design Portable computer terminal Portrait & Place Mat
materials Leather, ceramics, aluminium
dimensions h 5cm w 23cm L 30cm
h 2in w 9in L 11⅞in
manufacturer Philips/Olivetti Experimental Project, Italy
(One-off)

79 Alessandro Chiarato
design Portable computer terminal Magic Carpet
materials Kevlar
dimensions h 5cm w 30cm L 50cm
h 2in w 11⅞in L 19⅝in
manufacturer Philips/Olivetti Experimental Project, Italy
(One-off)

80 Michele de Lucchi with Cubo Musahiro
design Portable computer terminal Tool Panel
materials Aluminium
dimensions h 107cm w 200cm L 10cm
h 42⅛in w 78¾in L 4in
manufacturer Philips/Olivetti Experimental Project, Italy
(One-off)

The Philips/Olivetti joint project was intended to develop new semantic vocabularies for computer and communication products: it can be seen in this sense as an extension of Michele de Lucchi's Citizen Office project for Olivetti, which took as its starting point the dynamics of home-working, hot-desking and other contemporary work cultures. The new joint project is much more speculative. It set out to develop metaphors from domestic contexts into workplace uses. So the throw rug, for example, is the model for Magic Carpet, an electronic work space that can literally be spread on the floor. Similarly the place setting and the home work-bench formed starting points for new approaches to computer and information terminals.

81 SMh Italia SpA
(designs by SMh Italia design team unless otherwise credited)

design top row, left to right
Swatch Watch Automatic
Swatch Watch Chrono
Swatch Watch
Swatch Watch Chrono
Swatch Watch
Swatch Watch Scuba
lower row, left to right
Swatch Watch
Alessandro Mendini
Swatch Watch MusiCall
Paolo Bortoghesi
Swatch Watch
Nuola Goodman
Swatch Watch
Linda Graedel
Swatch Watch

materials All watches plastic with leather or plastic straps

dimensions L 22cm di 3.5cm
L 8⅝in di 1⅜in

manufacturer Swatch SA, Switzerland

82 Sottsass Associati

design Wristwatches Sottsass Collection

materials Stainless steel, calf leather

dimensions L 23cm di 3.7cm
L 9in di 1⅜in

manufacturer Seiko, Japan
(Limited edition)

83 Shinkichi Tanaka
design Briefcase Ex-Light LA-320
materials Aluminium
dimensions h 27cm w 37cm d 6.5cm
h 10½in w 14½in d 2⅝in
manufacturer Fuji Kowa Industry Co. Ltd., Japan
(Limited batch production)

84 Shinkichi Tanaka
design Suitcase Clutch EPO SE-A4, SE-B5
materials Span form
dimensions h 26.5cm, 22.5cm w 36.5cm, 29.5cm d 6.5cm, 7.5cm
h 10⅜in, 8⅞in w 14 ¼in, 11⅝in d 2⅝in, 3in
manufacturer Fuji Kowa Industry Co. Ltd., Japan
(Limited batch production)

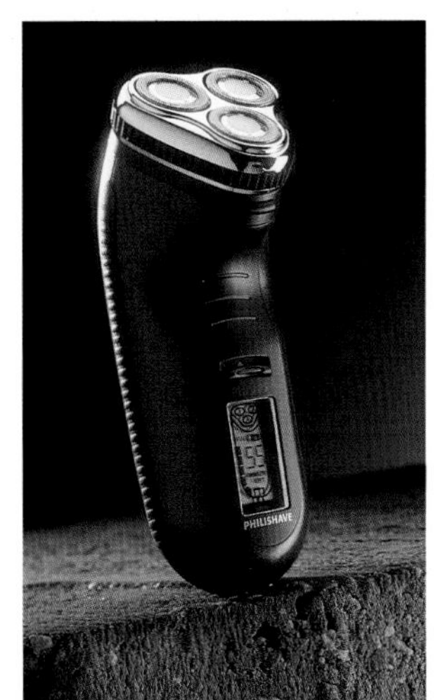

85 Philips Corporate Design
design Electric razor Philishave HS 990
materials ABS, chromed zinc bracket
dimensions h 6cm w 5cm L 14.5cm
h 2⅜in w 2in L 5¾in
manufacturer Philips Domestic Appliances & Personal Care BV, The Netherlands

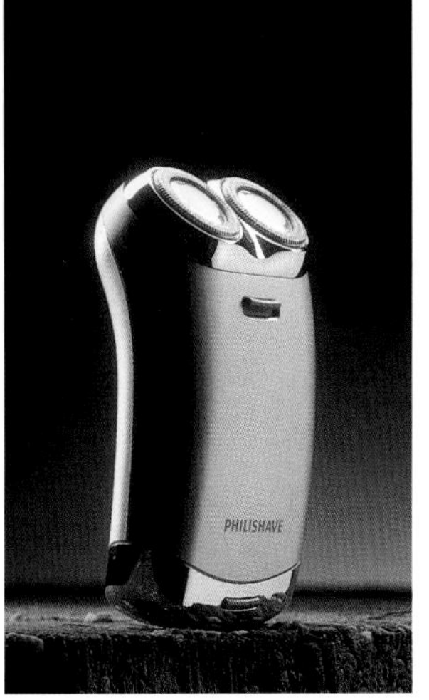
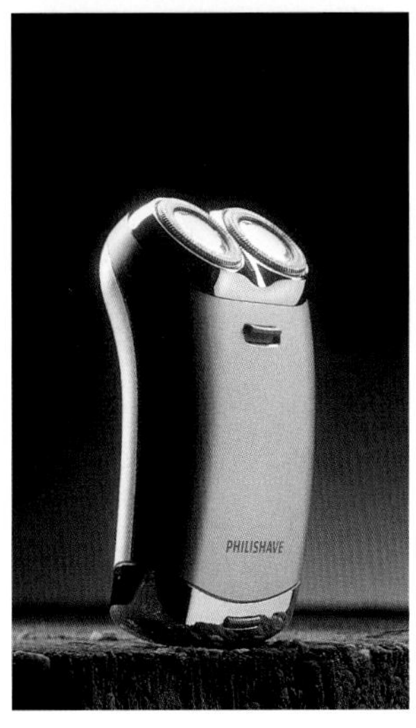

86 Philips Corporate Design
design Electric razor HS 190 compact shaver
materials ABS
dimensions h 5.3cm w 2.2cm L 9cm
h 2⅛in w ⅞in L 3½in
manufacturer Philips Domestic Appliances and Personal Care BV, The Netherlands

87 Kenneth Grange
design Razor Silk Effects
materials ABS Plastic
dimensions h 10cm w 4.5cm d 3cm
h 4in w 1⅜in d 1⅛in
manufacturer Schick Inc., USA

88 Philips Corporate Design
design Cleaner Triathlon
materials Polypropylene, ABS
dimensions h 47cm w 35cm L 49cm
h 18½in w 13¾in L 19¼in
manufacturer Philips Domestic Appliances & Personal Care BV, The Netherlands

89 Rainer Teufel, Diana Juratovac, Markus Mayer
design Gas barbecue grill Sunbeam
materials Cast aluminium, stamped steel
dimensions h 137cm w 61cm d 61cm
h 54in w 24in d 24in
manufacturer Sunbeam Leisure Products Co., USA

90 Kenneth Grange
design Toasters TT950, TT750, TT550
materials Moulded polypropylene casework
dimensions h 17.8cm L 42cm, 40.5cm, 31cm d 19cm, 13cm, 18.5cm
h 7in L 16½in, 16in, 12¼in d 7½in, 5⅛in, 7¼in
manufacturer Kenwood Ltd., UK

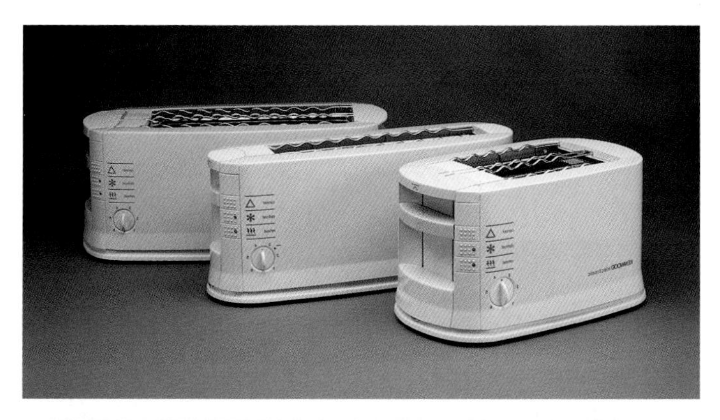

91 Kenneth Grange
design Electric Can Openers, C0600/C0300
materials Moulded polypropylene casework
dimensions h 23.6cm, 18.6cm di 13.4cm
h 9½in, 7⅜in di 5½in
manufacturer Kenwood Ltd., UK

92 In house design group
design Sponge mop, dust mop, broom, roller mop
O-Cedar 2000 Line
materials Polypropylene, polyethylene, acetal
dimensions h 137cm w 25.5cm
h 54in w 10in
manufacturer O-Cedar/Vining, USA

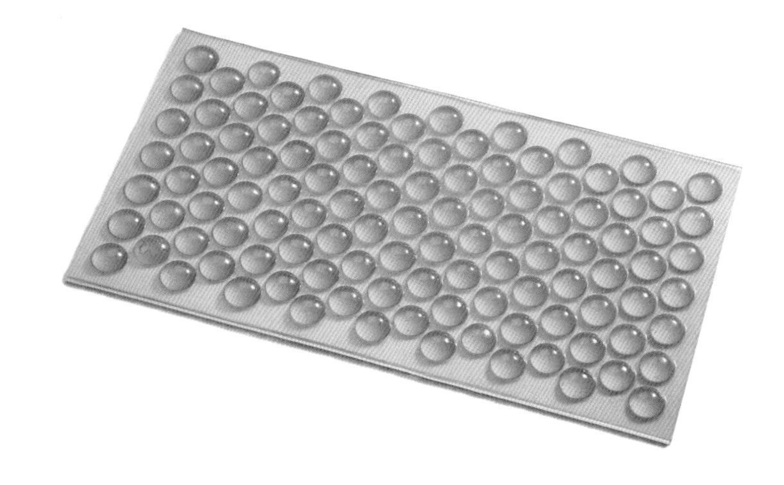

93 Hella Jongerius
design Flooring Bath mat
materials Polyurethane rubber
dimensions w 54cm L 60cm
w 21¼in L 23½in
manufacturer Droog Design, The Netherlands
(Limited batch production)

94 Winfried Scheuer
design Paperbin
materials Polypropylene
dimensions h 36cm w 36cm d 20cm
h 14⅛in w 14⅛in d 7⅞in
manufacturer Aero, London

95 Hiroshi Kobayashi
design Binoculars Nikon Muette
materials Polycarbonate, rubber, polypropylene
dimensions h 3.7cm w 11cm L 6.8cm
h 1⅜in w 4⅜in L 2¾in
manufacturer Nikon Corporation, Japan

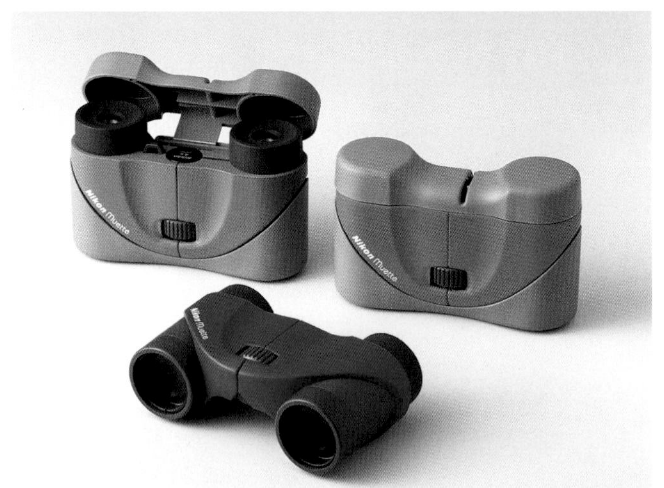

96 Stephan Doesinger
design Pen and card holder Bürobutler
materials Zelfo
dimensions h 3.2cm w 14cm L 32cm
h 1¼in w 5½in L 12½in
manufacturer Zellform GmbH, Austria
(Limited batch production)

Zelfo is a new material made from waste paper, cellulose, natural resins and starches, linseed oil and non-toxic pigments. The mix can be moulded using low-energy presses, and the finished items are lightweight, shock-resistant and non-conducting: since it is an organic material it can be wholly recycled. The Bürobutler is a demonstration piece for the new material, to develop applications in electronics, furniture and packaging.

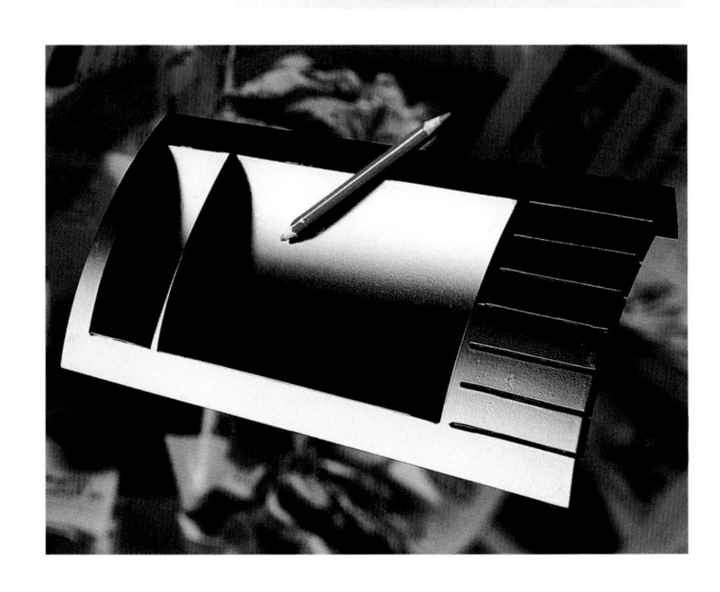

97	Nicolai Canetti
design	Softphone TM
materials	Plastic case covered with E.V.A.
dimensions	h 21.5cm w 7cm d 2.6cm
	h 8½in w 2¾in d 1⅛in
manufacturer	Recyco Inc., USA

98	Kazuo Kawasaki
design	Kitchen timer Cano
materials	ABS
dimensions	h 2.9cm di 7.5cm
	h 1⅛in di 3in
manufacturer	Takata Lemnos Inc., Japan

99	Plus Corporation
design	Plus tape printer
materials	Plastics
dimensions	h 12.5cm w 7.5cm d 3.4cm
	h 4½in w 3in d 1¼in
manufacturer	Plus Corporation, Japan

100 Yoshitaka Sumimoto, Mitsushige Sumimoto
design Saw Silky Topgun 660
materials SK-4 steel, vulcanized rubber
dimensions h 20cm w 3cm L 100cm
h 7⅞in w 1⅛in L 39½in
manufacturer UM:Kogyo Inc., Japan Topyu 660
(Limited batch production)

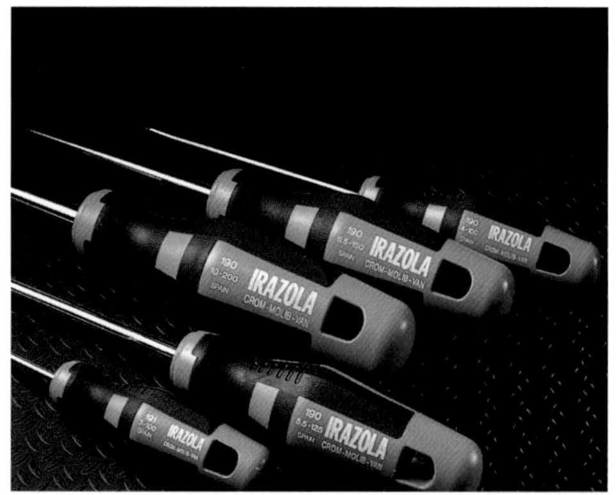

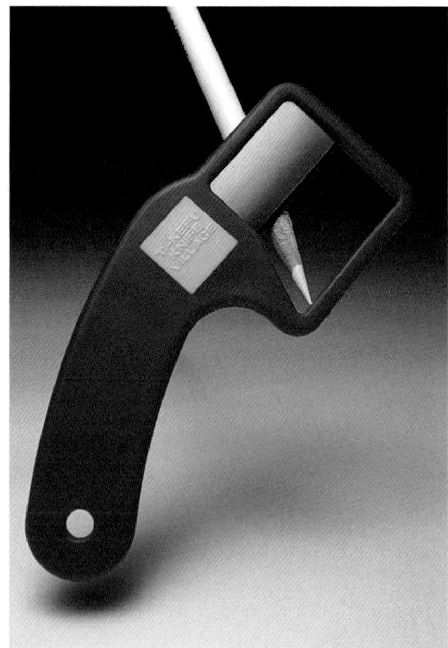

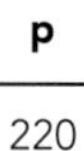

101 DCA Design International
design Screwdrivers Irozola Premium Range
materials Polypropylene, elastomer, steel
dimensions Various sizes
manufacturer Irozola SA, Spain

102 Kazuo Kawasaki
design Pencil sharpener PlaSchola
materials ABS laminated stainless steel
dimensions h 4cm w 4.9cm L 12cm
h 1⅛in w 1⅞in L 4¾in
manufacturer Takefu Knife Village Assn., Japan
(Prototype)

Jean Nouvel liked the ergonomic form of this pencil sharpener, which combines the concept of a traditional pen-knife (rather than the inexact rotary sharpener) into a new form. The open box over the blade not only serves to prevent accidents, but also helps the user's eye to guide the pencil nto the correct position for sharpening.

103 S. H. Hauser Associates Inc.
(John von Buelow, Ernesto Quinteros, Vincent Razo)
design Cymbal Holder Super Crown
materials Injection moulded polythene, thermoplastic elastomer
dimensions w 3.4cm L 13.3cm
w 1⅜in L 5¼in
manufacturer Cymbal Crown, USA

104 John Koenig, Jeff DeBord, Diana Juratovac, Rainer Teufel
design Boxes Fishing tackle boxes
materials Polypropylene
dimensions h 25cm w 25cm L 39.4cm
h 11in w 11in L 19in
manufacturer Rubbermaid, USA

105 Mike Nuttall
design Fishing reels New Generation Fishing Reel Combo Family
materials Recyclable ABS-blend and EVA-injected moulded plastic
dimensions Nibbler: h 7.5cm L 20.3cm d 5cm, h 3in L 8in d 2in
Jammer: h 7.5cm L 25.5cm d 5cm, h 3in L 10in d 2in
Lightning: h 8.9cm L 27.9cm d 6.3cm, h 3½in L 11in d 2½in
manufacturer Berkley Outdoor Products, USA

106 Tada Futoshi
design Fishing Line Connector National
materials ABS plastic
dimensions h 8.7cm w 12.2cm d 2.9cm
h 3⅜in w 4⅞in d 1⅛in
manufacturer Matsushita Battery Industrial Co. Ltd., Japan

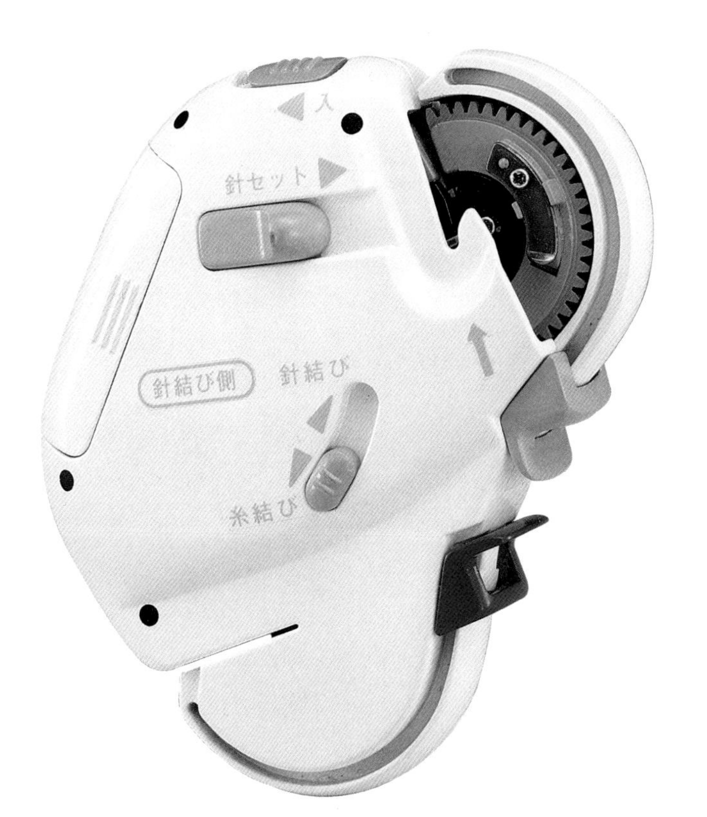

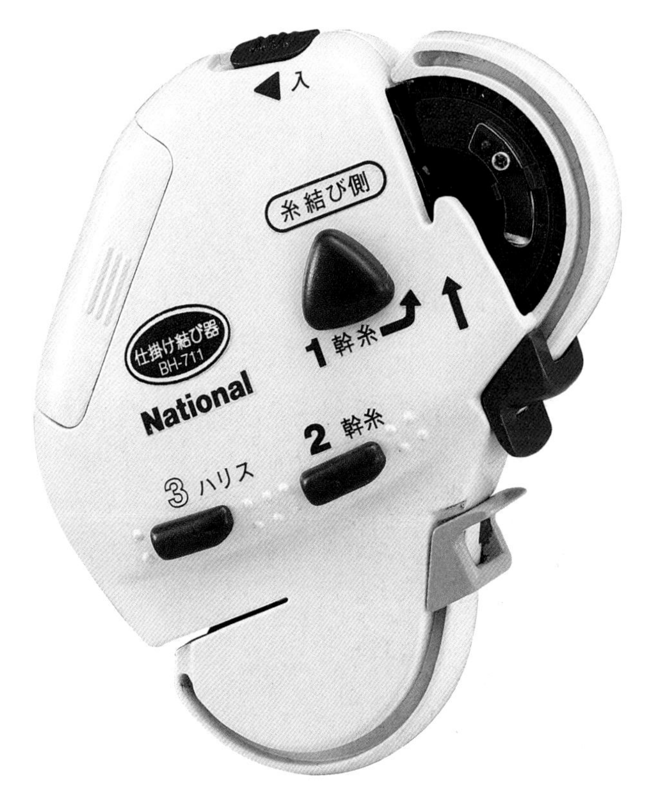

The application of new technologies to sports has mainly been towards improving performance at the top end of the sport: Olympic racing cycles are high on Nouvel's list of key contemporary products. These technologies percolate down, as in the range of new materials now available for amateur tennis rackets, for example. In this object by Tada Futoshi, design imagination, rather than high technology, has been applied to the fiddly problem of joining fishing lines together, each side of the object handling different types of knot.

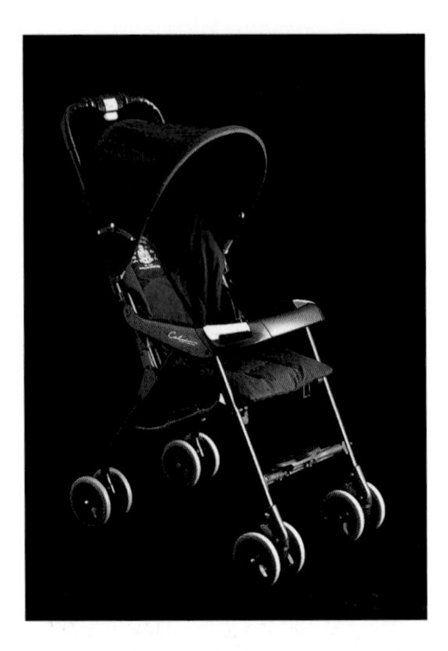

107 Tomihiro Kaneko for Orb Inc.
design Child seat Baby Stroller
materials Aluminium, plastic, cloth
dimensions h 92cm w 40cm L 60cm
h 36½in w 15¾in L 23½in
manufacturer Combi Co. Ltd., Japan

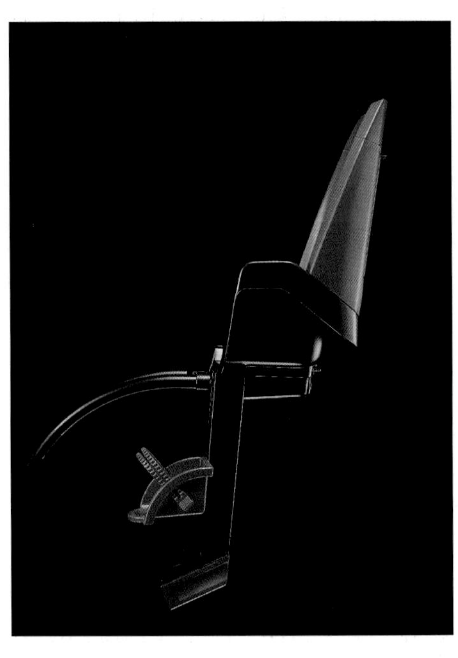

108 ninaber/peters/krouwel industrial design
design Child's bicycle seat Discovery
materials PP, PA recyclable plastics
dimensions h 53.4cm w 31.7cm d 17.6cm, h 21in w 12½in d 6⅞in
h 89.6cm w 37.8cm d 21.4cm, h 35¼in w 14⅞in d 8¾in
manufacturer Hamax AS, Norway

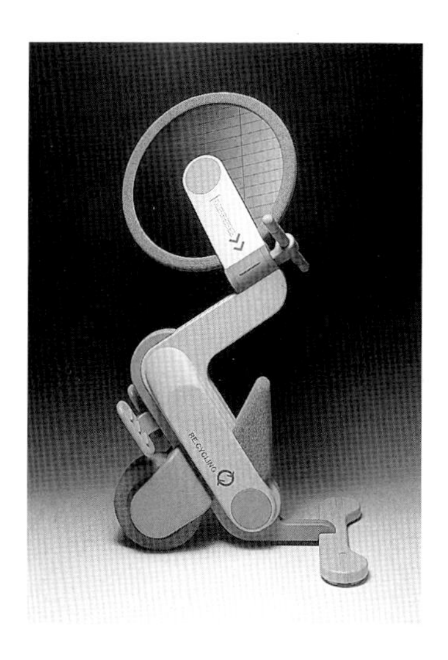

110 Shinichi Sumikawa
design Cycle Solar Bike (1/5 scale model shown)
materials Plastic, aluminium
dimensions h 15cm w 15cm
h 6in w 6in
manufacturer Shinichi Sumikawa Design Studio, Japan
(Prototype model)

109 ninaber/peters/krouwel industrial design
design Wheel straightener Tacx Scorpio
materials Steel, polyamide
dimensions Folded in: h 6cm w 27.7cm L 35.8cm, h 2⅜in w 10⅞in L 14in
Folded out: h 35.8cm w 19.7cm L 22.7cm, h 14in w 7¾in L 8⅞in
manufacturer Technische Industrie Tacx, The Netherlands

Cycles are an efficient and non-polluting means of transport, and these objects show designers working to develop new versions and applications, from child seats by ninaber/peters/krouwel, adjustable to different ages of the child, to a machine for straightening bent or distorted wheels. Japanese designer Shinichi Sumikawa has combined technologies with a Solar Bike, on which the front wheel stores up solar energy for the lighting system when the cycle is parked in the open.

BIOGRAPHIES

Werner Aisslinger was born in Nördlingen in 1964 and studied industrial design at the HdK, Berlin. Before creating his own design studio in 1992 in Berlin he worked with Jasper Morrison in London and for Studio de Lucchi, Milan. In 1993 he started an experimental design collaboration with Axel Kufus in Berlin. *f 1*

Lamberto Angelini, born in Bologna in 1949, studied mechanical engineering. For many years he worked in the automobile industry, notably for Volkswagen Style Centre, where he contributed to the development of the Golf Rabbit Mk. 2. He has been a freelance industrial designer since 1980 and has exhibited his work internationally. p 34

Ron Arad, born in Tel Aviv in 1951, studied at the Jerusalem Academy of Art and the Architectural Association, London (from 1974 to 1979). In 1981 he founded One Off Ltd with Dennis Groves and Caroline Thorman and in 1983 designed One Off's first showroom in Neal Street, Covent Garden. In 1988 he won the Tel Aviv Opera Foyer Interior Competition with C. Norton and S. McAdam, and the next year formed Ron Arad Associates in order to realize the project, moving premises to Chalk Farm, London. As well as the design and construction of the new One Off Design Studio, furniture gallery and workshop in 1990, recent projects have included furniture design for Poltronova, Vitra, Moroso and Driade, the design of various interior installations and domestic architectural projects such as the house in Schopfheim for a German publisher. Ron Arad was the editor of the 1994 *International Design Yearbook* and is a guest Professor in the H.S.F.A.K in Vienna. *f 71-81, t 15*

Junichi Arai was born in Kiryu City, Gunma Prefecture, Japan in 1932. Since the mid-50s he has developed new techniques for weaving with metallic fibres and was given the International Trade Industry Minister's award in the Grand Fair of Synthetic Fibres in Japan in 1961. Arai works with both Japanese and international fashion designers and has exhibited internationally most recently in the 'Textiles of the World' show at the Saint Louis Art Museum. His work can be seen in the permanent collections of the Fashion Institute of Technology, USA; the V&A, London; Museum of Art, Rhode Island School of Design, USA; Cooper Hewitt Museum, USA and the Okawa Museum, Kiryu, Japan. In 1987 Arai was awarded honorary membership of the Royal Designers for Industry, UK. *tx 17-31*

Josep Aregall was born in Barcelona in 1957 and since 1979 has designed and built commercial spaces, houses and offices. He has also designed exhibitions and temporary constructions, and has been Professor of Window Dressing and Temporary Constructions at the EINA Design School since 1985. He collaborated in the Barcelona Cinema Festival in 1987, 1988 and 1990 and the EINA 20 Years Exhibition. He designed the travelling exhibition for the presentation of the 1992 Barcelona Paralympic Games as well as collaborating on the interior design for part of the Industry and Energy Pavilion at EXPO'92 in Seville. *l 49*

Francesco Armato was born in Marsala in 1962 and studied architecture in Palermo where he came under the influence of Umberto Riva and Andrea Branzi. He received his degree in interior decorating and design in Florence under Professor Paolo Galli with whom he has been collaborating as assistant since 1990. His work includes the design of various country homes and since the beginning of 1994 he has been Art Director for Cerva. *l 10*

Jan Armgardt, who was born in 1947, trained initially as a cabinetmaker and later in interior design. After gaining practical experience in a firm involved in furniture design, he opened his own furniture studio in Bensheim, Germany, in 1974. He collaborates with companies such as de Padova, de Sede, Knoll and Wittman, and besides furniture also designs kitchen and table accessories, office equipment and lamps. He has been the recipient of numerous awards and prizes. *f 60-63*

Sigeaki Asahara was born in Tokyo in 1948 and studied in Turin. Italy. Since 1973 he has worked as a freelance industrial designer in Tokyo. He exhibits internationally, and one of his projects is on permanent show at the Brooklyn Museum of New York. His work has received much acclaim including a Compasso d'Oro. *l 44*

Paul Atkinson was born in Leeds in 1952 and was educated at the Loughborough College of Art and Design; the Leicester Polytechnic School of Industrial Design and the Royal College of Art, London. He established Atkinson Design Associates in 1982 and today clients number GEC, Knoll International, Rosenthal GmbH as well as British Rail, London Underground Ltd and Concord SLI. He has exhibited his work in Japan and the US. Atkinson is visiting lecturer at numerous universities in the UK including the Royal College of Art. *l 22*

Hiroshi Awatsuji, born in Kyoto, Japan in 1929, graduated from Kyoto City University of Art. In 1964 he began his collaboration with the Fujie Textile Co. Ltd. In 1988 he became a professor at the Tama University of Arts. He has participated in exhibitions worldwide and is internationally recognized for his work. He received an Outstanding Award at the 3rd International Textile Competition in Kyoto in 1992 and later that year a Gold Award at the 38th ID Annual Design Review in the USA. *tx 33-4*

Nelson Au joined IDEO in 1984 since which time he was worked on numerous projects for such clients as Apple Computer, Tandem, Compression Labs, Hewlett-Packard, Xerox, Norand and Silicon Graphics. While at IDEO he was been awarded an IDE Bronze award for the GRID PalmPad and a 1987 ID Annual Design Review award for the Presentation Technology Image Maker. Au received his BSID in 1984 from San José State University. *p 35*

Russell Bagley studied Product Design in West Sussex in 1981 and worked as a freelance interior designer developing an interest in furniture and lighting. In 1987 Bagley designed a number of special feature lights for Peter Gabriel's 'Real World Group'. This commission led to the creation of Box Products Ltd and the development of a range of furniture and light fittings, a partnership with the Real World Group which lasted for four years. In 1991 Russell Bagley joined William Alsop's practice as Product Design Associate. *l 45*

Gijs Bakker was born in Amersfoort, Holland in 1942. He studied at what is now the Rietveld Akademie, Amsterdam in the Department of Jewellery Design, and later at the Konstfackskolan Department of Industrial Design in Stockholm. Until 1986 Bakker was a freelance designer, as well as teaching at the Academie van Beeldende Kunsten at Arnhem. From 1987 to 1989 he was a partner in the design studio BRS Premsela Vonk in Amsterdam. Today he is head of the 'Man and Living' Department of the Academy of Industrial Design at Eindhoven, and design advisor for Cor Unum. In 1993 Bakker established Keizersgracht 518 in Amsterdam. His work can be seen in major design collections, including the Stedelijk Museum; the Denver Museum of Art; the Cooper-Hewitt Museum, New York and the V&A, London. *f 88*

Bang Design was founded in Sydney in 1989 by Bryan Marshall and David Granger. Both are graduates of industrial design, with degrees in environmental design from the School of Environmental Design at the University of Canberra. Before forming their own company, they spent six years working for manufacturers and design consultants. Bang Design's work has been exhibited and published widely in Australia. *f 36*

Beata Bär was born in 1959 and studied interior design and architecture in Mainz. In 1987 she founded her own design studio BÄR - Design before undertaking an extensive study period in Rome. In 1991 she began a collaboration with Hartmut Knell. Clients number Artifort, Thonet and Steelcase Strafor and she has exhibited her work widely within Europe. *f 59*

Roger Bateman was born in 1965 and educated at the Ravensbourne College of Design and Communication and the Royal College of Art. He established Square One in 1992 and has exhibited his work extensively in the UK. He lectured for a period of two years at the Liverpool Institute of Higher Education. *f 67*

François Bauchet was born in 1948 and today practises interior and furniture design in Saint Etienne, France. Interior design projects include the reception areas of the Musée d'Art et d'Industrie, Saint Etienne and the Centre d'art de Vassiviére in Limousin. He has exhibited his work in Europe and Japan and has had several one-man shows at Galerie Néotù, Paris. His work can be seen in the permanent collection of the Musée des Arts Décoratifs in Paris. *f 91*

Heinz Baumann, born in 1957 in Switzerland, designs and produces single pieces and limited editions of furniture in his own atelier and works with companies to produce designs for industrial production. In 1992 he was awarded a federal Scholarship and a Foundation from IKEA. *f 52*

Sally Beardsley is an American graphic designer currently living in Copenhagen. She graduated from the Rhode Island School of Design and before moving to Denmark worked in design studios both in Italy and England. Her book *Conversations at the Interface: Product-People Communication* is published by the Danish Design Centre. She is currently also a UN guest lecturer at the Central Academy of Arts & Design in Beijing, China. *p 43*

Yves Behar was born in Switzerland in 1967 and studied industrial design at the Art Centre College of Design in Switzerland. Before moving to San Francisco and working for Lunar Design as product designer he spent time with Bruce Burdick on exhibit design projects. *f 84-5*

Gwen Bertheau-Suzuki was born in Paris in 1956 and received a Diploma from the Institute of Architecture, Tournai, Belgium and a Masters Degree from Tokyo University. After working for Arata Isozaki & Associates for 4 years he established his own practice in Tokyo (1988). His designs include numerous architectural buildings, interiors and furniture products. He is Assistant Professor at Japan University, Faculty of Engineering. *l 52*

Franco Bettonica lives and works in Milan where he graduated from the Faculty of Architecture in 1953 forming his own company, Frattini which from 1954 collaborated with OPI (later to be known as Cini & Nils). His work can be seen in the permanent collection of MoMA, New York. *l 1*

John Betts joined Henry Dreyfuss Associates in 1984 as Senior Designer since which time he has been promoted to senior Project Manager in 1988 and Associate in 1989. He graduated in 1978 from the University of Illinois, Urbana with a BFA in Industrial Design and worked for several design consultancies in the USA before joining Henry Dreyfuss Associates. Today he provides design and project management for various clients including Polaroid cameras and is a member of the Industrial Designers Society of America. *p 39*

Mark Biasotti has been a senior industrial designer at IDEO since 1988 and has worked on major design projects for companies such as Tandem, Apple Computers, GRID and Hughes Aircraft. He received his BSID degree from the San José State University and before joining IDEO worked for Atari and Hewlett-Packard Corporate Industrial Design Division. *p 42*

Dr. Alison Black, Head of Human Factors, IDEO, London, is a human factors psychologist with a degree in Experimental Psychology and a PhD from the MRC Applied Psychology Unit in Cambridge. She has published articles and books on human computer interaction and information design, and lectures at the Royal College of Art and the London Business School. She is a member of the Association for Computing Machinery SIGCHI, and the British Psychological Society. *p 44*

Florian Borkenhagen was born in Frankfurt in 1959 and studied at the Academy of Fine and Applied Arts. He specializes in interior, set, exhibition, furniture and object design, and in 1990 set up his own studio in Como. *l 51*

Paul Bradley, senior industrial designer at IDEO, has been with the firm since 1985. Much of his work has focused on human factors and industrial design of computer input devices. He has served as the lead designer for many consumer and computer design efforts, resulting in products for Alps, Apple Computer, Logitech etc. He was the lead industrial designer for the IDEO team that created the Microsoft mouse. He received his BSID degree from Ohio State University. *p 36*

Alain Brux and **Philippe Gourdon** formed their lighting design partnership in 1987 since which time they have worked for clients in France, Italy, Switzerland and Germany. They have received a number of prizes for their work throughout Europe and are extending their interests to include the lighting of public buildings, most notably the international centre of Euro-Disney/Marne-la-Vallée, and to window and door design. *l 47*

Colin Burns, Interaction Designer, Interval Research, has a BSc in Industrial Design from the Royal College of Art. After working as a freelance designer and then in a partnership called Designers in Production, joined IDEO from 1988 to 1992. Colin Burns is a fellow of the Royal Society of Arts and is currently working with Interval Research, Palo Alto as well as lecturing in the Computer Related Design Department at the Royal College of Art. *p 46*

Nicolai Canetti graduated with a masters degree in design. He has worked in a large variety of capacities including teaching design, product development, manufacturing, consulting, graphic design, magazine design, advertising and publishing his own photography books. He has created numerous businesses including the design-related international consulting firm Canetti Design Group, in 1974; the Photo Library Inc with retail photo gallery in New York and the Madison Avenue Magazine and Singles World Magazine, and finally in 1982, Canetti Inc, an outlet for manufacturing, marketing and distribution of his own products. *p 97*

Pierangelo Caramia was born in 1957 in Cistermino, Italy. After graduating in architecture, in 1986 he got a masters degree in Urban Design under Prof. Andrea Branzi from the Domus Academy, Milan. He has designed products for numerous manufacturers including XO, Sawaya and Moroni, Arredaesse, Cassina and Alessi as well as designing the interior of 'Doublet' a flag factory in Lille and the 'Bond Street Café' with Alec Locadia in New York. He is currently Professor of Design at the Ecole des Beaux Arts in Rennes and has exhibited his work widely both nationally and internationally most notably at the 3rd International Architecture Exhibition at the Venice Biennale. *f 22*

Achille Castiglioni, born in Milan in 1918, began his career immediately after World War II with his brothers Livio and Pier Giacomo. He is well known for his innovative designs in interiors, furniture and lighting and his clients include Flos, Phonola, Bernini, Cassina, de Padova, Fontana Arte, Interflex, Kartell, Marcatre, Olivetti, Up & Up and Zanotta. Castiglioni is one of the foremost talents in Italian design and has been honoured nine times with the Compasso d'Oro. His work is in the collections of the V&A, London; MoMA, New York; Israel Museum, Jerusalem, and in museums in Prague, Zurich, Munich, Düsseldorf, Cologne, Hamburg and Helsinki. He is currently Professor of Industrial Design and Decoration at the University of Milan. *f 11, l 8*

Pierluigi Cerri, architect and founder member of Gregotti Associati was born in 1939. He is a member of the AGI. He is a member of the staff of *Rassegna* and *Casabella* magazines as well as the Graphic Art Director of *Pagina*. He is responsible for the image campaign of Palazzo Grassi in Venice, and has arranged various international art and design exhibitions. In addition Cerri designs objects and furniture for Unifor, B&B Italia, FontanaArte, Fusital and Rosenthal and also designed for the ships *Costa Classica* and *Costa Romantica*. *f 21*

Chérif was born in 1962 and studied at the Ecole des Beaux Arts in Algeria as well as at the Ecole Nationale Supérieure des Arts Décoratifs de Paris. Since graduation she has exhibited for VIA in France and abroad and in 1994 created a collection of furniture, objects and jewellery. *f 123*

Alessandro Chiarato graduated in architecture from Rome University after which he worked for Autonautica Sport and International Boat Italia. In 1983 he sat a masters degree in Design at the Domus Academy under Mario Bellini after which he worked with Olivetti SpA in their consumer products department. Today he is a consultant for Studio de Lucchi. *p 79*

Tommaso Cimini was born in 1947 and trained in lighting design. After graduation he worked for seven years with Artemide and in 1978 founded his own company. *l 2*

Kevin Clay, industrial designer, Hauser Associates, was born in 1956 and graduated from the Art Center College of Design in 1987 with a BS degree in Industrial Design. Prior to joining SGH he worked for Bartlett Design Associates. *p 12*

Christian Clerc was born in 1954 and for the last 15 years has been vice-president of the fashion house, Jean-Louis Scherrer. *f 125*

Franco Clivio was born in 1942 and studied at Ulm College of Design from 1963-8. Since graduating he has been product designer for Gardena, Ulm as well as carrying out freelance commissions for other companies such as ERCO, Siemens and the International Building Exhibition Emscherpark. Today he is a lecturer in product design at the College for Design Zurich and is a frequent guest lecturer at design colleges in the United States, Finland and Germany. *l 42*

Lluis Clotet, born in Barcelona in 1941, studied at the Escuela Tecnica de Arquitectura in Barcelona, graduating in 1965. In 1964 he founded Studio PER with the architects Pep Bonet, Christian Cirici and Oscar Tusquets and has collaborated in numerous projects with them. He is a founder member of Bd. Ediciones de Diseño, for which he still designs furniture and objects. He received the FAD award for the best interior in Barcelona in 1965 and 1972, and for the best building in 1978 and 1979. He has also received the Delta de Oro on three occasions for his industrial design. He exhibits widely both nationally and internationally. *l 23-4*

Nigel Coates was born in 1949 in Malvern, England. He studied at the University of Nottingham and at the Architectural Association where he has lectured since his graduation in 1974. In 1985 he co-founded Branson Coates with Douglas Branson. He is known for his belief that architecture can be odd and amusing as well as extremely well-built and durable, and his projects include work for Jasper Conran and Katherine Hamnett. He has also designed restaurants in Japan, including the Nishi Acabu Wall in Tokyo and the Sea Hotel in Otaru. His most recent projects include the restaurant at Schipol Airport. *t 11*

Carlo Colombo, born in Carimate in 1967, graduated in architecture from Milan Polytechnic with a specialization in industrial design. Work experience during this time was gained from Benetton. He started his professional career with Studio Pusinelli in Como and worked on projects in Africa and Russia. From 1990-92 he worked in photography and designed objects which resulted in his later collaboration with Cappellini. Other clients include YCAMI Edizioni, Flexiform and Vittorio Bonacina. He is also active in architecture and interior design, as well as in design teaching. *f 7*

Christopher Connell was born in Melbourne, Australia in 1955 and was educated in graphic design, applied art and interior design. He designed retail and commercial interiors before founding Modin Australia in 1990 and MAP (Merchants of Australian Products) with partner Raoul C. Hogg, in 1991, dealing with furniture and object design and design development. In 1994 he exhibited his work with 'Zeus' at the Milan Furniture Fair. *f 35*

Barry Cook graduated in 1990 with a BSc Hons. Degree in Engineering Product Design from the South Bank University in London. He specializes in contemporary lighting and is currently working as senior lighting designer for Basis Design Ltd. *l 38*

David Cruz, Project Manager, Hauser Associates, is an honours graduate of California State University at Long Beach, holding a BSID. Before working for Hauser he was Project Manager with PA Consulting Group in Princeton, New Jersey. *p 8*

Thomas Dair, Vice President of Smart Design Inc, holds a BID from Syracuse University (1977) and before joining Davin Stowell (later Smart Design) in 1979 he designed computer and medical products as a consultant. Dair teaches product design at Parsons School of Design in New York. *p 45*

Riccardo Dalisi, the Italian avantgarde designer, was a member of the experimental design group Global Tools throughout the 1970s. He has written several books on architecture, and teaches architectural composition at the University of Naples. He was awarded the Compasso d'Oro in 1981 for a coffee-maker by Alessi. He has also worked with Baleri Italia, Oluce, Play Line and Zanotta. He has participated in many exhibitions, including the Venice Biennale and the Milan Trienalle. *f121*

Philip Davies, Senior Designer, IDEO, London, has a Masters in Industrial Design from the Royal College of Art, London. He joined IDEO in 1966. He is a specialist in consumer product design, and also is responsible for the company's graphics in London. Davies is a member of the Industrial Designers Society of America and lectures at the Royal College of Art and the University of Kingston upon Thames. He is also a juror on the Royal Society of Arts student awards panel. His work has been exhibited in Japan and the UK. *p 46*

DCA was founded in 1958 and today is one of Europe's largest design groups employing over 50 industrial designers, graphic designers, engineers, electronic experts and modelmakers. *p 101*

Jeff DeBord is an industrial designer at Design Central, a design consultancy located in Columbus, Ohio. He was born in Columbus in 1962 and received his BS degree in Industrial Design from the Ohio State University in 1990. *p 104*

Djoke de Jong was born in Creil, in the Netherlands in 1960 and studied at the Academie Industriele Vormgeving in Eindhoven. He has exhibited at Droog Design, Milan; Dedalo, Amsterdam and 'Stroom op', Frankfurt. He has received the Herman Miller Award. *tx 10*

Michele de Lucchi was born in Ferrara, Italy in 1951 and graduated from Florence University in 1975. During his student years he founded the 'Gruppo Cavat', a group concerned with avantgarde and conceptual architecture. He worked and designed for Alchymia until the establishment of Memphis in 1981. Today he produces exclusive art-orientated handmade products, industrial consumer items and furniture in wood, metal, stone and other materials for companies serving specialized markets. His architectural activities range from shop design to large-scale office buildings and private apartment blocks. De Lucchi's work has received many awards and he has published and exhibited widely and internationally. Due to his activities and vast experience in the most important period of Italian design de Lucchi has lectured at design schools and universities such as Domus Academy, Milan and the University of Detroit. *f 43, l 37, p 66-77*

Delo Lindo was created in 1985 by Fabien Cagani and Laurent Matras who were both born in France and received Diplomas from the ENSAD, Paris. Their expertise covers interior design, exhibition design, and furniture for clients such as Soca Line and Cinna as well as tableware for Algorithme. *f 119*

Bernhard Dessecker, born in 1961 in Munich, studied interior architecture. From 1983 to 1984 he worked at Studio Morsa, New York and since 1984 has been a freelance designer, collaborating with the design team of Ingo Maurer. *l 19*

Tom Dixon was born in Sfax, Tunisia in 1959 and moved to the UK when he was four. From 1981 to 1984 he was involved in nightclub promotions and event organization. He now works on designing stage sets, furniture, sculpture, architectural installations and numerous other objects. His clients number Cappellini, Comme des Garçons, Nigel Coates, Ralph Lauren, Vivienne Westwood and Terence Conran. He has exhibited his work most recently in *A New Century in Design* at the National Museum of Modern Arts, Tokyo. His designs can be found in the Musée des Arts Décoratifs and the Pompidou Centre, Paris; the Vitra Chair Museum, Basle; the V&A, the Crafts Council and the Design Museum, London; and the Brooklyn Museum, New York. *f 118*

Stephan Doesinger was born in 1968 in Salzburg, Austria. He studied industrial design in Linz from 1988. In 1992 he studied architecture at the University of East London under Pascal Schöning, and the same year founded his own studio for graphic and product design with Doris Kropfreiter in Linz. He has recently been working freelance with Laurids Ortner, Kiska Industrial Design, Salzburg, Alessandro Mendini, Italy and Ron Arad in London where he is undertaking postgraduate studies at the Architectural Association. *p 96*

Donato d'Urbino and **Paolo Lomazzi** were born in Milan in 1935 and 1936 respectively. In the 1960s they created a series of inflatable designs, which culminated in their inflatable chair, Blow, in 1967. They continued with similar designs, working for Acerbis, Artemide, Driade, Disform and others. They recently extended their work to include architecture, product and lighting design, and their output is documented in books on Italian design, as well as in major international publications on industrial architecture and design. Examples of their work can be found in the permanent collections of MoMA, New York; the V&A and the Design Museum, London; the Pompidou Centre, Paris; the Kunstgewerbe Museum, Zurich; the Staatliches Museum für Angewandte Kunst, Munich; and the Jerusalem Museum, Israel. *f 19*

Guy Dyas, born in 1968, trained at the Chelsea School of Art and the Royal College of Art, London. He has worked as a product and industrial designer for several companies, notably the Sony Corporation in Tokyo. Since 1992 he has combined his work for Sony with freelance consultancy. He has exhibited his work in Japan. *f 83*

Giancarlo Fassina was born in Milan in 1935 and trained at the Superior Engineering Institute in Fribourg and the Milan Polytechnic where he graduated in architecture. In 1970 he joined Artemide, working closely with Enzo Mari in the design of the 'Aggregate System'. Recently he has collaborated with Marco Zanuso in the lighting of the new Fossati Theatre in Milan and with Mario Bellini for the lighting of the Milan Triennale. *l 36*

Maurizio Favetta, born in Bolzano in 1959, studied architecture in Milan. From 1985 to 1991 he was a member of Matteo Thun Associates after which he worked freelance, in particular being responsible for the development of Swatch stores worldwide. In 1994 he founded King Size, a consultant company for image and design which produces its own furniture collection. Favetta has published books on design most notably *Descendant of Leonardo da Vinci*, *Italian Design* and *The Italian Interior* (Graphic Sha, Japan). *f 104, 116*

Andrè Feldmann (born 1964) and **Arne Jacob Schultchen** (born 1965) have worked as a team since their first encounter at the Hochschule für Bildende Künste, Hamburg from which they graduated in industrial design in 1992/93. In 1994 they established their own studio in Hamburg. The range of their work runs from product-design, furniture, lighting and interior design to graphics, packaging, exhibition design and experimental works. *f 125*

Maurizio Ferrari was born in Monza, Milan in 1957 and received a Diploma from IPSIA, Lissone, followed by a degree in architecture from the Polytechnic of Milan and a Masters in Museography also from Milan. He started his professional career in 1984 since which time he has collaborated with several lighting companies. *l 43*

Maria Grazia Fiocco was born in Verona in 1956 and qualified at the Polytechnic of Milan. In 1978 she started a design associated company and in

1981 opened her own studio in Verona. Clients include Guy Laroche, Moulinex, Marazzi Ceramiche, Biesse, TVS and Morinox. *t 8, 21*
Enrico Franzolini was born in Udine in 1952 graduating from Venice University in 1979. Today his studio deals mainly in restoration and residential architecture as well as industrial design. *l 32*
Tosten Fritze was born in 1959 in Germany but moved to London in 1981 to study industrial design engineering at the Central School of Art, followed by studies in design management at the Domus Academy and marketing at the Bocconi University whilst working for Olivetti and King Miranda Associates. In 1988 he moved to San Francisco, as Senior Designer for frogdesign and then to the Netherlands, as Design Manager for Philips Corporate Design. Today he lives and works in Milan, as Principal for POOL and on design management at Studio de Lucchi. *p 78*
Tada Futoshi was born in Osaka in 1959 and graduated from the Kyushu Institute of Design. He entered Matsushita as an industrial designer and has designed for general, audio and TV products. He is currently working on battery-operated equipment for Matsushita. *p 106*
Shaun Fynn, industrial designer, Hauser Associates, is an honours graduate from Central St Martins School of Art and Design in London. Before joining SGH he worked in Milan and London. *p 8*

Piero Gilardino was born in 1960 in Milan. He started his furniture design career working for various Italian manufacturers before attending management, sales and marketing lectures and joining Pallucco Roma as Assistant Manager, later becoming Marketing and Sales Manager. In 1990 he founded USO Maison Gilardino where today he works as Managerial Director, Product Manager and furniture designer. *f 24*
Antonio Pio Giovanditto, born in Italy in 1958, graduated in architecture in 1986. Until 1989 he was assistant in industrial design at Pescara University after which he moved to Milan and started a collaboration with Sergio Calatroni working in Italy and Japan. In 1993 he joined forces with Maurizio Favetta and today is active in the fields of residential building, interior and industrial design. *f 116*
Stefano Giovannoni was born in La Spezia in 1954 and graduated from the Faculty of Architecture of Florence in 1978. He is the founder of the Bolidist movement and of King-Kong Productions. In 1991 he designed the Italian Pavilion at the *Les Capitales Européennes du Nouveau Design* exhibition at the Pompidou Centre, Paris. His work has been displayed in exhibitions in Italy and abroad. *t 31*
Ernesto Gismondi (who works also as Örni Halloween) was born in San Remo on 25th December, 1931 and studied aeronautical engineering at the Milan Polytechnic and missile engineering at the School of Engineering in Rome. He joined Artemide and together with Sergio Mazza developed new product lines. *l 11, 36*
Gaspar Glusberg was born in 1959 graduating in architecture from the Buenos Aires National University where today he is Assistant Professor in the School of Architecture. Glusberg is also a Member of the Design Department at the Centre of Art and Communication, Buenos Aires as well as being Director of the Design Department of Modulor SpA. In 1986 he started a programme of collaborative work with the designer Andrea Branzi. *l 14*
Linda Graedel-Sherman was born in San Francisco in 1941 and attended the Art Center School in Los Angeles. She continued her artistic education in Vienna and Paris, before finally settling in Switzerland in 1962. She ran a children's painting studio on the principles of Arno Stern and from 1980 onwards she has regularly illustrated cultural events in newspapers and magazines. She has held exhibitions in various towns in Switzerland and in 1994 created two Swatch watches. *p 81*
Kenneth Grange was educated at the Willesden School of Art, London and served in the Royal Engineers as a technical illustrator. He established his own industrial design practice in 1959. A founder-partner of Pentagram in 1972, his work includes mass production items ranging from small appliances to the Intercity 125 train. In 1969 he was appointed Royal Designer for Industry and in 1984 was awarded the CBE. He holds Honorary Doctorates from the Royal College of Art, London and Heriot Watt University, Edinburgh and has served as Master of the Faculty of Royal Designers for Industry (1985-7), as well as being the President of the Chartered Society of Designers (1987). He has been the recipient of major design prizes including 10 annual Design Council Awards. *p 87, 90-1*
Constantin Grcic is a German furniture designer who is at present working freelance in London and Munich. He was born in 1965 and trained as a cabinetmaker continuing his education at the John Makepeace School for craftsmen and the Royal College of Art, London. *f 90*
Monica Guggisberg and **Philip Baldwin** trained as glassblowers in Sweden at the Orrefors Glass School and with the Studio of Ann Wurff and Wilke Adolfsson. In 1982 they established their own design and glassblowing studio north of Lausanne in the French part of Switzerland. They divide their time between hand-blown production glass, table top glassware, free blown, one of a kind sculptural work; and design for the glass industry, namely Rosenthal since 1985 and Steuben since 1989. *t 4*

Dominic Habsburg (H.R.H. Archduke Dominic of Austria) was born in 1937 in the family castle of Sonnberg near Vienna. Forced into exile by World War II, he studied in Austria, Rumania, Switzerland, Argentina and the USA graduating from the Rhode Island School of Design as an industrial designer. As well as running his own studio he was director for product research and development of Semperit AG and an expert for the United Nations and the World Bank. The Archduke specializes in work with crystals and has developed his own mould-making technique for shaping the surface of mouth-blown glass three-dimensionally. *t 2*
Koji Hamai was born in Japan in 1964 and graduated from the Bunka Fashion College. He believes strongly in the importance of the textile in fashion design and is well known for producing highly fashionable fabrics. He initially joined Miyashin Corporation in Hachioji where he acquired his knowledge of textile production. In 1986 he moved to the Issey Miyake Design Studio where he stayed until 1991, leaving to work as a freelance fashion designer. He has received many awards within Japan. *tx 1-4*
David Hales is a leading designer for Smart Design, New York. *p 45*
Stuart Harvey Lee was born in North Yorkshire in 1965 and after working briefly at the steelworks in Sheffield, studied mechanical engineering at the Imperial College of Science and Technology in London and industrial design at the Royal College of Art. He has worked in Europe, Japan and the United States and is currently a senior designer at Smart Design Inc. His work has been published internationally and exhibited in London at the Design Museum and the Aram Design Gallery, and in New York at Gallery 91. *p 45*
Harry Haun is an in-house designer for S&W Medico Teknik AS in Copenhagen, Denmark specializing in the design of hospital equipment. Haun has shown at numerous design exhibitions and has won several awards including the Danish ID prize in 1979 and 1988. *p 43*
Trix Haussmann studied at the Swiss Institute of Technology, Zurich graduating in architecture and urban planning in 1963. Since 1967 she has worked together with **Robert Haussmann**. Robert Haussmann studied in Zurich and Amsterdam. Today he is Professor at the Academy of Art in Stuttgart. *f 86-7*
Haute Hause was founded by Dwight Huffman (born 1967) and John Rantanen III (born 1961). They specialize in 'reconstruction' furniture design which integrates new perceptions of form and space with the use of low impact materials such as locally harvested wood. Their work is widely available within the United States. *f 89*
Matthew Hilton was born in 1957. He studied furniture design at Kingston Polytechnic, London until 1979, then, after working for several years as an industrial designer in London, he started his own design work in 1984. At present he is designing for SCP, disform, XO, Idée and Alterego. He regularly exhibits his work at the Milan and Cologne Furniture Fairs. *f 23*
Yoshiki Hishinuma is a fashion and textile designer who was born in Sendai, Japan in 1958. He has presented collections since 1984, showing both in Japan and Europe. In 1992 he became the subject of a monograph *Here and There* and exhibited his work at EXPO '92 Seville. Since 1993 he has been costume director of Universiade '95, Fukuoka. *tx 5-9*
David Hoard, Interface and Product Designer, Hauser Associates, graduated from the Art Center College of Design in 1992. At Hauser he works on computer, medical and consumer electronic projects. *p 9*
Hans Hollein was born in 1934 in Vienna, Austria. He is an artist, architect, planner, designer, teacher, writer and winner of the Pritzker Architecture Prize, USA, in 1985. *f 103, t 16-17*
Martyn Hoogendijk was born in 1970 in Berg Ambacht, the Netherlands. He attended the Academie Industriele Vormgeving in Eindhoven and exhibited his work for Droog Design. After his military service he plans to open his own studio. *f 27*

Takenobu Igarashi was born in 1944 in Takikawa City, Japan. His major works include desktop accessories for Raymay Fujii Corporation, lighting fixtures and stainless dinnerware for Yamada Shomei Lighting Company and clocks for Oun Design Corporation. Many of his products can be found in permanent collections of various museums. He created sculptures for the Nissan 'Infiniti' showrooms in the US and the 'Hibiki' sculpture at the entrance of the Suntory Concert Hall in Tokyo. In 1989 he received the Katsumia Masaru Design Award and in 1993, the Industrie Forum Design Hanover Award.
James Irvine was born in London in 1958 and graduated from the Royal College of Art in 1984. He then moved to Italy, working as a consultant designer for Olivetti with Ettore Sottsass and Michele de Lucchi. He participated in '12 New Memphis 86' and became a member of the group Solid. In 1988 he opened his own studio in Milan designing interiors, furniture and industrial products with various companies including Alessi, Cappellini and Fantini. In 1990 Irvine taught as a visiting lecturer at the Domus Academy, Milan. *p 69*

Ehlen Johansson was born in 1958 and started work as a designer at IKEA in 1984. *f 122*
Hella Jongerius was born in 1963 and attended the Academie Industriele Vormgeving in Eindhoven. She has exhibited at Le Vent du Nord in Paris and at Droog Design in Milan. *p 93*
Diana Juratovac is Vice President of Design Central, an Industrial Design Consultancy in Columbus, Ohio. She was born in Ohio in 1963 and received her degree in Industrial Design from the University of Cincinnati in 1986. *p 89, 104*

Shiu-Kay Kan is an architect who specializes in lighting design. Projects include a shopping centre in Malta, a nightclub in London and a conference center in Beijing. *l 50*
Nazanin Kamali is a Persian refugee and a graduate of the Royal College of Art. Her intricate work has gained her much acclaim. *f 14*
Tomihiro Kaneko founded Kaneko Design Office in 1975 which today is known as Orb Inc. He was born in 1943 and graduated from Kuwazawa Design School in industrial design. Currently involved in teaching design, he has received various awards within Japan including the Industrial Machine Design Award, the Japan's Inventor's Association award and the Good Design Mark award (G Mark). *p 107*
Masafumi Katsukawa is a young Japanese designer currently living and working in Milan. *l 20-1, 34*
Kazuo Kawasaki, one of Japan's leading industrial designers, was born in Fukui, Japan in 1949. Following his graduation from Kanazawa University in 1972, he joined Toshiba. In 1980 he founded eX-DESIGN, INC., where he was engaged in both design theory and practice, dealing with areas from business strategies to community revitalization and from traditional crafts to interior designs and computers. He is the director of Kazuo Kawasaki Design Formation. He has received many awards, including the 1992 I.C.S.I.D. Excellence Award. The Mainichi Design Award was awarded to his products for the handicapped. His work is in the collection of the Cooper-Hewitt Museum and the Musée des Arts Décoratifs. *t 26, p 98, 102*
King Kong was founded in 1985 by Stefano Giovannoni (born 1954) and Guido Venturini (born 1957) who both graduated in architecture from Florence University. Since 1979 they have taught and carried out research at the Florence Faculty of Architecture and at the Domus Academy. Their interest is focused on cartoons, science fiction, celluloid mythology, areas of the imaginary and of artificial fiction. King-Kong have exhibited at events including the Paris Biennale, the Venice Biennale, the Barcelona Biennale and the Milan Triennale as well as in Brazil and Japan. *t 31*
Toshiyuki Kita was born in Osaka in 1942. He has been working on environmental product design since 1969 in Milan and Japan, and is also involved in traditional Japanese craft design. In 1987 he took part in the celebration of the Pompidou Centre's 10th anniversary, and in 1990 was awarded the Delta de Oro in Spain. In 1991 Kita designed the interior and the chairs for the revolving theatre for EXPO '92.His work is in the collections of MoMA, New York and the Design Museum, London. *f 106*
Hiroshi Kobayashi is Assistant Manager of Chiba University in charge of measuring instruments, compact cameras and binoculars. *p 95*
John Koenig is a Senior Designer at Design Central, a Design Consultancy in Columbus, Ohio. He

was born in Cincinnati, Ohio in 1964 and received his degree in industrial design from the University of Cincinnati in 1988. *p 104*

Peter A. Koloski was born in 1960 and attended the Ohio State University, Department of Industrial Design and the Columbus College of Art and Design. Before joining Design Central as Project Manager for Industrial Design he worked for various product design companies in the USA. *p 101*

Makoto Komatsu was born in 1943 in Tokyo and from 1970 to 1973 was Assistant to Professor Stig Lindberg at Gustavsberg Porcelain in Sweden. He has achieved national acclaim through various design awards and his work can be seen in the permanent collections of MoMA, New York and the V&A, London. *t 7*

Osamu Kondo was born in 1962 in Aichi and attended the Aichi College of Art. In 1985 he joined the General Audio Division Design Sector of Matsushita and today works for their AV Design Centre.

Thomas Krause, born in 1959 in Copenhagen, is a Bachelor in furniture design from Denmark's Design School. Before working for Lego Toy Company he was a freelance industrial designer working for Tuborg, IKEA, Royal Copenhagen and Post & Telegraph. *f 98*

Masahiko Kubo was born in Aichi-ken in Japan and graduated from Tokyo University of Fine Arts and Music. From 1981-91 he worked for Pola Cosmetics Co. in Japan before moving to Italy. He has been working for Studio de Lucchi since 1991. *p 80*

David Laituri, Senior Industrial Designer, Lunar Design, holds a BSc in industrial design from Ohio State University and undertook postgraduate studies at the Staatliche Akademie der Bildenden Künste in Stuttgart and at the Center for Creative Studies in Detroit. His main responsibility at Lunar Design is generating concept products for Apple Computer. He has received a number of awards from the Industrial Designers Society of America. He was a member of the faculty of the Center for Creative Studies in Detroit, MI. *p 1-2*

Romolo Lanciani was born in 1945. His collaboration with Walter Posern began in 1983 with the formation of Neostudio (dissolved in 1992). During the time they spent together they dealt with industrial, graphic and interior design, the design of light fittings, the preparation of stands for exhibitions and catalogues, for clients such as Luce, Mandelli, Punto and Luxo Italiana. From 1993 Romolo Lanciani has continued to work with Luxo. *l 3,4*

Vico Magistretti, born in Milan in 1920, graduated in architecture in 1945. A member of the Academy of San Luca since 1967, he teaches at the Domus Academy and is an honorary member of the RCA, London. The recipient of numerous major awards including the Gold Medal at the 9th Milan Triennale in 1951, the Compasso d'Oro in 1967 and 1979 and the SIAD Gold Medal in 1986, Magistretti's furniture, lamps and other designs are found internationally. He has worked for companies such as Alias, Artemide, Cassina, De Padova, Fiat, Knoll International, and Rosenthal. He has exhibited widely, and his work can be seen in many design collections worldwide. *f 28-33*

Erik Magnussen was educated at the Danish School of Arts and Crafts. Today he has his own design studio and is a partner of Eleven Design active in furniture, product and industrial design. Clients include Bing and Grondahl, Royal Copenhagen and Stelton and his work is exhibited at museums worldwide. Magnussen has also worked as a lecturer at the Royal Danish Academy of Fine Arts. *f 5*

Christian Maier was born in 1963 in Schwaz, Austria and studied industrial design at the College for Creation, Linz. From 1986 to 1990 he worked as a freelance interior and industrial designer after which he started to develop lighting prototypes for Planlicht, Austria. *l 35*

Chiaki Maki was educated at the Rhode Island School of Design and received a Bachelor of Fine Arts in Textile Design in 1985. Before creating Maki Textile Studio in 1989, she worked for clothing companies in New York and Tokyo. She was a finalist in the International Textile Contest sponsored by the Japanese Fashion Foundation in 1986, 1987 and 1990, and has exhibited her work widely. *tx 12-13*

Kaori Maki was educated at the Rhode Island School of Design and received a B FA in Textile Design in 1988. She then began a professional internship with Jack Lenor Larsen in New York. Before joining her sister Chiaki Maki in the Maki Textile Studio in 1992, she worked as a freelance textile designer in New York, Thailand and Japan. In 1987 she was nominated for the Grand Prix in the American section of the International Textile Design Contest and was again a finalist in 1988. *tx 11*

Enzo Mari was born in Novara in 1932 and studied at the Academy of Fine Art in Milan. He has taken part in several Biennales in Venice and in the Triennale, Milan. In 1972 he participated in *Italy: The New Domestic Landscape* at MoMA, New York. Mari is involved in graphic and industrial design, publishing and the preparation of exhibitions. He has recently been occupied with town planning and teaching and has organized courses for the History of Arts faculty at Milan Polytechnic. He has been awarded the Compasso d'Oro on three occasions. His work is to be found in the permanent collections of various contemporary art museums including the Stedelijk Museum, Amsterdam, the Musée des Arts Décoratifs, Paris, and the Kunstmuseum, Düsseldorf. *f 12-17, 25*

Ingo Maurer was born in 1932 on the island of Reichenau, Lake Constance, Germany and trained in typography and graphic design. In 1960 he emigrated to the United States, working as a freelance designer in New York and San Francisco before returning to Europe in 1963. He founded Design M in Munich in 1966, and since then his lighting designs have achieved world recognition, He has exhibited widely, including *Ingo Maurer: Making Light* at the Museum Villa Stuck, Munich and *Licht Licht* at the Stedelijk Museum in Amsterdam, and his work forms part of the permanent collections of many museum, including MoMA, New York. *f 82, l 25-8*

Markus R. Mayer is a designer and model maker at Design Central, a design consultancy in Columbus, Ohio. He was born in Tetnang, Germany in 1962. After a tool and die making apprenticeship, he finished his studies at the Art and Design school at Pforzheim and received a diploma in industrial design in 1991. *p 89*

Mario Mazzer was born in 1955 and was educated in Milan at the Polytechnic Design School, obtaining a degree in Architecture in 1978. In 1990 he founded his own practice in industrial and architectural design. He has collaborated with companies such as Acerbis, Busnelli, Morphos, and Zanotta and his work can be found in a number of design museums. Mario Mazzer has received several special mentions in *Young & Design* in '87-'89 and '91, being awarded the 2nd prize in the latte year. *f 100*

Hilton McConnico was born in Memphis Tennessee, USA in 1943 and worked as a stylist for Ted Lapidus, Jacques Heim and Yves St Laurent before moving into film and showbusiness design, being responsible for the decor in films such as *La lune dans le caniveau* and *Diva*. In the late 80s he expanded his interests to include textile and lighting as well as painting and photography. *tx 32*

Steve McGugan was born in Vancouver in 1960 and studied product design at the Art Centre College of Design from 1979 to 1981. He has worked as an in-house designer for Bang and Olufsen and David Lewis Industrial Design. In 1988 he formed his own design consultancy in Copenhagen, working in all areas of product design. He has received the Danish Design Competition for the best plastic product in production. His work is displayed in the permanent collection of MoMA, New York. *p 43*

Alberto Meda, born in Como, Italy in 1945, graduated in mechanical engineering from Milan Polytechnic in 1969. He worked at Magneti Marelli, and at Kartell as executive producer before starting a freelance practice collaborating with a number of clients including Gaggia, Kartell, Centrokappa, Lucifero, Cinelli, FontanaArte, Luceplan, Anslado, Mondedison, Mandarina Duck and Carlo Erba. He has been awarded numerous international prizes including the Compasso d'Oro in 1989 and Design Plus in 1992. *f 69*

Friedbert Meinert was born in 1953 in Germany. He trained as an engineering patternmaker in Stuttgart and moved to London In 1974. He studied product design at the Middlesex Polytechnic and also has a postgraduate teaching diploma. He was managing director of Aktiva Systems from 1988 to 1991. He is now managing director of Basis Design which specializes in lighting design manufacture and light planning. Recent projects include specialist library lighting for St Johns College Cambridge, display lighting for Ford with Imagination and retail lighting for Harrods, London. *l 41*

Mario Melocchi was born in Parma in 1931 and founded OPI (later Cini and Nils) in 1956. Today he works in packaging and product design designing collections for restaurants, the home and the office. He works with the architect Franco Bettonica and their clients number Lancôme, L'Oreal, Nestlé and Philips. *l 1*

Alessandro Mendini is the publisher of the design magazines *Casabella*, *Modo* and *Domus*. For many years he has been the theorist of avantgarde design, co-founding the Global Tools Group in 1973 as a counter-movement to established Italian design. In 1978 he started his collaboration with Studio Alchymia in Milan and developed the so-called 'Banal design' which sought to change items in daily use into new and ironical objects. In 1983 he became Professor of Design at the University of Aplied Art in Vienna. In the last few years he opened Atelier Mendini with his brother the architect Francesco Mendini designing projects such as the Gronigen Museum and, with Yumiko Kobayashi the Paradise Tower, Hiroshima. *l 55, p 81*

Eiji Miyamoto was born in the textile manufacturing city of Hachioji, Japan, in 1948, graduating from the Hosei University in Tokyo in 1970. He joined his father's textile firm, Miyashin Co. Ltd., and is today the Managing Director. In 1988 he joined the Hachioji Fashion Team. He has exhibited his designs within Japan, most notably in a series of one man shows from 1980 -1993. He lectures at the Bunka Fashion College. *tx 16*

Koji Mochizuki was born in Osaka in 1961, graduating from the Salesian Polytechnic in 1976 where he majored in industrial design. In 1981 he joined the Tape Recorder Division of Matsushita and today works for their AV Design Centre. *p 58*

Carlo Moretti was born in 1934 on the island of Murano, Italy. After cutting short his law studies in Padua he joined his father in his glass workshop. After a brief period he left to co-found his own die-decorated glass kiln with his brother Giovanni where he now constantly develops new techniques and glass finishes, collaborating with young designers and architects. *t 5*

Kenneth Mori, born in Los Angeles in 1965, received a BSc in Industrial Design from California State University Long Beach in 1990, He has collaborated with Xerox Corporation, Patton Design and Ashcraft Design. *p 51,53*

Jasper Morrison was born in London in 1959 and studied at the Kingston School of Art and the Royal College of Art, winning a Berlin scholarship in 1984. In 1986 he established his own design office in London. Amongst others he designs for SCP, Cappellini, Alias and Vitra and lectures at the Hochschule der Kunste, Berlin and Saarbrüken, the European Institute of Design, Milan and the Royal College of Art, London. He has exhibited widely in Europe and the UK, most notably for Vitra in Milan, at the Kunstmuseum in Düsseldorf and at Galerie Néotù, France. *f 2-4, t 25*

Pascal Mourgue was born in 1943 in Neuilly-sur-Seine, Paris and is a graduate of the Ecole Nationale Supérieure des Arts Décoratifs . Since 1969 he has been designing furniture, carpets, tableware and even trimarans. He has exhibited his work widely within Europe and in 1984 was elected 'Designer of the Year' by the Salon du Meuble de Paris, as well as receiving the Grand Prix de la Création de la Ville de Paris in 1992. His work can be seen in the permanent collection of the Musée des Arts Décoratifs in Paris. *f 109-112*

Sarah Murrey graduated from the Furniture Design Department of the Royal College of Art, London in 1994. *f 105*

Paul Newman is a British furniture designer and founder of Aero with architect Rob Whyte. *l 5*

Marc Newson was born in Sydney in 1963 and graduated from the Sydney College of Art in 1984. In 1985 the Powerhouse Museum, Sydney acquired some of his designs, at the same time offering him a Craft Council Grant to devise new work. Since 1987 he has worked periodically in Japan for Idée, creating, amongst others, the Rattan and Felt series. Marc Newson lives and works in Paris and is currently working on new designs and for exhibitions in New York and Los Angeles. *f 117-7a, 128, l 13, t 24*

ninaber/peters/krouwel Industrial Design was established in 1985 by Bruno Ninaber van Eyben, Wolfram Peters and Peter Krouwel with the aim of producing a wide variety of line assembly and mass-produced products for the consumer and professional market. Ninaber graduated from the Maastricht Art Academy in 1971, Peters and Krouwel from the Delft Technical University in 1978. They have won recognition both within the Netherlands and abroad, and their work can be seen in the permanent collections of MoMA, the Stedelijk Museum, and the Design Museum, among others. In 1990 nine of their products received Gute Industrieform awards. *f 39, p 57, 108-9*

Mike Nuttall is the director of industrial design for IDEO's US offices. He has designed numerous award-winning high-technology products, including the Microsoft mouse and all of Silicon Graphic's bold computer enclosures. He holds a degree in industrial design from Leicester College of Art &

Design and an MA degree from the Royal College of Art in London.

Matias Ocana, Prototype Manager for Hauser Associates, was born in Ambato, Ecuador and studied engineering at the University of Ambato. He emigrated to America in 1982 where he continued his training and is currently studying mechanical engineering at El Camino College. He has model making experience in the fields of aerospace and architecture as well as industrial design. *p 30*

Katsuhiko Ogino was born in 1944 graduating from Musashino University of Art in 1966. From that year until 1969 he was a lecturer at the Japan Design School after which he established various practices - Mono-Pro Kogei (1972); Humpty Dumpty Ltd (1976) and Time Studio Ltd (1978). He has received national recognition for his work and in 1986 was made a member of the Craft Center Japan of which he is now director. *f 6, 93*

Ondine and **Culture Shock Ltd** were both created by Julia Shua-King Cheng who holds diplomas in art, design and music from the Ecole Nationale Supérieure des Beaux Arts, Paris, the Royal Conservatory of Music, Toronto and the University of Toronto. Since graduation she has carried on her artistic aspirations as well as branching out into tableware and furniture design. She has shown her work in Europe and now has a studio in Paris. *p 1*

Luciano Pagani and **Angelo Perversi** were born in Milan in 1950 and graduated in architecture from Milan Polytechnic. Before setting up their design studio they worked individually in the fields of architecture and lighting design for companies such as Flos, and for Mondadori and Rizzoli. They have received international acclaim for their work being awarded the Compasso d'Oro in 1987 and the Product Design Award IBD in 1992. Pagani and Perversi started working with Zanotta in 1993. *f 18*

Roberto Pamio has worked near Venice since graduating in architecture in 1968. His projects include both domestic and industrial design for clients such as Cadel, Matteograssi and Leucos. He has worked in the USA, Australia, Mexico and Japan as well as in Italy. *l 54*

Francesco Pascali was born in 1957 and studied architecture at the Architectural Institute of Venice. From 1987 he has completed several public and private architectural commissions for interiors. *f 64*

Doug Patton graduated from California State University, Long Beach, with a BS in Industrial Design. Today he is principal of Patton Design which specializes in human interface design, mechanical engineering and industrial design. His clients include Apple Computer, Hewlett Packard, Hitachi, Mitsubishi, Philips and 20th Century Fox. He has been awarded over 70 design awards and patents, and his work can be seen in the permanent collection of the Smithsonian Institute. *p 51, 53*

Luke Pearson was born in 1967 and studied furniture design at the Royal College of Art, graduating in 1993. He is currently a freelance designer and has worked for Ross Lovegrove, Jasper Conran, and Habitat. In 1992 he was responsible for the seating design at the Kings Head Theatre, London. *p 49*

Pelikan Design was founded in 1978 by Nils Gammelgaard and Lars Mathiesen. This design team concentrates mainly on furniture and product design. Working with several Danish and international manufacturers they have earned worldwide acclaim. *f 20*

Jorge Pensi is a Spanish architect and industrial designer, born in 1946 in Buenos Aires. He has worked in Barcelona since 1977, specializing in the design of furniture, lighting, fittings and product image. He has achieved wide acclaim for his designs, most notably the Toledo chair for which he was given the first Award Selection SIDI-1988, two silver Deltas and an Award Design-Auswahl 90 from the Stuttgart Design Centre. Since 1989 he has worked with companies from Italy, Germany, Finland and the USA on product design. *f 99*

Karin Pesau, born in 1963, studied product design at the Hochschule für Angewandte Kunst under Prof. Carl Aubeck since which time she has won considerable recognition for her range of Snodo lamps edited by Woka Lamps. She has exhibited her work in Vienna, Munich, Linz, Bulgaria, Berlin and New York. *l 39*

Marlan H. Polhemus is an industrial design consultant specializing in product design, innovation and development. Before becoming Senior Vice President and Principal of Goldsmith Yamasaki Specht Inc, he held positions at General Motors, Harley Earl, Inc., and at Dave Chapman, Inc. He has gained recognition through various national design awards. *p 41*

Paolo Portoghesi was born in 1931 in Rome where he graduated in 1957. From 1967-1977 he taught at the Faculty of architecture at the Milan Polytechnic and he was Rector from 1968-1976. At present he is a Professor at the Sapienza University in Rome. As an architectural historian, his best known books are monographs on historical and modern architects. As designer, he has created furniture and various objects for Poltronova, Alessi, Ceramiche Montesanto and also for Swatch. In 1983 Portoghesi was Chairman of the Biennale in Venice. *p 41,81*

Walter Posern was born in Graz, Austria in 1944 and studied at the Brera Academy of Design, Milan. In 1985 he co-founded Neostudio with Romolo Lanciani, specializing in lighting design. In 1992 Neostudio was dissolved and Posern formed the company Walter Posern DAG, enlarging his activity to include technical and illustrative graphics and exhibition as well as industrial design. Today he lives and works in Milan. *l 3 - 4*

Thierry Poubeau studied at the Ecole Boulle in Paris followed by a furniture specialization at the Musée des Arts Décoratifs . Today he works as a freelance industrial designer. *f 38*

Kuno Prey lives and works in San Candido in the Dolomite Mountains where he was born in 1958. He studied at the Domus Academy in Milan and after graduating in 1984 he started working with furniture manufacturers. Kuno Prey is an R & D consultant for various companies and has designed a multitude of successful products, many of which have received international awards. *f 115*

Andrée Putman, the Parisian interior designer, initially studied music at the Paris Conservatoire with François Poulenc. After several years as a stylist and journalist, she founded the design company Créateurs et Industriels. Today, her own enterprise, Ecart International, focuses on the production and revival of classic furniture design and modernist accessories. Her interior design projects have brought her world fame. These include the Morgans Hotel, New York; the Wasserturm Hotel, Cologne; Le Lac, Japan; offices for the French Minister of Culture; an art museum in Rouen; and the Museum of Modern Art in Bordeaux. Work carried out in 1993/1994 includes the headquarters of Air France, the Hotel Sheraton, Paris-Roissy and the concept for the chain of Bally shoeshops worldwide. *f 65-6*

Pol Quadens is a freelance furniture designer who lives and works in Bruggen, Brussels. Recently he has started working for Italian companies as a consultant and also produces work by other Belgian designers. *f 94*

Enrico Quell has a degree in industrial design and since 1981 has worked in professional studios gaining experience in both industrial design and graphics. In 1984 he began to work as an industrial design consultant for Olivetti in Milan. Then in 1990 he founded his own industrial design studio with Fabrizio Galli. He has participated in various exhibitions, and his work has been published both in Italy and abroad. *p 77*

Ernesto Quinteros, designer, Hauser Associates, graduated from California State University, Long Beach, with a BS degree in Industrial Design. Before working with SG Hauser he spent many years in advertising and commercial graphics as well as in residential architecture. *p 30*

Karim England Rashid received a Bachelor of Industrial Design degree in 1982 from Carleton University in Ottawa, Canada. He did his graduate studies in Italy under Ettore Sottsass and Gaetano Pesce, then moved to Milan for a one-year scholarship at the Studio of Rodolfo Bonetto. On his return to Canada he worked for seven years with KAN Industrial Designers in Toronto. Since 1991 he has been principal designer for Karim Rashid Industrial Design. Projects include furniture, lighting, houseware and product designs. Rashid has been a faculty member at the Ontario College of Art and a fulltime assistant professor at the Rhode Island School of Design and today is assistant Professor of industrial design at the Pratt Institute, New York and at the University of the Arts, Philadelphia. His work has received international recognition. *t 13*

Vince Razo, mechanical engineer, Hauser Associates, is an industrial design graduate of California State University. He worked for several industrial design firms before joining SGH. *p 8-9, 103*

Aldo Rossi was born in Milan in 1931 and studied architecture at Milan Polytechnic. In 1960 he became Director of *Casabella* and a year later founded his own studio. In 1965 Rossi became Professor at the Milan Polytechnic and subsequently in the Architectural Institute of Venice. He has lectured in Zurich, Harvard and Yale. In 1988 he received the first prize in the design competition for the National Museum of History, Berlin and in 1990 the Pritzker Prize. Rossi has designed furniture for Molteni and Unifor and products for Alessi. *f 37, 102, l 15*

Alejandro Ruiz was born in Bahia Bianca in 1958 and took a degree in industrial design at the Faculty of Fine Arts of UNPL, Argentina. He worked as a design researcher for UNPL until 1985 when he moved to Milan and worked with Andrea Branzi, Aldo Cibic and Massimo Morozzi on courses at the Domus Academy. Before setting up his own design studio in 1989 he taught at the European Design Institute and at the Summer School of the Architectural Faculty of the Milan Polytechnic. *t 30*

Hirose Ryuichiro was born in 1957 in Kumamoto, Japan. He attended the Nihon University College of Art, joining the 'Tokyo Stereo' Division Design Sector of Matsushita in 1980. Today he works in their AV Design Centre. *p 63*

Lino Sabattini is an Italian silversmith born in 1925. His metalwork first attracted international attention in 1956 when it was exhibited in Paris. Since then, Sabattini has continued to be closely associated with a simple, sculptural approach to metal and glassware, working for companies such as Rosenthal AG in Germany and Zani Metalwares in Italy. He exhibited several times at the Milan Triennale, being awarded the Compasso d'Oro in 1979. His works are in the permanent collections of the British Museum and V&A, London, MoMA and the Cooper-Hewitt Museum, New York. *t 10*

Rolf Sachs studied business administration in London and San Francisco but his interest in art, design and film resulted in a career in furniture design. He has held one man shows in Germany and exhibited in Germany, Austria and Paris. *f 54-8*

Marc Sadler graduated in industrial design in Paris after which he carried out extensive research in the use of new plastic materials, specializing in the design of sports equipment and accessories. After an extended trip to the Orient he moved to the USA and opened a studio in New York. At the same time he created a workshop in Asolo staffed with a team of model makers and technicians where he developed a new multiuse product 'Totem' and began his collaboration with Far Eastern manufacturers. Among his current clients he numbers Cartier, Dainese, Ebel Swiss, Fiorucci, Reebok and Intersport Swiss. *l 29-30*

Yoshihito Saitou was born in Tokyo in 1964, graduating from the Tokyo National University of Fine Arts and Music Design Course in 1987. In the same year he joined GK Industrial Design Associates where today he is chief designer in the Design Development Department and also the Product Design Department. In 1989, 92 and 93 his work was cited by MITI, Japan. *p 11, 27*

Masatoshi Sakaegi was born in 1944 in Chiba-ken, Japan. In 1938 he founded the Masatoshi Sakaegi Design Studio which specializes in ceramic and melamine tableware and ceramic sculpture. He has won many awards for his work, most recently at the Japan Design Forum '93. In 1991 he became an Assistant Professor at the Art University of the Province of Aichi. *t 23*

Thomas Sandell was born in Jakobstad in Finland and started his architectural training at the KTH in Stockholm. Since 1985 he has been employed by the architectural office of Professor Jan Henriksson and has worked on several projects within Sweden, including the café for the National Museum of Cultural History in Stockholm and the Eden Hotel, also in Stockholm. *f 70*

William Sawaya was born in Beirut in 1948 and graduated in 1973 from the National Academy of Arts. Before moving to Italy in 1978 he worked in the USA and France. In 1984 he founded Sawaya & Moroni with Paolo Moroni where he is artistic director and project manager. *f 107-108*

Winfried Scheuer was born in Calw, Germany in 1952. He worked as a trainee in the styling department of Mercedes-Benz in Sindelfingen, before studying at the Royal College of Art, London from 1979 to 1981. He has worked in London as a self-employed industrial designer since 1986 and has exhibited his work at Documenta Kassel and the Luci Exhibition, Memphis, Milan. He is visiting lecturer at the Royal College of Art, London and the Hochschule der Künste, Berlin. *p 94*

Hagai Shvadron was born in Israel in 1958 and graduated from the Holon C.T.E Tel Aviv University with a degree in industrial design and with a teaching diploma. He moved to Italy in 1984 and studied at the Domus Academy completing a thesis entitled 'The Home Computer of the Nineties'. In 1986 he started working as a design consultant to Olivetti with Mario Bellini and is responsible for the design of Olivetti's portable computers line with Michele de Lucchi. Today he has his own practice working with clients worldwide such as Panasonic, Japan and Aminach, Israel. His work has been exhibited and published internationally and he has taught at the Holon University, Domus Academy and at the Bezalel Academy of Jerusalem. *p 67*

Mamoru Shiozaki was born in Kyoto in 1955 and attended the Musashino University College of Art. In 1979 he joined the Air Conditioning Division Design Sector of Matsushita and today works for their AV Design Centre. *p 20*

Dieter Sieger established his own architectural firm in Munster Albachten, Germany, following his graduation as an architect from the Dortmund School of Arts and Crafts in 1964. From 1965 to 1976 he was occupied with the design and construction of terraced houses and single family houses in Greece, Spain, France, the USA and Saudi Arabia. An interest in sailing led to his interior designs for sailing and motor yachts, which in turn has resulted in a collaboration with Dornbracht, and designs for modern equipment for private bathrooms. In recent years he has also ventured into ceramic design. Sieger has been awarded state prizes in Japan, Northern Westphalia and the Netherlands and his work has been exhibited worldwide. *t 19-20*

Borek Sipek was born in Prague in 1949. After taking a furniture design course at the School for Arts and Crafts in Prague he moved to Germany in 1968 where he studied architecture at the High School for Art in Hamburg and took a philosophy course in Stuttgart. Before moving to Amsterdam in 1983 he taught design theory at the University of Essen and was scientific assistant at the Institute for Industrial Design at the University of Hannover. Since starting his own architecture and design studio in 1983 he has had solo exhibitions at the Musée des Arts Décoratifs, the Stedelijk Museum, the Vitra Design Museum and the Museum for Decorative Arts in Prague. His work can be seen in the permanent collections of the major design museums worldwide and he has been honoured with the Ordre des Arts et des Lettres from the French government in 1991 and with the Prins Bernard Fonds Prize for Architecture and Applied Arts in 1993. Borek Sipek is senior lecturer in Architecture at the Prague Academy of Applied Arts. *f 113, t 9*

Karel Slovacek, mechanical engineer, Hauser Associates, was originally educated at the Technical College, Hranice, and the University of Mechanical Engineering Brno, Czechoslovakia before moving to San Francisco where he trained at the City College. Prior to joining SGH, Karel Slovacek was the primary engineer for Holbrook Design. *p 12*

Sottsass Associati, established in 1980, has international clients in the fields of architecture, interior design, industrial design, graphics and corporate identity, including Apple Computer, Olivetti, Alessi, Coca Cola, Mitsubishi, Matsushita, and Cassina. Sottsass Associati's partners are Ettore Sottsass, Marco Susani, Johanna Grawunder, Mike Ryan, James Irvine and Mario Milizia. *f 45-7, l 56-9, p 82*

Ayala Sperling-Serfaty was born in Israel in 1962. Following early education and military service in Israel, she studied Fine Art at the Middlesex Polytechnic and Art History and Philosophy at the Tel-Aviv University, being awarded a scholarship from the Sharet Fund, Israel in 1984 and presented with first prize in the Annual Furniture Design Competition in Israel in 1993. She has exhibited her work in Israel and has been published in Israel, Japan and Italy. *f 130-31*

Peter Spreenberg, Senior Interaction Designer, IDEO, San Francisco, has a degree from the Illinois Institute of Technology. His design experience includes international design, graphic design and typographic font design for medical equipment, computer software, consumer products and multimedia. He has won awards for his designs and been published in magazines such as *Abitare* and *ID*. He is a member of the American Centre for Design and the Association for Software Design. *p 44*

Henk Stallinga was born in 1962 in Tietjerksteradeel, the Netherlands and studied at the Academy of Industrial Design and the Gerrit Rietveld Academy in Amsterdam. He has exhibited his work at furniture fairs in Italy, Belgium, Spain and Germany. *f 101, l 18, t 28*

Philippe Starck was born in Paris in 1949. After a period of activity in New York, he returned to France where he has since built up an international reputation. He has been responsible for major interior design schemes, including François Mitterrand's apartment at the Elysée Palace, the Café Costes; and the acclaimed Royalton and Paramount hotels in Manhattan, New York. He has also created domestic and public multipurpose buildings such as the headquarters of Asahi Beer in Tokyo. As a product designer he works for companies throughout the world, collaborating with Alessi, Baleri, Baum, Disform, Driade, Flos, Kartell, Rapsel, Up & Up, Vitra and Vuitton. His many awards include the Grand Prix National de la Création Industrielle. His work can be seen in the collections of the major design museums. *f 40-2, l 9,33*

Davin Stowell, President of Smart Design, founded Davin Stowell Associates in 1978, then along with Tom Dair, Tamara Thomsen and Tucker Viemeister founded Smart Design Inc. in 1985. Stowell holds a Bachelor of Industrial Design from Syracuse University (1976) and after graduation worked for Corning Glass Works Consumer Products Division. His work has been honoured within the United States. *p 45*

Studioquadrifoglio Arch. Ass. was founded by Gianni Menguzzato (39), Michele Villis (39) and Claudio Nascimben (36) who all graduated from the University of Architecture in Venice. Clients number Casamania by Frezza, AGV, MDS, Boeri, Lem, Brancale, Medico Italia Spa, Serma Elettronica and Orna SpA. Originally involved in product design, the company has expanded to include architecture and interior design. *f 92*

Reiko Sudo was born in Ibaragi Prefecture, Japan and educated at the Musashino Art College. Before co-founding Nuno Corporation in 1984 she worked as a freelance textile designer and has since designed for the International Wool Secretariat, Paris and for the clothing company Threads, Tokyo. At present she is Director of Nuno Corporation and a lecturer at the Musashino Art University. She has exhibited both nationally and internationally, and her work can be seen in the permanent collections of MoMA and the Cooper-Hewitt Museum, New York; the Museum of Art Rhode Island School of Design; the Philadelphia Museum of Art; the Museum of Applied Arts, Helsinki; and the Montreal Museum of Decorative Arts. *tx 14-5*

Minoru Sugahara was born in Tokyo in 1940 and graduated from Waseda University. He joined the Sugahara Glassworks Inc., in 1963 and since 1973 has headed the design team which has developed approx. 2,000 items of glassware in 20 years. *t 12*

Shinichi Sumikawa was born in Tokyo in 1962 and graduated from Chiba University Industrial Design Department in 1984. From 1984-1991 he was a member of the Sony design team working both in Japan and America. In 1992 he established Shinichi Sumikawa Design Studio in Tokyo and has received second prize at the Nagoya Design Competition in 1993 and 1994. *p 5, 110*

Mitsushige Sumimoto was born in Ono City, Hyogo in 1955 and graduated from Kober University, Department of Civil Engineering in 1978. He entered Design EMI Associates in 1982 and became Managing Director in 1987. *p 100*

Yoshitaka Sumimoto was born in Ono City, Hyogo Prefecture in 1953. He graduated from Osaka University of Arts in 1975 and established Design EMI Associates in 1980, becoming its President and Managing Director in 1987. He was awarded the Good Design Prize for products of small industry in 1985 and today is producing designs for Mitsubishi and other clients. *p 100*

Kioshi Suzuki was born in Kyoto in 1946, graduating in product design from the Tama College of Art. In 1970 he joined the TV Division Design Department of Matsushita Electric Industrial Co. and currently works for their AV Design Centre. *p 65*

Barry Sween, industrial designer, Hauser Associates, received a BS degree in Industrial Design from California State University at Long Beach in 1991. He also studied at the University of Essen, Germany, and has received numerous awards for his design including recognition from the Industrial Design Society of America. *p 15*

Kyle Swen holds an industrial design degree from San José State University. He has been employed professionally by Lunar Design, Tandem Computers and Moss Design during the past seven years. Swen is currently working as a designer for Astro Products, Inc., a startup company based in Palo Alto, California. *p 8*

Yoichi Takahashi was born in Oita, Japan in 1952 and attended the Oita Tsurusaki Industrial College of Art. In 1971 he joined the House Equipment Design Sector of Matsushita and today works for their AV Design Centre. *p 21*

Shinkichi Tanaka was born in Fukuoka, Japan in 1950 and graduated from the Kuwazawa Design Institute in 1972. His product design company, Zero-one Design, was founded in 1978 before which he worked for AIWA, Japan and undertook an extensive tour of Denmark to research Danish design. He is a member of the Japan Design Association and lectures at the Kuwazawa Design Institute. *p 83-4*

Marc Tanner, Manager of Industrial Design, IDEO, London, has a degree in industrial design from Newcastle University. As well as working in London he has worked at both the San Francisco and Boston offices of IDEO. He lectures at the Royal College of Art, and is also a juror on the Royal Society of Arts student awards panel. He is a member of the Chartered Society of Designers and the Industrial Designers Society of America. *p 44, 46*

Rainer B. Teufel is President of Design Central, a design consultancy based in Columbus, Ohio.He studied industrial design at the Hochschule für Bildende Künste in Hamburg and at the Ohio State University. Before joining Design Central he was Senior Associate at Richardson/Smith and instructor at the Ohio State University. *p 89, 104*

Brandt Thompson is an American designer born in 1965. He graduated in 1991 in product design from Art Center College of Design, Pasadena. He currently works at Patton Design. *p 31*

Roberto Tosso and **Noti Massari** are lighting designers now working with Leucos, Venice. *l 53*

Luigi Trenti was born in Florence in 1965 and studied industrial design, CAD and presentation techniques. His work has been published in international magazines like *Area* and in text books such as *Se Dici Design*. A member of the ADU, Trenti is at present Chief Designer for Targetti Sankey. *l 46*

Mario Trimarchi has been collaborating with the Domus Academy for several years first as Director of the Master Course in Industrial Design (1990-1993) and now as the Coordinator of the Domus Design Agency. He has also developed research programmes for companies such as Secco, Nuove Ceramiche Ricchetti and Seleco as well as working for Olivetti Design Studio where he designs personal computers and automatic bank terminals. In 1990 he received the Industrial Design SMAU Award for the Olivetti Cash Dispenser designed with Michele de Lucchi. *p 70,72-5*

Kati Tuominen was born in 1947 in Helsinki and studied there at the School of Industrial Arts and the University of Industrial Arts. Since 1980 she has been employed by the Art Department of Arabia. She has exhibited her work widely in Europe, the States and Japan and in 1993 was awarded a State Artist's scholarship for five years. Examples of her designs can be seen in the permanent collections of the Nationalmusuem., Stockholm, the Hetjens Museum, Düsseldorf, the V&A, London, the Museum of Applied Arts, Helsinki, the Arabia Museum, Helsinki and the Israel Museum, Jerusalem. *t 22*

Olivier Védrine was born in Perpignan in 1962 and studied at the School of Architecture in Montpellier and at the Ecole de Paris-la-Villette where he was awarded an architecture diploma in 1987. In 1988 he was given a scholarship by the French government and carried out research at the University of Waseda in Japan. He has exhibited his work in Paris and Japan. *t 18*

Tucker Viemeister, Vice-President of Smart Design Inc, was born in Ohio and graduated from the Pratt Institute. He worked in his father's design studio before forming Smart design in 1985 along with Davin Stowell, Tom Dair and Tamara Thomsen. Mr Viemeister has juried, lectured and taught around the world. He is on the faculty of Yale and Parsons and is a juror for the Rotterdam Prize. He will be the Chair of the Industrial Designers Society of America's 1995 convention in Santa Fe. *p 45*

Massimo Vignelli was born in Milan and studied architecture in Milan and Venice. He went to the United States from 1957-1960 on fellowships from design firms. In 1960 he established Vignelli Office of Design and Architecture in Milan with Leila Vignelli, later becoming Vignelli Associates in 1971 and Vignelli Designs in 1978. His work includes graphic and corporate identity programmes, publication designs, architectural graphics and exhibition, interior, furniture and consumer product designs for many leading American and European companies and institutions. His work can be seen in the permanent collections of the leading design museums internationally and he has been awarded many prizes worldwide including the Gran Premio Triennale di Milano in 1964 and the Compasso d'Oro also in 1964. *t 3*

Arnout Visser was born in 1962 in Middelburg, the Netherlands and studied at the Art College in Arnhem (1984-1989) and at the Domus Academy in Milan (1990-1991). Since graduation he has been working freelance making designs in glass, metal and recycled materials. t 27

Burkhard Vogtherr was born in 1942 and after serving an apprenticeship as cabinet maker studied industrial design at the Werkkunstschule Kassel und Wuppertal. His work has received significant acclaim within Germany and has been published both nationally and in the USA. *f 48*

John von Buelow, Project Manager, Hauser Associates, is a graduate of San Jose State University with a BS degree in Industrial Design. Prior to joining SGH in 1981 he gained corporate and consulting experience at Bunker Ramo and two Southern California design consulting firms. *p 12, 103*

Bernard Vuarnesson is an interior, furniture and objects designer. Trained as an engineer in the wood industry, he started an office in Paris calculating roof fabrics. In 1972 he founded Sculptures-Jeux and designed playground equipment with his wife Ariane Vuarnesson. From 1975 until 1980 he was consultant at the Ecole Camondo, Paris. *f 50*

Köbi Wiesendanger was born in Switzerland and studied at the Kunstgewerbeschule. He has been Art Director for Young and Rubicam, TBWA and since 1976 for Avant de Dormir. *f 95, 97*

Akira Yamamoto currently works with Sigeaki Asahara and numbers Lucitalia among his clients. *l 44*

Max Yoshimoto, Studio Manager/Vice President of Lunar Design, holds a Bachelor's degree in industrial design from the San José State University. Before joining Lunar Design he was principal of his own firm where he specialized in industrial design for electronics and medical technology companies. Max Yoshimoto has received a number of awards from the Industrial Designers Society of America and his work has been widely published. *p 15*

Hans Zaugg was born in Derendingen in 1936 and trained as a joiner in his father's firm. In 1980 he set up his own company which he refers to as a 'school of innovation'. He was responsible in part for the creation of the Swatch watch. *f 121*

SUPPLIERS

Acerbis International SpA., Via Brusaporto 31, 24068 Seriate, Italy. *Outlets:* Belgium: Artiscope-Zaira Mis, 35, Bd. St. Michel, 1040 Brussels. Far East: Valentino Renda, Piazza Roma 84, 22066 Mariano Comense. France: Francis Helven, Chateau Le Mouchet, 26260 Chavannes. Germany: Hoffenhauser Hermann Niels, Bergstrasse 61, 69259 Wilhelmsfield; Holke Florin, Am Schwarzen Meer 118, D-28205 Bremen, Weis & Weis, Von Merveldt Str 12, D-48336 Sassenberg. The Netherlands: Kees Biermans, Parkstraat 9, 4818 Breda. Scandinavia: Interstudio, Ludersvej 4 Frihavnen, 2100 Copenhagen, Denmark. Spain: Carrasco Ignacio, Plaza Conde Valle Suchil 9, 28015 Madrid. Switzerland: Gianni Franco Fedrigo, Via G. Washington 102, 20146 Milan. UK: Environment, The Studio, 120 High Street, South Milford, Leeds LS25 5AQ; Environment Flos Ltd., 31 Lisson Grove, London NW1 6UV. USA: I. L. Euro Inc. - Ivan Luini, 900 Broadway No. 902, New York NY 1003.

Aero Ltd., 96 Westbourne Grove, London W2 5RT, UK.

Alessi SpA.,Via Privata Alessi 6, 28023 Crusinallo, Novara, Italy. *Outlets:* Denmark: Gense AS, 17 Maglebjergvejm 1800 Lyngby. Finland: Casabella OY, 24 Yliopistonakatu, 20100 Turku. France: Société Métallurgique Lagostina, 62 rue Blaise Pascal, 93600 Aulnay-sous-Bois. Germany: Van der Borg GmbH, Sandbahn 6, 4240 Emmerich. Japan: Italia Shoji Co. Ltd., 5-4 Kojimachi, 1-chome, Chiyoda-ku, Tokyo 102. The Netherlands: Interhal BV, 8 Zoutverkoperstraat, 3330 CA Zwijndrecht. Sweden: Espresso Import, 10E Furasen, 42177V Frolunda. Switzerland: Guido Mayer SA, 9 rue du Port Franc, 1003 Lausanne. UK: Penhallow Marketing Ltd., 3 Vicarage Road, Sheffield S9 3RH. USA: The Markuse Corporation, 10 Wheeling Avenue, Woburn, MA 01801.

Alias Srl., 29 Via Leonardo de Vinci, G. del Monte, Italy. *Outlets:* Austria: Design Agentur Herbeckstrasse 27, Vienna. Belgium: Kreymborg 66 av Moliere, Brussels. France: Roger Von Bary, 19 rue Lafitte, 75009 Paris. Germany: Hans Jorg Taubert, Nerostrasse 40, Wiesbaden. Greece: Hadzimihals, 13th National Road, Athens. Holland: Eikelenboom Keienbergweg 54, Amsterdam. Hong Kong: Le Cadre Gallery, G/F Ruttonjee H., 11 Duddel Street. Japan: Casatec Ltd., 2-9-6 Higashi, Shibuya-ku, Tokyo 150. The Netherlands: Kreymborg 63 Minervaalan, 1077 Amsterdam. Sweden: Design Distribution, 38A Doebelnsgatan 11352 Stockholm. Switzerland: Renato Stauffacher, 2 Capelli, 6900 Lugano. UK: Artemide GB Ltd. 17-19 Neal Street, London WC2H 9PU. USA: International Contract Furniture, 10 Maple Street, Norwood, New Jersey; Luminaire, 7300 S. W. 45th Street, Miami, Florida. ; Mossa, 1214 Washington Av. St. Louis, Missouri; Domus, 6438 Dawson Blvd, Norcross, Georgia.

Akaba SA., Kale Nagusia 56, 20160 Lasarte, Gipuzkoa, Spain.

Altana Arte, 23/3 Via Carozzani, 30027 S. Donà di Piave (Ve), Italy

Alterego, Via Marconi 20, 25080 Cariago, Italy. *Outlet:* UK: Viaduct 10 Summer's Street, London.

Anibou Pty Ltd., 726 Bourke 2016, N. S. W. Australia.

Anritsu Corporation, 1800 On-Na, Atsugi-shi 243, Kanagawa, Japan.

Apple Computer, 20525 Mariani Ave., Cupertino, California, 95015, USA.

Arabia, Hämeentie 135, 00560 Helsinki, Finland.

Ron Arad Studio, 62 Chalk Farm Rd., London NW1 8AN

Ardi, 2 Chemin Beauchet, 78490 Méré, France.

Ark Telecom, 124 Carmen Lane, Suite K, Santa Maria 93454, California, USA.

Jan Armgardt, 45 Grieselstr, 64601 Bensheim, Germany

Arredaesse, Via SM Maddalena 37, 22060 Arosio (Co), Italy

Art Andersen & Co. 3 Keld Langesgade, Copenhagen 1367, Denmark.

Arteluce (Division of Gruppo Flos SpA). Via Angelo Faini 2, Bovezzo, Brescia 25073, Italy. *Outlets:* Belgium: Flos SA, Gossetlaan 50, 1720 Groot Bijgaarden. France: Flos GmbH, Am Probsthof 94, 5300 Bonn 1. Japan: Flos Co. Ltd., PMC Building, 1-23-5 Higahi-Azabu, Minato-ku, Tokyo 106. Spain: Flos SA, c/Bovedillas 16, San Just Desvern, 08960 Barcelona. Switzerland: Flos SA, 75 Blvd St-Georges, 1025 Geneva. UK: Flos Ltd., The Studio, 120 High Street, South Milford, Leeds, Yorks. LS25 5AQ. USA: Flos Inc., 200 McKay Road, Huntington Station, New York, NY 11746

Artemide SpA., Via Bergamo 18, 20010 Pregnana Milanese, Italy. *Outlets:* Australia: Ornare, 14 Ormond Avenue, 5072 Magil. Austria: Vertreter Design Agentur R. Greinecker, Herbeckstrasse 27, 1183 Vienna. Belgium/The Netherlands/Luxembourg: Horas SA, Beemstraat 25, 1601 Ruisbroek. Canada: Artemide Ltd. 9200 Place Picasso, Montréal (ST Léonard), Québec H1P 3JB. Cyprus: HC Furniture and Art Ltd., 24 Pindarou Str., PO Box 586, Nicosia. Denmark/Finland/Sweden/Norway: Renzo d'Este, H. E. Teglersvej 5, 2920 Charlottenlund. France: Artemide E. u. r. l., 6-8 rue Basfroi, 75011 Paris. Germany: Artemide GmbH, Ltterpark 5, D-4010 Hilden. Greece: Habitat - K Frampton & Co., 9, Herodotou Street, Athens 10674. Hong Kong: Artemide Ltd. 102-103 Ruttonjiee Centre, Duddel Street. Japan: Artemide Inc., 2nd Floor Axis Bldg, 5-17-1 Ropongi, Minato-ku, Tokyo 106. Korea: Kunyang Trading, Kangnam-Gu, Yeoksam-Dong 721-39, PO Box 7594, Seoul 135-080. New Zealand: ECC Lighting Ltd., 39 Nugent Street, PO Box 291, Auckland. Portugal: FNI - Fabbrica Nacional de Iluminaçao SA, Avenida Leite De Vasconcelos, Lote 16, Apartado 3, Alfragide, 2700 Amadora. Singapore: Concept Lighting Pte. Ltd., 356 Alexandra Road, 0315 Singapore. Spain: Artemide SA, C/ Ripolles 5 y 7 08820 Prat de Llobregat, Barcelona. Switzerland: Artemide Illuminazione AG, via Trevano 72, 6900 Lugano. Turkey: Fil Mimari AS, Spor-Cad, 159 Akaretier, 80680 Istanbul. UK: Artemide GB Ltd., 17-19 Neal Street, London WC2H 9PU. USA: Artemide Inc., National Sales and Customer Service Center, 1980 New Highway, Farmingdale, NY 11735.

Ascom Radiocom Ag., Weissensteinstr, Solothurn 4503, Switzerland.

Atmosphère, 22 rue Washington, Paris 75008, France. *Outlet:* USA: Sak's Fifth Avenue, 611 5th Avenue, New York, NY 10022.

Avant de Dormir, 3 via Turati, 20121 Milan, Italy.

Bang & Olufsen Technology A/S, Peter Bangsvej 15, 7600 Struer, Denmark

Bär & Knell Design, 30 Hauptstr, D-74206, Bad Wimpen, Germany. *Outlets:* Cyprus: Cocoon Furniture, PO Box 1126, Limasol. Italy: Delafabro SNC., Mobili di Casa, Via dei Ponti 7, 330967 Spilimbergo; AGF Srl, Via Madonna Della Neve 24 Bergamo; Marmi & Graniti, Zantedeschi, Via A. de Gaspari, 37015 Domegliara; Dilmos s. a. s, Piazza San Marco, 20121 Milan. South Africa: Innovation Furniture Contracts, 179 Loop St., Cape Town, 8001. Switzerland: Interni, Emmentalstr 240, 3414 Oberburg; Kluge AG., Dufourstrasse 138, 8008 Zürich. UK:

Space, 28 All Saints Road, London W11.

Basis Design Ltd., Unit 18, 109 Bartholomew Road, London NW5 2BJ.

Bd Ediciones de Diseño, 291 Mallorca, 08037 Barcelona, Spain. *Outlets:* Austria/Germany: IMD Inter Marketing Distribution AG. Flöthbruchstrasse 11, 4156 Willich 2, Anrath, Germany. Belgium: Quattro, 25 rue de la Regence, 1000 Brussels. Canada: Triede, 460 McGill, Montreal, Quebec H2Y 2H2. France: 8 rue des Quatre Fils, 75003 Paris. Greece: Varangis Avepe SA, 40 M Botsari, GR 15121 Pefki. Holland: IMD Inter Marketing Distribution AG, Beverweerdlaan 22, 6825 AE Arnhem. Hong Kong: Le Cadre Gallery, 8 Sunning Road G/F, Causeway Bay. Italy: Zoltan. Via Alesandria 5, 20144 Milan. Japan: Art Front Gallery, Daikanyama Edge 3F, 28-10 Sarugaku-cho, Shibuya-ku, Tokyo. Portugal: Arquitectonica, Rua da Escola Politécnica 94, 1200 Lisbon. Singapore: Galeria Ecletique, 58 Tanjong Pagar Road. Switzerland: IMD Marketing Distribution AG, Eebrunnestrasse 26, 5212 Hausen (AG). UK: Interior Marketing, 2 Woods Cottages, Hartfield Broad Oak, Bishop's Stortford, Herts CM22 7BU. USA: Luminaire, 7300 Southwest 45th Street, Miami, Florida 33155; Current 1201 Wester Avenue, Seattle, WA 98101; Di-zin, 1320 Main Street, Venice, CA 90291.

Yves Behar, 1049 Market St. Suite 605, San Francisco 94103 California, USA.

Berkeley Outdoor Products, One Berkley Drive, Spirit Lake 51360-1041, Iowa, USA.

Branson Coates Architecture Ltd., 23 Old Street, London EC1V 9HL.

Bruno Longhoni, 73 Via Giovanni da Cermenate, 22063 Cantù, Italy

Canon Inc. 3-30-2, Shimomaniko 146, Tokyo, Japan. *Outlets:* Australia: 1 Thomas Holt Drive, North ryde, Sydney NSW 2113. Belgium: Bessenveldstraat 7, 1831 Diegem. Finland: Kornetintie 3, 00380 Helsinki. France: Centre d'Affaires Paris-Nord, 93154 Le Blanc-Mesnil Cedex. Germany: Hellersbergstr 2-4, W-4040 Neuss. Italy: Via Mecenate 90, 20138 Milan. Japan: 11-28, Mita 3-chome, Minato-ku, Tokyo 108. Latin America: Apartado 7022, Panama 5, Rep. de Panama. The Netherlands: Bovenkerkerweg 59-61, 1185 XB Amstelveen. Spain: Calle Joaquin Costa, No. 41, 28002 Madrid. Sweden: Stensätravägen 13, S-127 88 Skärholmen. Switzerland: Industriestrasse 9, 5432 Neuenhof/AG. UK: Canon House, Manor road, Wallington, Surrey, SM6 OAJ. USA: One Canon Plaza, Lake Success, New York, NY 11042.

Cappellini Arte. Via Marconi 35, 22060 Arosio, Italy. *Outlets:* Austria: Wolfgang Bischof OHG, Judenplatz 6, 1010 Vienna. Belgium: Rika Andries, Turnhoutsebaan 144b, 2200 Borgerhout. France: Cerutti Giuseppe, Loc. Gran Chemin 1, 11020 Saint Christophe. Germany: Novus, Gartenstrasse 26, 7959 Achstetten Bronnen 3. Greece: Aveope SA, 40 M. Botsari, G - 151-21 Pefki. The Netherlands: Hansje Kalff Meubelagenturen, Puttensestraat 8, 1181 Je Amstelveen. Portugal: Galante Interior Design, Rua Borges, Carneiro 49/55, P - 1200, Lisbon. Spain: Santa & Cole, Blames 71, E - 8440 Cardedeu Barcelona. Sweden: Mobile Box AB, Nybrogatan 11, 11439 Stockholm. Switzerland: Yves Humbrecht Diffusion, Mon Repos 3, 1066 Epalinges. UK: SCP Ltd. 135-139 Curtain Road, London EC2. USA/Canada: I. L. Euro Inc., 9000 Broadway 902, New York.

Casamania by Frezza Srl., Via Ferret 11/9, 31020 Vidor (Treviso), Italy.

Cassina SpA., Via Luigi Businelli 1, Meda 20036 Milan, Italy. *Outlets*: France: Sanda 168 rue de Faubourg Saint Honoré, 75008 Paris. Germany: Pesch GmbH & Co., KG., Kaiser Wilhelm Ring 22, 5000 Cologne 1. Japan: Cassina Japan Inc., 2-9-6 Higashi, Shibuya-ku, Tokyo 150. The Netherlands: Mobica, 31 Middenweg, 3401 Ijsselstein. Spain: Mobilplast, 40 calle Milagro, 08028 Barcelona. UK: Marcatré, 179 Shaftesbury Avenue, London WC2H 8AR. USA: Atelier International Inc., The International Design Centre, 30-20 Thomson Avenue, Long Island City, NY 10001, New York.

Cerva, Via Faentina 171, 50010 Caldine, Fiesole (Firenze), Italy.

Chérif, 2 Square Paul Bert, 96260 Asnières, France.

Ciatti SpA., Via del Botteghino, Loc, Borgo ai Fossi, 50010 Badià Scandicci (Florence), Italy.

Cicena, 150 East 58th Street, New York, NY 10155-2998, USA.

Cini & Nils Srl., Via Francesco Ferrucio 8, 20145 Milan, Italy. *Outlets:* Austria: Jandl Wohnbedarf, Boltzmanngasse 12, Vienna. Belgium/Luxembourg: Sig. Hugo Vleminckx, Rayo, O. L. Vrouwstraat 78, Mechelen. Germany (postal districts 1/2/3): Klaus Siemensen, Segeberger Strasse 127, Neumunster. (postal districts 4/5): Klaus Jansen, Stuting str 63, Gevelsberg. (postal districts 6/7/8): Folker Jahnke, Schertlinstrasse 20, Schondorf. Holland: Hansje Kalff, Puttensestraat 8, Amstelveen. Spain: Sig. Higueras Paseo Colon 102-104, Cardedeu, Barcelona. Switzerland: Catherine Corremans , Ipso Facto, 6 rue Joseph Girard, Geneva.

Le C. I. R. V. A., 62 rue de la Joliette, 13002 Marseille, France

Combi Co. Ltd., 3-16-9 Uchikanda, Chiyoda-ku, No. 101, Tokyo, Japan.

Concord Lighting Ltd., 174 High Holborn, London WC1V 7AA, UK. *Outlets:* France: S L I France, Tour Neptune, 20 Place De Seine, Courbevoie Cedex 20, 92086 Paris. Germany: S L I Lichtsysteme GmbH, Zeiss Strasse 2, D-50859 Cologne. Italy: Tecnolyte SpA., Via Nazionale 193, 00184 Rome. Japan: Light Cube Ltd. 1-2, Shiba, 5-chome, Minato-Ku, Tokyo. The Netherlands: Indoor B. V., Paulus Potterstraat 22-24, Amsterdam 1071 DA. Scandinavia: Hovik Lys AB, Telefonstigen 2, S-13141 Nacka, Stockholm.

Cor Unum, P. O. Box 311, 'S 5201 AH Hertogenbosch, The Netherlands. *Outlets:* Italy: Cecilia Flegenheimer, 3 via dal Pazzo, 20132, Milan. Germany: Teunen en Teunen, Postfach 36, 6222 Geisenheim 2. The Netherlands: Carlo Wanna, P. O. Box 1035, 3330 Zwijndrecht.

Cymbal Crown, 13423 Blanco, Suite 190, San Antonio 78216, Texas, USA.

DDM, 193 Lindwurmstr, 80337 Munich, Germany

DMD-Developing Manufacturing Distribution, Partweg 14, 2271 AJ Voorburg, The Netherlands.

Design Gallery Milan, Via Manzoni 46, 20121 Milan, Italy

Design House AWA, 1-21-1 Jingumae Shibuya-ku, 150 Tokyo, Japan

Draenert Studio GmbH., Steigwiesen 3, D- 88090 Immenstaad/Bds, Germany. *Outlets:* France/Belgium: Gérard van Houtteghem, 28 Impasse Belle Image, F-60802 Crepy en Valois Cedex. Scandinavia: Interstudio AS, Lüdersvej 4, Frihavnen, 2100 Kobenhavn. UK: Ramchester Furnishings Int. Ltd., 63 Buckingham Gate, London SW1 E6AS

Driade SpA., 12 Via Padana Inferiore, 29012 Fossadello di Caorso, Piacenza, Italy. *Outlets:* France: Arturo Del Punta, 7 rue Simon Le France, 75004 Paris. Germany: Stefan Müller, Bereiteranger 7, 8000 Munich 90. Japan: Ambiente International Inc., Sumitomo Semei Bldg, 3-1-30 Minami-Aoyama, Minato-ku, Tokyo. The Netherlands: Espaces & Lignes, Nassaulaan 2A, 2514 The Hague. Scandinavia: Design Distribution, Doebelnsgatan 38A 1, 11352 Stockholm, Sweden. Spain: Bd Ediciones de Diseño, 291 Mallorca, 08037 Barcelona. UK: Viaduct Furniture Ltd.

Droog Design, Noordeinde 31, 2611 KE Delft, The Netherlands. *Outlets:* . Italy: Cecilia Flegenheimer, 3 Via del Pozzo Toscanelli, 20132 Milan. The Netherlands: DMD Parkweg 14, 2271 AJ Voorburg

Ecart, 111 rue Saint Antoine, 75004 Paris, France

é de Padova, 14 Corso Venezia, 20121 Milan. Italy. *Outlets:* Belgium: Rika Andraes, 144 Thurnhoutsebaan, 02140 Antwerp. *Outlets*: Germany: Sabine Rick, 14a Leo-Statzstr, 40474, Düsseeldorf. Japan: Casatec Ltd., 9-6 Higashi 2-chome, Shibuya-ku 150 Tokyo. The Netherlands: Hansje Kalff, 8 Purrensestraat, 01181 Je Auisterveen, Holland. Spain: Giberna SL Indefil, Trestorres 11,1 08017 Barcelona. UK: Aram Design Ltd., 3 Kean Street, Covent Garden, London WC2 4AT. USA: Luminaire, 7300 SW 45th Street, Mismi, FL 33155.

ERCO Leuchten GmbH., 80-82 Brockhauser Weg, 58507 Lüdenscheid, Germany. *Outlets:* Australia: Spectra Lighting Pty., Ltd., 15 Industrial Avenue, Wacol, Quensland 4076. Austria: Erco Leuchten GmbH, Zweigniederlassung Wien, Modeceter Str 14/4. OG/BC A-1030, Vienna. Belgium: Erco Lighting Belgium Bvda/SPRL, Avenue Molière 211 B-1060 Brussels. Cyprus: J. N. Christofides Trading Ltd., PO Box 1093, 29a Michalakopoulou Str., Nicosia. Denmark: Lightmakers AS, Indiavej 1, Sondre Frihavn 2100 Kobenhavn O. Finland: OY Hedengren AB, Lauttasaarentie 50, SF-oo 200 Helsinki, Postilokero 190. France: ERCO Lumières, SARL., 6ter rue des Saints Péres, 75007 Paris; Succursale Lyon, 4 rue V. Lagrange, 69007 Lyon. Germany: ERCO Leuchten GmbH., Postfach 2460, 58505 Lüdenscheid. Greece: Christos Vakirtzis (Ltd.), Rizari 17, Athinai 11634. Hong Kong: Architectural Lighting (HK) Ltd., 3F. Shing Dao Industrial Building, 232 Aberdeen, Hong Kong. Iceland: Segull Ltd., Eyjaslod 7, 101 Reykjavik. Ireland: ERCO Lighting Ireland Ltd., 289 Harolds Cross Road, Dublin 6. Italy: ERCO Illuminazione Srl., Via Cassanese 224, Palazzo Leonardo, 20090 Segrate (Milan); ERCO Illuminazione Srl., Via Dei Colli Portuensi 345, 00151 Rome. Japan: ERCO TOTO Ltd., 3-44-1 Mukoujima, 131 Tokyo Sumida-ku. Korea: Al-Omar Electrical Lights Est., PO Box 6512, 32040 Hawalli . Malaysia: Seng Hup Electric Co. Snd Bhd., 44-2 et 44-3 Jalan Sultan Ismail, 50250 Kuala Lumpur. The Netherlands: ERCO Lighting Nederland BV., Gooimeer 13, NL-1411 DE Naarden. Norway: ERCO Belysning AS, Industriveien 8B, N-1473 Skarer, Postboks 83 Ellingsrudsen, 1006 Oslo 10. Oman: Delta Ltd., PO Box 4537, Ruwi. Portugal: Omnicel Tecnicas de Illuminaçáo, SA., rua Castilho, 57-5. Dto. 1200 Lisbon. Qatar: Rafco, PO Box 831, Old Rayyan Road, Doha. Saudi Arabia: Technolight, PO Box 12679, Jeddah 21483, Singapore: De. De Ce Design Centre c/o Kliktube Electrical Systems, Pte Ltd., 11 Keppel Road, Singapore 0409. Spain: Erco Illuminazione SA, Poligono El Plà, c/ El Plà s/n (Parcela 28), 08750 Molins de Rei. Sweden: Aneta Belysning AB, Box 3064, 35033 Växjö. Switzerland: Neuco AG, Würzgrabenstrasse 5, 8048 Zürich. Thailand: Palicon, Pro-Art Lighting Ltd., 4th Floor, 29-4 Sukhumvit 31, Phrakanong, Bangkok 10110. Turkey: Total Aydinlatma Mümessillik, Sanayi ve Ticaret AS, Tevukiye Caddesi No. 73/3 80200 Istanbul. United Arab Emirates: Scientechnic, PO Box 325, Dubai. UK: ERCO Lighting Ltd., 38 Dover Street, London W1X 3RB.

Farallon Computing, 2470 Mariner Square Loop, Alameda, California 94501, USA.

Fiam Italia SpA., Via Ancona 1/b, 61010 Tavullia, Pesaro, Italy. *Outlets:* Austria: Manfred Prunnbauer, 10 Selzergasse, 1150 Vienna. France: Guy Favali, 15 rue Reynaud de Trets, 13010 Marseille. Germany (North): Conzept Beckord kg., Lehmkuhlstrasse 21, 32108 Bad Salzuflen; (South): Riexinger Handelsagentur, Vorstadt 7, 71116 Gaertringen. Japan: Italprogramm, 43/A E. Bertini, 47100 Forli, Italy. The Netherlands: Mobica BV, 50 Gossetlaan, 1702 Groot Bijgaarden, Belgium. Spain: Gibarna SL., 11 Tres Torres, 08017 Barcelona. Switzerland: Humbrecht Diffusion, CP 4277, 1110 Morges. UK: Bianchi Furniture Traders, 2 Manley House, High View, Hitchin, Herts SG5 2HL. USA: Forma & Design, Shore Point, One Selleck Street, 06855 Norwalk, CT.

Flos SpA., Via Angelo Faini 2, Bovezzo 25073 Brescia, Italy. *Outlets:* Belgium: Flos SA, Gossetlaan 50, 1702 Groot Bijgaarden. France: Flos SARL, 23 rue de Bourgogne, 75007 Paris. Germany: Flos GmbH, Am Probsthof 94, 5300 Bonn 1. Spain: Flos SA, c/Bovedillas 16, San Just Desvern, 08960 Barcelona. UK: Flos Ltd., The Studio, 120 High Street, South Milford, Leeds LS25 5AQ Yorks. USA: Flos Inc., 200 McKay Road, Huntingdon Station, New York, NY 11746.

FontanaArte, Alzaia Triest 49, 20094 Corsico, Italy. *Outlets:* Austria: Kilga Markus, Seilergasse 15, 6020 Innsbruck. Belgium/Luxembourg: D'Acan Srl 36 Avenue Beau Séjour, 1410 Waterloo. France: Rousselin & Pecnard, 42 rue des Poissonniers, 92200 Neuilly sur Seine. Germany (North): Sabine Picx, Leo Statz Strasse 14a, 40474 Dusseldorf. Germany (South): Achim Reich, Elisabethenstr 50, 61348 Bad Homburg. The Netherlands: Andrée Kok, Pilatus 4, EK 1186 Amstelveen. Spain: Fabio Ballabio, Calle Remei 37/41 1020, 08028 Barcelona. Switzerland: Karl Kasper, Loewengraben 24, 6000 Lucerne 5. UK: Clemente Caviguoli, 86 Ladbroke Grove, London W11 2HE. USA: Ivan Cuini, I. L. Euro Inc., 900 Broadway 902, New York, NY 10003.

Foscarini Murano SpA., 1 Fondamente Manin, Murano, Venice 30141, Italy. *Outlets:* France: Horas International, 150 rue Championnet, Paris. Germany: Alta Linea GmbH, 6 Sandhof, 4040 Neuss 21 Norff. The Netherlands: Horas International, Beemdstraat 25, Ruisbroek 1610. UK: Liaison, 917-919 Fulham Road, London SW6 5HU.

Fuji Kowa Industry Co. Ltd., 3-23-3 Shinmachi, Setagaya-ku 154, Tokyo, Japan

Fujitsu, 1015 Kamikodanaka, Nakahara-ku 211, Kawasaki, Japan.

G. B. S. Co. Ltd., 6-13-4 Minami-Aoyama, Minato-ku 107, Tokyo, Japan.

Grundig AG., Kurgartenstr 37, D-90762 Fürth/Bayern, Germany. *Outlet:* UK: Grundig International Ltd., Mill Road, Rugby, Warwickshire SV 21 1PR.

Koji Hamai, 303 1-15-6 Kamitenjaku, Mitaka-City, Tokyo 181.

Hamax AS., Postuttak, N-1601 Krakeroy, Norway.

Fritz Hansen A/S., Allerodvej 8, 3450 Allerod, Denmark

Haute House, 1428 Danby Rd.,Ithaca, New York, NY 14850. *Outlets:* France: Néotù Gallery, 25 rue de Renard, 75004 Paris. Japan: N. Vision, 29-16 Midori, Gaoka, 6-chome, 228 Zama-skhi. USA: Néotù Gallery, 84 Wooster, NY 10012, New York.

Hishinuma Institute Co. Ltd., 5-41-2 Jingumae

Shibuya-ku 150, Japan.
Hughes Network Systems, 10450 Pacific Centre Court, San Diego 92191, California, USA.

Idée Co., Ltd. 5-4-44 Minami-Aoyama, Minato-ku Tokyo 107, Japan. *Outlet:* France: Idée Europe, 21 rue Danielle Casanova, Paris 75001.
Ikea of Sweden, Box 702, 34381 Almhult, Sweden.
Iralzola SA., Pol. Ind S/N, Placencia de las Armas, E-20590 Guipuzcoa, Spain.
ITA (Industria Tavoli e Affini), Via Aquileia 8, I-33050 San Vito al Torre, Udine, Italy
Itozen Co., 2-816, Sakaino, Kiryu 376, Gumma, Japan

Jovian Christie Inc., 3-4249-5 Hirosawa, 326 Kiryu, Gumma, Japan

Källemo AB., Box 605, 331 26, Värnamo, Sweden. *Outlets*: Denmark: P. Thorsen Mobler A/S, Viborgvej 175, 8240 Aarhus. Germany: MGM Möbel GmbH, Burg Mödrath, Köolnerstr 151, 50171 Kerpen. Japan: Swedish Furniture Group, Sweden Center Building, PO Box 40 6-11-9, Roppongi, Minato-ku, Tokyo 106.
Kartell SpA., Via dell Industrie 1, 20082 Noviglio (Milan), Italy. *Outlets:* Australia: Plastex, 85 Fairbank Road 3168 Clayton, Victoria. Austria: Eugen Leopold, Fielderstrasse 2-4, 4020 Linz. Belgium: Tradix SA, 90-02 rue du Mail, 1050 Brussels. Denmark: Collection Creative Danas Plads 15, 2000 Frderiksberg. France: C & D Diffusion SARL, 3 avenue du Bois Vert, 77240 Vert-Saint-Denis. Germany: Gotthilf Riexinger, Vorstadt 7, 7034 Gärtingen. Hong Kong: William Artists International Ltd. 232 Aberdeen Main Road, 3/F Shing Dao, Aberdeen. Israel: Goldberg and Co., 21-10 Haorgim Street, 58857 Holon. Japan: Interdecor Inc., 2-9-6 Higashi, Shibuya-ku, Tokyo 150. Lebanon: Vent Nouveau SARL, PO Box 233, Jal El Dib, Beirut. The Netherlands: Modular Systems, Bosboom Toussaintstraat 24, 1054 Amsterdam. Portugal: Grup Dimensao SA, Av. Eng. Arantes E Oliveira 5, 1900 Lisbon. Spain: Jordi Rotger, Zaragoza 62, 8008 Barcelona. Sweden: Claes Brechensbauer, Möbelagentur, Kyrkoköpinge Pl. 26, 23191 Trelleborg. Switzerland: Gatto Diffusion, 30 rue Des Cahvannes, 2016 Cortaillod. Turkey: Mood, Akkavak Sok. 47/2 Nisantasi, 80220 Istanbul. UK: Environment, The Studio, 120 High Street, South Milford, Leeds LS25 5AQ, Yorks. USA: I. L. Euro Inc., 900 Broadway 902, New York, NY 10003.
Kay Tay Co., 1-7-18 Motomachi, Katsuyama 911, Fukui, Japan.
Kenwood Ltd.,New Lane, Havant Hampshire PO9 2NH, UK. *Outlets:* France: Société Kenwood France, 13 rue du Pont des Halles, 94150 Rungis. Germany: Kenwood Elektro Gerate GmbH. Dornhosstrasse 18, 63263 Nev-Isenburg. Hong Kong: Kenwood Appliances Hong Kong, Ltd., 6D HK Spinners Industrial Building Phase 5, 760 Cheung Sha Wan Road, Kowloon. Italy: Singer Italia SpA., Via Trnto 59, 20021 Ospiate di Bollote, Milan, Italy. Japan: Aikosha Manufacturing Co. Ltd. 7-10-8 Chuo, Warabi-shi, Saitama 335. The Netherlands: Beska Nederalnd BV, PO box 2009, Moeskam PWEG 20, 5202 Cas Hertogenbosch. Scandinavia: Kenwood AS, Brogrenen 8, 2635 Ishoj Copenhagen, Denmark. Spain: River International SA., Beethoven 15, Atica 7A, 08021 Barcelona. USA: The Rival Co., 800 East 101 Terrace, Kansas City MO 64131.
Kimura Glass, 3-10-7 Yushima, Bunkyo-ku 113, Tokyo, Japan.
King Size, Via Tortona 26, 20144 Milan, Italy.
The Knoll Group, 105 Wooster Street, 10012 New York, New York, USA.
U. M. Kogyo Inc., 1015-1 Kishi-cho, Ono City 675-13, Hyogo, Japan. *Outlet:* The Netherlands: De Wild, 54 DeMeeten, 4700 BD Roosendaal.
Thomas Krause & Phipip Ludvigsen ,19 Bag Sondermarken, 2000 Frederiksberg, Denmark
Kron SA., S/No Camino Ancho, 28814, Daganzo, Madrid, Spain. *Outlets:* Belgium: Interoffex. Betaardlaan 15, 1850 Grimbergen. France: Pluralys, Les Monts, 74540 Hery-sur-Alby. Germany: Office Design, Berliner Ring 89, 64625 Bensheim. Japan: Shukoh Co. Ltd., 2-2-10 Tokyo-to Ohta-ku, Yaguchi 146. UK: Office Realisation, Old Lakers Farm, Mill Road, West Chilting, Sussex RH20 2PZ.

Leucos Srl., Via Treviso 777, Scorze, Venice, Italy. *Outlets:* France: Artemide SARL, 6-8 rue Basfroi, Paris 65011. Germany: Leucos Deutschland GmbH, Bunsenstrasse 5 Martinsried, B. Munich 8033. Japan: Arflex Japan Ltd., 4565 Kodachi Kawaguchiko-cho, Minimisuru-gun-Yamanashi. The Netherlands: Kreymborg BV, Minervalaan 63, 1077 Amsterdam. Spain: Forum International, Venida de Salvert 25, 46018 Valencia. UK: MW United, 3 Willow Business Park, London SE26 4QP. USA: Leucos USA Inc., 70 Campus Plaza, Edison, NJ 08837.
Lifeline Systems Inc., One Arsenal, Market Place, Watertown 02172, Massachusetts, USA.
Ligne Roset SA., 01470 Briord, France. *Outlets:* Germany: Roset Möbel GmbH, 51 Industriestrasse, 79194, Gundelfinaen. Italy: Roset Italia, 43 Boccaccio, 20123 Milan. Japan: Dreambed Co. Ltd. Sasai-Yachiyo-cho, Takata Gun, Hiroshima-ken, 731-03. UK: Roset UK, 95a High Street, Great Missenden Bucks, HP19 OBA. USA: Roset USA Corp., Suite 604. 200 Lexington Avenue, New York NY 10016.
Lisar SpA., Via Boccaccio 68/72, 22070 Carbonate (Co), Italy.
Logitech Inc., 6505 Kaiser Drive B3, Fremont 94555, California, USA.
Lucitalia SpA., 50 Via Pelizza da Volpedo, Cinisello B., 20092 (ML), Italy. *Outlets:* Asia: Casa Luce Inc., 2-16-12 Sotoranda, Chiyoda-ku, Tokyo 101, Japan. Argentina: Luz Y Colorm srl., Sarmiento 1164, 1041 Beunos Aires. Austria/Germany: Luci Leuchten GmbH, Buerglen 16, 88090 Immenstaad/Bodensee, Germany. Benelux: Quattro Benelux SA, Haltenaken 11, 3320 Hoegaarden, Belgium. Canada: Scangift-821, Tecumseh Road, Pointe Claire, Que Hor 4XB. Denmark: Taifo Buying Agencies A/S, Studsgade 35, Box 720, 8100 Aarhus. France: Luxo France SA., 96 Bd Auguste Blanque, 75013 Paris. Greece: Habitt - K. Frampton & co., 9, Herodotou Street, Kolonaki, 10674 Athens. Iceland: Heimsljos, Kringlan, 8-17-Reykjavik 103. Italy: Showroom and Projects Development, Lucitalia, via Brera 30, 20121 Milan. Israel: Y. Wallish Technologies Lt., Kehilat Saloniky Str., 69513 Tel Aviv. Lebanon: Memas SARL, Dora Gate, Beirut. Switzerland: Gatto Diffusion, rue des Chavannes 30, 2016 Coraillod. USA: Illuminating Experience Inc., 233 Cleveland Ave., Highland Park, NJ 08904. Venezuela: Lamparas Diana Dos SA., Av. 4 de Majo, Isle Margarita Porlamar.
Lumina, Via Casorezzo 63, 20010 Arluno (Mi), Italy. *Outlets:* Austria: Jandl Wohnbedarf, Boltzmanng 12, 1090 Vienna. Australia: Euroluce Australia Pty Ltd., 820 Parramatta Road, Lewisham, NSW 2049. argentina: Distribuidora G5 Srl., Thames 744, 1414 Buenos Aires. Belgium: Ardeco International, Avenue de General de Gaulle 39, 1050 Brussels. Canada: Agences Volt - Pierre Boulais, 68 rue Alie, Dollard des Ormeaux, Quebec. Denmark: Domus Interieur, Osterbrogade 60, 2100 Copenhagen. France: Objectique, BP 114000, 13793 Aix-en-Provence Cedex 3. Greece: Christos Vakirtzis, 7 Rizari Street, 116 34 Athens. Holland: Eikelenboom BV, Keienbergweg 54, 1101 GC Amsterdam. Israel: D. I. Lighting Fixtures Ltd., PO Box 21330, 61213 Tel Aviv. Norway: Expo-Nova, Bygdoy All'e 59, 25 Oslo. Spain: Avenida de Sala Vert 25,5,9A, 46018 Valencia. Switzerland: Lumina Design GmbH, Forchastr 149, 8132 Egg. UK: Forma Lighting Ltd., Unit 3, Mitcham Industrial Estate, 85 Streatham Road, Mitcham, Surrey CR4 2AP; Forma Lighting Ltd., Business Design Centre, Units 310-311, 52 Upper Street, London N1 9QH.. USA: Frederick Ramond Inc., 16121 So. Carmenita Road, 90701 Cerritos, CA; Current, 1201 Western Avenue, Seattle WA 98101-2960; D.I.V.A., 8818 Beverley Bl, 90048 Los Angeles, CA. Luminaire, 2331 Ponce de Leon Blvd., Coral Gables, FL 33134; Lee's Int. Furniture Gallery, Inc. Lee's Studio, 1069 Third Ave., 10021 NY, New York. Venezuela: Cedrin C. A., C. C. C. Tamanaco P. B., Local 43-Q-03 - 2DA Etapa, Caracas; Lamparas Diana, Avenida 4 de Mayo, Centro Elvi Local A - Porlamar; Servi-Fer CA., Centro Commerciale Ventura, Calle 75 Entre AV. 12 Y 13, Maracaibo.
Luxo Italiana SpA., 1 Via della Mone, 24030 Presezzo, Bergamo, Italy

Maki Textile Studio, 899-7 Totohara, Itsukaichi Machi 190-01, Nishitama, Tokyo, Japan.
Map Pty Ltd., 570 Chapel St., Sth Yarra 3141 Melbourne, Victoria, Australia.
Marsberger Glaswerke Ritzenhoff. Paulienstr 84, 34431 Marsberg, Germany. *Outlets:* France: 3D Diffusion, 1 Ave. Alphand, 75116, Paris. Germany: Van der Borg, GmbH, 5 Ossenbruch, 46446 Emmerich. Italy: Carlo Giannini SpA., 9 Via Caporalino, 25060 Cellatica (Brescia). The Netherlands: Interhal Select B. V. 8 Zoutverkopersstr, 3334 KJ Zijndrecht. Mexico: Mexico Importadora N. I. S. A. de C. V., 103 Av. Sonora, Col Roma, 06700 DF Mexico. Spain: M. Echevarria S. L., 159 Entenza, 08929 Barcelona. Switzerland: Guido Mayer SA, Case Postale, 1312 Eclèpans-Gare VD. UK: Penhallow Marketing Ltd., 3 Vicarage Road, Sheffield S9 3RH. USA: Oggetti, 48 Northwest, 25th Str. 33127 Miami, Florida.
Matsushita Battery Co. Ltd., 1 Matsushita-cho, Moriguchi, Osaka 570, Japan.
Matsushita Communication Industrial Co. Ltd., 600 Yokohama 226, Kanagawa, Japan.
Matsushita Electric Industrial Co., Ltd., 1-4 Matsuo-cho, Kadoma-City 571, Osaka, Japan. *Outlets:* Canada: Matsushita Electric of Canada Ltd. 1475 The Queensway, Toronto M8Z IT3, Ontario. France: Panasonic France SA, 932/8 Avenue de Président Wilson, La Plaine Saint Denis 270 Cedex. Germany: Panasonic Deutschland, 22525 Winsbergring Hamburg 54. Hong Kong: Shun Hing Electronic Trading Co. Ltd. New East Ocean Centre 14th - 15th Floor, 9 Science Museum, Kowloon. Italy: Panasonic Italia SpA., No. 19 Via Lucini, 20125 Milan. Scandinavia: Panasonic Svenska AB, Fitta Backe 3, Norsborg 145, 84 Stockholm. Spain: Panasonic Sales Spain SA, 20-30 Plantas 4, Josep Taradellas, 5Y608029 Barcelona. UK: Panasonic House, Willoughby Road, Bracknell, Berkshire RG12 8FP. USA: Matsushita Electric Corporation of America, 1 Panasonic Way, Secaucus 07094, New Jersey.
Matsushita-Kotobuki Electronics Industries Ltd., Office Equipment Office, 247 Fukutake, Saijo City 793, Ehime, Japan. *Outlet:* USA: Panasonic Company, Division of Matsushita Electric Company, One Panasonic Way, Secaucus, NJ 07094.
Ingo Maurer GmbH., 47 Kaiserstrasse, 80801 Munich, Germany. *Outlets:* France: Altras SARL 24 rue Laffitte, 75009 Paris. Japan: Studio Noi Co., Ltd., Rangee Aoyama Bldg, No 710, 1-4-1 Kita-Aoyama, Minato-ku, Tokyo 107. The Netherlands: inter collections b. v., 2 Bosrand Schiedam 3121 XA. Scandinavia: Mr Finn Sloth, 1 Heilsmindevej DK 2920 Charlottenlund, Denmark. Spain: Santa & Cole, 71 Balmes, 08440 Carcedeu, Barcelona.
Metalarte SA., 4 Avda. Barcelona, 08970 St. Joan Despi, Barcelona, Spain. *Outlets:* Argentina: Tecnoilar Sa, Nicolás A. Caputo, Paraquay 792 5, 1057 Buenos Aires. Australia: Tangent, 6-36 Boronia St., Redfern NSW 2016. Austria: Molto Luce, Europastrasse 45, 4600 Wels. Belgium: Light SA, Boulevard M. Lemonnier 99, 1000 Brussels. Brazil: Design Alternativo, Rua Marques do Herval 66, CEO 90570-Porto Alegre RS. Canada: Angle International, 460A rue McGill, Montreal, Quebec H2Y 2A3. Chile: Interdesign, Isodora Goyenechea 3200, Santiago de Chile. France: Electrorama, 11 boulevard Saint Germain, 75005 Paris. Germany: Altalinea, 6 Sandhof, 41469 Neuss 21 Norf. Hong Kong: Teamwork Design Studio Ltd., 6A Kiu Yin Commercial Building, 361-363 Lockhart Road, Wanchai. The Netherlands: Hooge Products Verlichting, Moeskampweg 10, 5222 s' Hertogenbosch. Italy: Barovier & Toso Srl, Fondamenta Vetrai 28, 30141 Murano, Venice. Mexico: Marca Interiores SA de C. V., Insurgentes Sur 1180 Col. del Valle, 03210 Mexico D. F. Portugal: Electro Ravd, Rua da Trindade 1-29, 4002-Porto. Singapore: Relex Electric (F. E.) PTE Ltd., 605b MacPherson Road, 07-14 Citimac Industrial Complex. Switzerland: U. S. W. SA, Château D'Affry 33, 1762 Givisiez, Fribourg. UK: Mr Light HMP Group Ltd., 275 Fulham Road, London SW10 9PZ. Uruguay: Artesanos Unidos SA, José E Rodo 2174, Montevideo. USA: Hinson Lamps, 27-35 Jackson Avenue, Long Island City, NY 11101-2817. Venezuela: Illuminación Helios CA, Parque Central, Edif. Anauco, Sotano 1, Local DS-42, Caracas 1015
Meliconi SpA., 8-10 Via Minghetti, 40057 Bologna, Italy.
Mercury Personal Communications, Elstree Way, Borehamwood WD6 1DT, Herts.
Miyashin Co. Ltd., 582-11 Kitano-cho, Hachiôji-shi, Tokyo 192
Modulor SA., 4070 Elpidio Gonzalez, Buenos Aires 1407, Buenos Aires, Argentina.
Möbelmanufaktur, 15a Bahnhofstr. CH-9450 Altstätten, Switzerland.
Molteni & Co. SpA., 50 via Rossini, 20034 Gussano, Italy. *Outlet:* UK: Orchard Associates, Box No. 65, Teddington, Middx TW11 9ED.
Carlo Moretti Srl. 3 F. Ta Manin, 30141 Murano-Venezia, Italy.
Mori Produzione Inox SpA., 90 Via Brescia, Lumezzane Termine 25066, Brescia, Italy.
Moroso SpA. 60 via Nazionale 33010 Cavalicco/ UD, Italy. *Outlets:* Australia: Canberra Flaor Pty Ltd., 8 Ipswick Street, Fyshwick Act. 2609. Austria: Michel Pilte, Via dei Colli 24, 33019 Tricesimo, Udine, Italy. Asia: Italmobil (Asia)Pte Ltd., 20 Kramat Lane, 04-06 United House, Singapore 0922. Belgium: Tradix SA, rue du Mail 90-92, 1050 Brussels. Denmark and Sweden: Interstudio A/S, Luedersvej, Frilhavnen, 2100 Kobenhavn, Denmark. Finland: Stanza OY, Annankatu 24, 00100, Helsinki. France: Chennouf Gilles, 15 rue de Petit Musée, 75004, Paris. Germany (postal codes 1-3): Thomas Graeper, Enzianstrasse 8, 4902 Bad Salzufluen; (postal codes 4-5): Walter J. Schiedermeier, Marienbergerweg 12, 5000 Cologne 71; (postal codes 6-8): Hubert Essenko, Maxim-Wetzgerstrasse, 8000 Munich 19. Greece: Avel Srl, 190 Klfsias Ave, 121 Athens 36. Hong Kong:

Le Cadre Gallery Ltd., 4B Sunning Road G/F, Causeway Bay. Hungary: Comester, Aranykez u 8, 1052 Budapest. Ireland: O'Hagan Contract, 101 Chapel Street, Dublin 1. Japan: Corrente Corporation, 3-2-chome, Kanda-Isukasa-cho Chiyoda-ku, Tokyo: The Netherlands: Ivo Verbeek Meubelimport, Johan Huizinhgalaan 288, 1065 JN Amsterdam. Singapore: Abraxas Design Pte Ltd., 4 Shenton Way, 01-01 Shing Kwan House, Singapore. Spain: Roger Sin Roca, Ronda Gral. Mitre 174-176, 08006 Barcelona. Switzerland: Oliver Ike, Kroenleinstrasse 31/a, 8044 Zurich. Turkey: Atelye Derin, Apdj Ipekci Caddesl 14/1, 80220 Nisantasl, Istanbul. UK: Atrium Ltd., Centrepoint 22-24, St Giles High Street, London WC2H 8LN. USA: Ernest Stoecklin, PO Box 208, 135 Fort Lee Road, 07605 Leonia, New Jersey.

Morphos (division of Acerbis Int SpA.), 31 Brusaporto, Seriate (BG), Italy. *Outlets:* Belgium: Artiscope-Zaira Mis, 35, Bd. St. Michel, 1040 Brussels. Far East: Valentino Renda, Piazza Roma 84, 22066 Mariano Comense. France: Francis Helven, Chateau Le Mouchet, 26260 Chavannes. Germany: Hoffenhauser Hermann Niels, Bergstrasse 61, 69259 Wilhelmsfield; Holke Florin, Am Schwarzen Meer 118, D-28205 Bremen, Weis & Weis, Von Merveldt Str 12, D-48336 Sassenberg. The Netherlands: Kees Biermans, Parkstraat 9, 4818 Breda. Scandinavia: Interstudio, Ludersvej 4 Frihavnen, 2100 Copenhagen, Denmark. Spain: Carrasco Ignacio, Plaza Conde Valle Suchil 9, 28015 Madrid. Switzerland: Gianni Franco Fedrigo, Via G. Washington 102, 20146 Milan. UK: Environment, The Studio, 120 High Street, South Milford, Leeds LS25 5AQ; Environment Flos Ltd., 31 Lisson Grove, London NW1 6UV. USA: I. L. Euro Inc. - Ivan Luini, 900 Broadway No. 902, New York NY 1003.

Nambe Mills Inc., 1127 Siler Rd., Santa Fé, New Mexico 87505, USA.

Néotù, 25 rue du Renard, 75004, Paris, France

Nikon Corporation, Fuhi Bldg., 2-3 Marunouchi, 3-chome, Chiyoda-ku, Tokyo 100, Japan. *Outlets:* France: Nikon France SA, 191 rue du Marché Rollay, 94504 Champigny-sur-Marne, Cedex. Germany: Nikon GmbH, Tiefenbroicher Weg 25, 40472 Düsseldorf 30, Germany. Japan: Nikon Optical Co., Ltd., 10-8 Ryogoku 2-chome, Sumida-ku, Tokyo 130. The Netherlands: Nikon Europe BU, Schipholweg 321, 1171 PL Badhoevedorp. UK: Nikon UK Ltd., 380 Richmond Road, Kingston, Surrey KT2 5PR.

Noto - Zeus, Via Vigevano 8, 20144 Milan, Italy. *Outlets:* France: Jean Gabriel Robin, Chemin des Sables, 69970 Chaponnay. Germany: Sabine Hainlen, Hermann Kurz Str 14, 7000 Stuttgart. Italy: Noto -Zeus, 8 via Vigevano, 20144 Milan. Japan: Ambiente Int. Minami Aoyama, 4-11-1 Minato-ku, Tokyo 107. The Netherlands: Miracles, 218 Prinsengracht, 1016 HD, Amsterdam. Scandinavia: Casalab, 19 Mosebakken, Virumy, 2836 Copenhagen. UK: Viaduct, 1-10 Summer's Street, London EC1R 5BD. USA: Luminaire, 7300 S. W. 45th Street, Miami, FL 33155.

Nuno Corporation, Axis B1 5-17-1 Roppongi, Minato-ku 106, Tokyo, Japan. *Outlet:* USA: Nuno N. Y., D & D Building 2nd Floor, 979 Third Avenue, New York, NY 10022.

O-Cedar/Vining, 1201 Kenton St., Springfield, Ohio 45505, USA.

Iris Ohyama Inc., 3-2-2, Shinjuku-ku, Shinjuku, Tokyo, Japan.

O Luce, 22 Via Conservatorio 22, 20122 Milan, Italy.

Ing. C. Olivetti & Co. SpA., 77 G. Jervis, Ivrea 10015, Turin, Italy.

Omni Cellular Ltd., 96 S. Madison, Carthage, Illinois 62321, USA. *Outlet:* UK: The Luxor Corporation, Luxor House, 2 Beach Road, Littlehampton, West Sussex BN17 5HT.

Ondine Industries Ltd., 12 rue Amélia, 75007 Paris.

Optelma AG., Gartenstrasse 7, Wiedlisbach 4537, Switzerland. *Outlets:* France: Optelma France SARL, 71 blvd Brandebourg, 94200 Ivry-sur-Seine. Germany: Agora Leuchten Vertriebs GmbH, Semerteichstr. 94, 44263 Dortmund. The Netherlands: Optelma Benelux, 21 Av. A. Giraudlaan, 1030 Brussels, Belgium. Spain: Tecnicas de Iluminacion C/. Jesus 77 Bajos 5, 46007 Valencia. UK: Optelma Lighting Ltd., 14 Napier Court, The Science Park, Abingdon, Oxfordshire OX14 3NB.

Patton Design, 8 Pasteur Suite 170, Irvine California 92718, USA.

Philips International BV., Building SX, PO Box 518, 1 Glaslaan, Eindhoven 5600 MD, The Netherlands. *Outlets:* Austria: Österreichische Philips Industrie GmbH, 64 Triester Strasse, 1100 Vienna. Belgium: NV Philips, 2 De Brouckereplein, PO Box 218, 1000 Brussels. Denmark: Philips Elapparat AS, 80 Pragsboulevard, 2300 Copenhagen. Finland: OY Philips AB, 8 Kaivokatu, Helsinki. France: SA Philips Industriale et Commerciale, 50 avenue Montaigne, 75380 Paris. Germany: Philips GmbH, Kilanstrasse 19, 8500 Nuremberg; Allgemeine Deutsche Philips Ind. GmbH, Steindamm 94, 2000 Hamburg. Italy: Philips Italia SA, Piazza IV Novembre 3, 20100 Milan. Japan: Philips Industrial Development and Consultants Co. Ltd., Shuwa, Shinagawa Bldg, 26-33 Takanawa 3-chome, Minato-ku, Tokyo 108. Norway: Norsk AS Philips, PO Box 5040, 6 Soerkedaksveien, Oslo 3. Spain: Philips Iberica SAE, 2 Martinez Villergas, Apertado 2065, 28027 Madrid. Sweden: Philips Norden AB, 11584 Stockholm. UK: Philips Electrical and Associated Industries Ltd., Arundel Great Court, 8 Arundel Street, London WC2 3DT. USA: North American Philips Corporation, 100 East 42nd Street. New York NY 10017.

Planlicht Ges. M. B. H. & Co. KG, Fiecht-au 25, 6130 Vomp, Postfach 44, Germany.

Playline by SCEP., 78 via Melitiello, 80017 Melito (NA), Italy. Outlets Belgium: Mobitec System SA., 11 Stockbergerwer, Eupen. France: Steph Simon, Hanry Machet, 40 rue de Chateaudun, 94200 Ivry-sur-Seine. Germany: D. D. S., 267 Offenbacherlandstr. 60599 Frankfurt/M.

Plus Corporation, 3-B22, Nakase 1-chome, Mihama-ku, Chiba 261-01 Japan. Outelts France: Carpentras, Parc d'Acrivités, Ragon 7av. Descartes 44119, Treillieres. Switzerland: Stilus, Via Passeggiata, 1-CH-6828 Balerna. UK: Rapesco Ltd., Rapesco House, Connections Business Park, Otford Road, Sevenoaks, Kent TN14 5DF.

Pol International Design Company SPRL., Av R. Vander Bruggen 85-87, 1070 Brussels, Belgium. *Outlets*: Belgium: Tradix SA, 90-92 rue du Mail, 1050 Brussels. France: Edifice, 27 bis Bld Raspail, 75007 Paris; Conran Shop, rue de Bac 75007, Paris. Holland: Bjart Design Group, De Smalle Zijde 4, 3903 Veenendael. Hong Kong: Ratio Mobili Ltd., Shops 318, 319 Prince's Building, Chater Road Central. Germany: D tec, Telleringstrasse 5, 40597 Düsseldorf. Taiwan: H. N. Lin, 1F, 32 Chin Shan S, Road SEC 1, Taipai. UK: The Conran Shop Ltd., Michelin House 81 Fulham Road, London SW3 6RD. USA: Linea, 8843-49 Beverley Blvd, Los Angeles 90048; Cumberland Furniture 30-20 Thomson Avenue, Long Island City NY 11101, New York.

Polaroid Corporation, 549 Technology Square, Cambridge, Massachusetts 02139, USA.

Porro Industria Mobili, 35 via per Cantù, 22060 Monte Solaro, Como, Italy. *Outlet:* Germany: Peter Pfeiffer, Novus-Wohnbedarf GmbH, Klaus-Graf Stauffenbergstr 11, Laupheim.

Porzellanfabrik Arzberg, Zweigniederl. der Hutschenreuther AG. 1-7 Jakobsburg, Arzburg 95659, Germany. *Outlets:* France: Intertrade France, Zone Industrielle, Rue Gay Lussac, Mitry-Mory 77290. Italy: Corrado Corradi SpA., 8 via Medici del Vascello, 20138 Milan. Japan: Hurschenreuther Japan Office, Aios Gotando Bldg. 302, 10-7 Higashi Gotando 1-chome, Shinagawa-ku, Tokyo 141. The Netherlands: Schott Zwiesel BV, Postbus 83, 2050 AB Overveen. Scandinavia/Sweden: Schott Serving AB, Box 14032, Gustavslundsvägen 153, 16114 Bromma. Spain: Riera Internacional SA, 72 Vilamari, 08015 Barcelona. UK: Hurschenreuther UK, Palmerston Business Centre, 11 Palmerston Rd, Sutton, Surrey SM1 4QL. USA: Hutschenreuther USA, 85 Price Parkway, Farmingdale, New York, NY 11735.

Practical Peripherals, 375 Conejo Ridge Road, Thousand Oaks 91361, California, USA.

Quart de Poil', 27 Rue de Bière, 75005 Paris, France. *Outlet:* Japan: Guichet M, 3-12-17 Naka-Ochici, Shinjuku-ku, Tokyo. USA/Canada: Kiosk Design Incorporated, 115 Dupont Street, Toronto, M5R 1V4, Ontario, Canada.

Recyco Inc., 18 Sargent Place, Mt. Vernon, New York, NY 10550. *Outlets:* Germany: Telesys, Siemensstrasse 6, 71101 Schonaich. Italy: Master Verophone, via Degli Arrotini, 19-57121 Livorno. Japan: Nason, 230 5th Avenue, NY 10001, New York. Singapore: Telecom Singapore, Kuek Chin Hing, 20 Pickering Street. Sweden: Telia, Televerket, 123-86 Farsta.

Robots, Via Galvani 7, 20082 Binasco (Mi), Italy

Rosenthal, 18 Casinostr, 1520 Selb/Bayern, Germany 8672

Rossana RB Srl., 49 Prvinciale, 61025 Montelabbate 61025, Presaro, Italy.

The Royal College of Art, Kensington Gore, London SW7 2EU.

Rubbermaid, 1147 Akron Rd., Wooster, Ohio 44691, USA.

Sabattini Argenteria SpA., 2 V. Don Capiaghi, 22070 Como, Italy.

Sabie, 648-1 Zen Shon in cho, 2-chome, Agawa dór, Teranouchi agann, Kamikyó-ku, Kyoto-shi, Japan.

Rolf Sachs Furniture, Yower House, 2 Fulham Park Road, London SW6. *Outlet:* Europe: Designer's Agency, Prinzregentenstr 2, 83022, Rosenheim, Germany.

Sakaegi Design Studio, 1-74 Nakamizuno-chou 489, Aichi-ken, Japan.

Thomas Sandell, c/o CBI 34 Birger Jarlsgatan, Box 26126, S10041 Stockholm, Sweden.

Sapsa Bedding, 62 Viale Rimembranze, 20099 Sesto San Giovanni, Milan, Italy. *Outlets:* Austria: Hukla Werke GmbH., Oberlaaerstrasse 246, 1100 Vienna. Belgium: Sapsa Bedding B. V., Gal. Porta Louise 203, Bte 7, Louizaport Gal. 203 - Bus 7, 1050 Brussels. Brazil: By Design Moveis e Asscessorios Ltd., R. Germaine Burchard 332, Fundos Perdizes - Sao Paulo. Denmark: Lillblund Agentur APS, Lille Standstraede 20, 1104 Copenhagen. Germany: Hukla Werke GmbH., Matratzen une Polstermöbelfabrikeu, 77723 Gergenbach/Baden. Greece: Media Strom-Athinaiki, Sdtromatopiia SA, 5 An Legaki (Rentis)18233 Piraeus. Hong Kong: Gruppo Mobilia Ltd., 1/F Casey Ind. Bldg., 20 Wong Chuk Hank Road, Wong Chuk Hang. Hungary: V. A. M. Design KFT., Visegradi Str 109, 1061 Budapest. Israel: S. Sides, 16, Shoken Street, Tel Aviv. Japan: Hukla Japan Inc., 9-12 Osaki 2-chome, Shinagawa KU, Tokyo 141. Korea: Shina Industrial Corp. 55-16 Nonhyun-Dong, Kangnam-Gu, Seoul. The Netherlands: Sapsa Bedding N. V., 26 Industrieweg 5, 4147 CS Asperen. Norway: Sonas Sovnsystem, Semsbyveien 118, 3170 SEM. Portugal: Districol, Rua Costa Cabral, 342-348, 4200 Porto. Spain: Sapsa Bedding SL., Escola Industrial 9 3o, 08201 Sabadell (Barcelona). Seden: Tibro Moebelindustri Intern AG., Fabriksgalan 7, 34322 Tibro. Switzerland: Swift AG., Melsenweg, 4552 Derendingen.

Sawaya & Moroni SpA., 11 Via Manzoni, 20121 Milan, Italy. *Outlets:* Belgium: Top Mouton, Obterrestraat 67-69, 8994 Poperinge/Proven. France: Dominique Devoto, 11 rue Azais Barthes, 34500 Beziers. Germany: Gisela Grimm. 20 Rosengartenstrasse, 70184 Stuttgart. Switzerland: Gehri c/o Mobil Form, 2 Saegegasse 3110 Muensingen.

Scarabas/Cumin Lugia, 54 Duca D'Aosta, 33044 Manzano (UD), Italy. *Outlet:* Belgium: Espace et Lignes, 55 Ulenstraat, Brussels.

Schick Inc., 10 Webster Rd. CTO6460-9001, Milford, Connecticut, USA. *Outlet:* UK: J. Walter Thompson, 40 Berkeley Square, London W1X 6AD. USA: J. Walter Thompson, 466 Lexington Ave. 6th Floor, New York, NY 10017.

Schopenhauer SpA. (Gruppo FontanaArte), 49 Alzaia Trieste, 20094 Corsico (ML), Italy. *Outlets:* Austria: Kilga Markus, Seilergasse 15, 6020 Innsbruck. Belgium/Luxembourg: D'Acan Srl., 36 Avenue Beau Séjour, 1410 Waterloo. France: Rousselin & Pecnard, 42 rue des Poissonniers, 92200 Neuilly sur Seine. Germany (North): Sabine Picx, Leo Statz Strasse 14a, 40474 Dusseldorf. Germany (South): Achim Reich, Elisabethenstr 50, 61348 Bad Homburg. The Netherlands: Andrée Kok, Pilatus 4, EK 1186 Amstelveen Spain: Fabio Ballabio, Calle Remei 37/41 1020, 08028 Barcelona. Switzerland: Karl Kasper, Loewengraben 24, 6000 Lucerne 5. UK: Clemente Caviguoli, 86 Ladbroke Grove, London W11 2HE. USA: Ivan Cuini, I. L. Euro Inc., 900 Broadway 902, New York, NY 10003.

Sculptures-Jeux, 1 rue Domat, 75005 Paris, France.

Sea & Sea, 3-2-10 Saiwaicho, Kawaguti-shi, Saitama 332, Japan.

Sega of America Inc., 255 Shoreline Drive, suite 200, Redwood City 94065, California, USA.

Seiko, 15-1 Kyobashi 2, Chomechuo-ku, 104 Tokyo, Japan.

Sharp Corporation, 22-22 Nagaike-cho, Abeno-ku, Osaka 545, Japan.

SKK, 34 Lexington St., London W1R 3HR.

Soca Line, 7 rue Vega, A La Belle Etoile, 44470 Carquefou, France. *Outlets:* Australia: Ke Zu Pty Ltd., 95 Beattie Street, Balmain NSW 2041. Belgium/Luxembourg/Holland: Quattro Benelux SA NV, Altenaken 11, 3322 Hoegaarden. Canada: Kiosk Mobilia, 115 Dupont Street, Toronto, Ontario M5R 1V4. Finland/Sweden/Norway: Design Distribution, Dobelnsgatan 38A, 1 TR S, 11352 Stockholm. USA: IDA Stein and Associates, 1337 Merchandise Mart, Post Office Box 3342, Chicago, Illinois 60654.

Solzi Luce Srl., 46 Via del Sale, 26100 Cremona, Italy. *Outlets:* Germany: Robert, Bunsenstrasse 5, Postf. 1229, 8033 Martinsreed. The Netherlands: Taifo 35 Box 220 Studsgade, Aarhus. UK: GFC, Westminster Business Square, Durham Street, London SE11 5JA. USA: Lighting Bug, 320 West 202 ND, 60411 Chicago Heights.

Sony Corporation. 6-7-35 Kitashinagawa,

Shinagawa-ku, Tokyo, Japan.

Ayala Sperling-Serfaty. 69 Maze'h St., 65789 Tel Aviv, Israel.

Steuben, 717 Fifth Avenue, New York NY 10022. USA.

Sugahara Glassworks Inc., 797 Fujishita, Kujukuri Sanbugin, Chiba, Japan. *Outlet*: USA: Tampopo, 410 Suite 100 Townsend, San Francisco 94107, California.

Sunbeam Leisure Products Co., 41010 Howard Bush Drive, Neosho, Missouri 64850-9164, USA.

Shinichi Sumikawa Design Studio, No. 205, 1-13-10 Sangenjaya, Setagaya-ku 154, Tokyo, Japan.

Swatch SA., Jakob-Stämpflistrasse 94, Biel 2500, Switzerland. *Outlet:* Ferdinand Menrad GmbH & Co. KG., Konrad-Celtis-Str. 81, 81369 Munich.

Takata Lemnos Inc., 511 Hayakawa, Takaoka, Toyama, Japan.

Takefu Knife Village Assn., Echizen no Sato-mae, Yokawa-cho, Takefu-shi, Fukaor 915, Japan.

Targa Italia, Via Orti 14, 20122, Milan, Italy.

Targetti Sankey SpA., 164 Via Pratese, 50145 Florence, Italy.

Tecta, Lauenförde 37697, Germany. *Outlets:* Austria/Germany: Alfred Reik, Ulrichstrasse 32, 73033 Göppingen. Belgium/the Netherlands: Ton J. de Geus, Gandel 17/23 8243 BV Lelystad. Denmark: Erling Nielsen, Viborgvej 175, 8210 Arhus V. France: Roger van Bary, 18 rue Laffitte, 75009, Paris. Italy: Frigerio Architettura, D'Interni - Divisione FAI, Corso. Italia 124, 20033 Desio-Milan. Spain: B. D. Ediciones de Diseño, C/Mallorca 291, Barcelona 37. Switzerland: Müller Innenarchitektur, Im Glockenacher 56, 8053 Zürich. UK: Aram Design Ltd., 3 Kean Street, London WC2B 4AT.

Kurt Thut AG., Möbelfabrik, CH-5115 Möriken, Switzerland.

Toulemonde Bochart, 7 Impasse Branly, 91320 Wissous, 2. 1. de Villemilan, France. *Outlets:* Germany: Design Focus, 1 Adenauer Str, 50374 Erftstadt. Italy: Pierre Frey, Via Vella 18, 10129 Turin. The Netherlands: Topolino, Postbus 70, 1260 AB Blaricurm. Scandinavia: Skanno, Aleksanteriulscetu 40, 00100 Helsinki. Spain: Camino de la Ereuita S/N, 08430 Santa Ines La Roca. UK: The Conran Shop. Michelin House, 81 Fulham Road, London SW3 6RD. USA: Luminaire, West Superior 310, Chicago Il 6810.

Trilux-Lenze GmbH & Co., Städtteil Müsten, Arnsberg 5760, Germany.

Trois Suisses, 12 rue de la Centenaire, 59963 Croix, France.

Unifor SpA., 1 via Isonzo, 22078 Turate, Como, Italy. *Outlets:* Australia: Unifor Office Systems Pty Ltd., 276 Devonshire Street, Surry Hills, Sysdney, NSW 2010. France: Unifor France SA, 6 rue des Saints Pères, 75007 Paris. Germany: Unifor Vertrieb, 32 Barer Strasse, 80333 Munich. Japan: Shukoh Co. Ltd., 2-10 2-chome Yaguchi, 146 Tokyo, Ohta-ku. The Netherlands: SV Design Office Systems BV, 137 Terbregse Recther Rottekade, 3055 XC Rotterdam. Scandinavia: Engelbrecht, 38 Skindergade, 1159 Kobenhavn K, Denmark. Spain: Ciento Quince SL, 115 Paseo de la Castellana, 28046 Madrid. UK: Ergonom Ltd/Langley Business Centre, Station Road, Langley SL3 8YN, Berks. USA: Unifor Inc/I. D. C. /Center Two-duite 706, 30-20 Thomson Av, Long Island City, New York, NY 11101.

UN Kogyo Inc., 1015-1 Kishicho, Ono City 675-13, Hyogo, Japan.

USO (Mobili Artigianali Contemporanei), Via Brera 11, 20121 Milan, Italy. *Outlets*: Benelux: Mr Pieter van Damme, Museumstraat 8, 2000 Antwerp. Greece: Varangis Avepe, M. Botsari, Pefki. Spain: Mr Casimiro Fernandex, Urbanizacion Soto de Llanera Casa No. 5, 33192 Pruvia, Principado de Asturias. Switzerland: Interni Rondelli, Emmentalstrasse 240, 3414 Villa Oberburg.

Venini SpA., 50 Fondata Vetrai, Murano, Venice 30141, Italy. *Outlets:* France: Collectania, 168 rue de Rivoli, Paris 75001. Germany: Graf Bethusy - Huc Vertriebs, 1 Hans-Sachs-Strasse, Krailling 8033. Hong Kong/Singapore: Lane Crawford Ltd., 28 Tong Chong Street, 8/F Somerset House, Hong Kong (Quarry Bay). Japan: Kitaichi Glass Co. Ltd., 1-6-10 Hanazono, Otaru, Hokkaido 047. Monaco: L'Art Vénitien, 4 Avenue de la Madonne, Monaco 98000. The Netherlands: Desideri, 50 Gossetlaan, Groot-Bijgaarden 1702, Belgium. Saudi Arabia: Khair M. Al-Khadra Trading Estate, PO Box 1376, Jeddah 21431. UK: Liberty Retail Ltd., Regent Street, London W1R 6AH. USA: Hampstead Lighting & Accessories, Suite 100, 1150 Alpha Drive, Alpharetta, GA 30201.

Verrerie de Nonfoux, 1417 Nonfoux, Switzerland. *Outlets:* France: Quartz Diffusion, 4 ruedes 4 Vents, 75006 Paris. Germany: Lichtenberg Studio Glass, Christel Schmidt-Allee 25, 22926 Ahrensburg. USA: New Glass Gallery, 345 West Broadway, New York.

Viaduct, 1-10 Summer's Street, London EC1R 5BD.

Virtual Vision Inc., 7659 178th Place NE, Redmond, WA 98052 USA. *Outlets:* Denmark: Tone A/S, Rugmarkon 36, 3520 Farum. France: N. B. S., 104-106 rue Rivay, 92300 Levallois Perret,. Germany: Quadral, Am Gerrenhauser Bahnhof 26-30, 3000 Hannover 21. Italy: Giucar Record, Via Remiglia 9, 40068 S. Lazzaro Di Savena (BO). Japan: Electori Co., Ltd., 1-19-3 Kamiochiai, Shinjuku-ku, Tokyo 161; Footwork International Inc., 4-14-3 Nishitenma, Kita-ku, Osaka 530; Triad-ship Corporation, 37-11 Udagawa-cho, Shibuya-ku, Tokyo 150. Spain: Euro AD. SI Ltd., Recinto Ferial, Avda. Jesus Santos Rein, Ed. Diana 1 Local 8, Fuengirola, Malaga 29640.

Vitra International AG., 15 Henric, 4010 Basle, Switzerland. *Outlets:* Austria: Vitra GmbH., Pfeilgasse 35, 1080 Vienna. Belgium: N. V. Vitra Belgium SA, Woluvelaan 140A, 1831 Diegem. France: Vitra SARL, 40 rue Violet, 75015, Paris. Germany: Vitra GmbH, Charles Eames-Str. 2, 7858 Weil am Rhein. Italy: Vitra Italia Srl, Corso di Porta Romana 6, 20122 Milan. Japan: Haller Japan Ltd., Canal Tower, 9-3 Koamicho Nihonbashi, Chuo-ku, Tokyo 103. The Netherlands: Vitra Nederalnd BV, Assumburg 73, 1081 GB, Amsterdam. Saudi Arabia: Vitra Middle East Ltd., PO Box 64 80, Dammam 31442. Spain: Vitra Hispania SA, Serrano No. 5, 404a, 28001 Madrid. UK: Vitra Ltd., 13 Grosvenor Square, London W1X 9FB. USA: Vitra Seating Inc., 30-20 Thomson Avenue, Long Island City, New York, NY 11101.

Voice Powered Technology, 19725 Sherman Way, Suite 295, Canoga Park 91302, California, USA.

Wogg AG., 16 am Grund, 5405 Baden, Aargan AG, Switzerland. *Outlets*: Austria: Dagmans Neuger Móbelagentur, 87 Kampenwandstr 87, 83229 Aschan. Germany: Stefan Górtitz, 7-9 Heinrich Barfnstr, 20146 Hamburg.

Yamada Shomei, 3-16-12 Sotokanda, Chyoda-ku 101, Tokyo, Japan. *Outlet:* Itlay: I Guzzini Illuminazione Srl, PO Box 39-59, 62019 Recanato.

Yamaha Corporation, 10-1, Nakazawa-cho, Shizuoka 430, Japan.

Zanotta SpA., Via Vittorio Veneto 57, 20054, Nova Milanese, Milan, Italy. *Outlets:* Austria: Giovanni Marelli, Via Guglielmo Oberdan 5, PO Box 148, I-20036 Meda (Mi), Italy. Australia: Arredorama International Pty Ltd., 1 Ross Street, Glebe, NSW . 2037. Austria: Prodomo, 35-37 Flachgase, 1060, Vienna. Belgium: Zaira Mis, 35 Boulevard Saint Michel, 1040 Brusels. France: Giuseppe Ceruti, Località Grand Chemin 1, I-11020 St Christophe (AO), Italy. Germany: Fulvio Folci, 14 Dahlienweg, 4000 Düsseldorf 30. Japan: Nova Oshima Co. Ltd., Sakakura Bldg, Akasaka, Minato-ku, Tokyo. The Netherlands: Hnasje Kalff, 8 Puttensestraat, 1181 Je Amstelveen, Holland. Norway/Denmark/Sweden: Poul Vigso, Bagovaenget 20, Skaerbaek. Spain: Angel Pujol, Av. República argentina 218, 08023 Barcelona; Fernandez Casimiro, Urbanizacion soto de Llanera, Casa No. 5, 33192 Pruvia, Oviedo. Switzerland: Peter Kaufmann, 123 Rychenbergstrasse, 8400 Winterhur. UK: The Architectural Trading Co. Ltd., 219-29 Shaftesbury Avenue, London WC2H 8AR. USA: International Contract Furnishings, 305 East 63rd Street, New York, NY 100210.

Zelform GmbH., Riederstr. 3, 4753 Taiskirchen, Austria.

Zerodisegno (Division of Quattrocchio), Via Isonzo 51, Alessandria 15100, Italy. *Outlets:* Austria: Rückl Jan, Via 2 Giugno 13, S. Biagio di Caltalta, Italy. Belgium/Luxembourg: Friday, Kon. Prinsstrrat 29, rue du Prince Royal, 1050 V Brussels. Denmark: Absolut Interior, Gravensgade 13, 9000 Aalborg. France: Inedit, 5 rue de Charonne, 75001 Paris. Germany: Present Perfect, 95 Frauenlobstrasse, 55118 Mainz. The Netherlands: Evat-Thea Verhoeven Design, 5/a Lambertusstraat, TB Hedikhuizen 5256. Spain: José Cunill Bonmam, San Jaun B. / La Salle 1. Esca 30, 29 Premia de Mar 08330, Barcelona. Switzerland: Pur Handelsgentur, Südstrasse 24, 4900 Langenthal. USA: Zero US Corporation, Industrial Circle, Lincoln, RI 02865.

Zumtobel Licht GmbH., 30 Schweizerstr, A-6850 Dornbirn, Austria. *Outlets:* France: Zumtobel - Agence Ile de France, 2 rue de la Cristallerie, 92310 Sèvres. Germany: Zumtobel Licht GmbH, 2-4, Achtzehn-Morgen Weg, 61242, Usingen. Italy: Zumtobel Staf Illuminazione Srl, 49 viale Bervera, 20162 Milan. Japan: Koizumi Sangyo Corp. 3-12, Kanda-Sakumacho, Chiyoda-ku, Tokyo 101. The Netherlands: N. V. Zumtobel Benelux S. A. 14 Cannaertserf, Breda 4824 GC. Scandinavia: Zumtobel Belysning AB, 140 A. Ulvsundavägen, 16130 Bromma/Stockholm. Spain: Lledo Illuminacion SA, 14, Cid Campeador, 28080 Mostoles (Madrid). Switzerland: Zumtobel Licht AG, 7 Riedackerstrasse, 8153 Rümlang. UK: Zumtobel Lighting Systems Ltd., Unit 5, The Argent Centre, Pump Lane, Hayes/Middlesex UB3 3BL. USA: Zumtobel Lighting Inc., 141 Buidling 16D, Lanza Ave., 07026 Garfield, New Jersey.

ACQUISITIONS

AUSTRIA

AUSTRIA

Austrian Museum for Applied Arts, Vienna

Donald Judd bookcase (1993)
Peter Kogler curtain, Amelse (1993)
Alessandro Mendini sofa, Bisanzio (1988)
Vico Padova chair (1991)
Roland Ralner chair, (redition 1993)
Kiki Smith 12 glass jars (1992/93)
Philippe Starck chair, Lang (1986), table, Titos Apost (1982)
Raymond Voogt sleeping box (1993)

CANADA

Musée des Arts Décoratifs, Montréal

Ron Arad chaise longue, London Papardelle (1992); shelves, One Way or Another (1989), *by* One-Off
Hiroshi Awatsuji plate Tsubaki (1991), *by* Nikko Co.; fabric, Fuumon (1990), *by* Fujie Textile Co. Ltd; fabric Hana (1989); fabric Hibiki (1989); fabric Kasane (c1990); fabric Kei (c. 1990); fabric Seki (c. 1990); fabric Sou (1989); plates, Seki, Hana, Nagare (c1990), *by* Design House AWA
Gijs Bakker lamp, Umbrella (1973), *by* Artimeta
Mario Bellini, table lamp Area (1975), *by* Artémide SpA.
Constantin Boym clock, Mona Lisa (1990) *by* Elika; vase, Recycle (1988); table lamp, Cheapest Lamp Possible (1985), *handcrafted by the designer*
Andrea Branzi 5 vases (1991), *by* Design Gallery, Milan
Livio Castiglioni & Gianfranco Fratini lamp, Boalum (1969), *by* Artémide
Eric Chan telephone, EC2 (1991), *by* ECCO
Tom Dixon chair, S; floor lamp, Cobra; armchair, Fat prototypes (1987)
Daniel Ebihara, table lamp, Maya (1984), *by* Rock Demon
Garouste & Bonetti chair, Imperial (1985), *by* Néotù
Frank Gehry lounge chair, Bubbles (1979), *by* New City Editions
Massimo Iosa Ghini pitcher, Stimulata (1989), *by* Design Gallery Milan
Peter Haas bench, Winged (1991), *handcrafted by the designer*
Takenobu Igarashi bowls, Triangle; Circle; Square (1989), *by* Yamasho Casting
Licio Isolani salt and pepper shakers (1992), *handcrafted by the designer*
Takamaichi Itoh, clock Spiral (1982), *by* Nichinan Corporation
Yonosuke Iwai, clock 91 (1991), *by* ODAKI-DOKI, Inc.
E. B. Jackson rug, Spiral (1984), *handcrafted by the designer*
Birgir Kaipiainien, charger (c 1964), *by* Arabia
Kiyoshi Kanai tissue box, Kleenext (1992); folding chair (1987), *handcrafted by the designer*
Kazuo Kawasaki ashtray, Symptoms III (1988); clock, Hola (1987), *by* Takata Inc.; kitchen knives, Fluctus (1986) knife, Culeus (1986), pencil sharpener, Schola (1986) *by* Takefu Knife Village; floppystand and book-end, Bini (prototype) (1991), fabricated *by* EX-Design Inc.
Kazuo Kawasaki and Echizen Wakasa scissors, &1, Round, Square, Triangle (1986), *by* Takefu Knife Village
Toshiyuki Kita floor lamp, 91 Holes (1991), desk accessories, Repro (1988), *by* IDK; bowls (1986), *by* Omukai Koshudo Co. Ltd.
Kenneth Krayer table and vase, Postal Porn (1991), *handcrafted by the designer*
Lisa Krohn & Martha Davis table lamp and wall sconce, Can & Able (1990), *by* ABle Inc.
Shiro Kuramata vase (1990), stool (prototype) (1965) *by* Ishimaru; clock, 2081 (1981), *by* Nichinan Corporation
Masayuki Kurokawa table lamp, Cobra (1973), *by* Yamagiwa; paperweight (1984), *by* Daichi Co. Ltd.; desk accessories, Gom (1973), *by* Fuso Gom Industry.
Marvin Lipofski vessel (1965) and vessel, California Sketch Series (1975), *handcrafted by the designer*
Locadia speaker (1988), *handcrafted by the designer* using Ramsa speaker
John Lonczak lamp, Hot Dog (1989), *by* Form Farm Inc.; lamp, Schleep (1991), *handcrafted by the designer*
Vico Magistretti coffee table, Dimitrio
Angelo Magistretti table lamp, Lesbo (1967), *by* Artemide
Umeda Masanori coffee set Mutsugoro (1984), *by* Yamaka International
Richard Meier, buffet plate, Signature black (1984), *by* Swid Powell
Howard Meister table, Signal (1991), *handcrafted by the designer*
Alessandro Mendini jewel case, Godezia (1993), *by* Design Gallery Milan
Alessandro Mendini, 2 vases, Stelleria; Alchemilla (1993) *by* Design Gallery Milano
Olivier Mourgue lounge chair, Bouloum (1968), *by* Airborne
Forrest Myers stool, Thicket (1991), *handcrafted by the designer*
M&Co speaker, Hug (1988), *handcrafted by the designer*
Kozo Okado boxes, Tsutusugata (1984), *handcrafted* at Kasubake Village
Sinya Okayama stool, Kaxzenoko (1984), *handcrafted by the designer* ; Crocodile (1983), *by* Sinya
Emilio Pucci vase (c1970) *by* Rosenthal AG
John Roth table lamp, Grasl Vulgaris (1973), *by* Ingo Maurer GmbH
Kozo Sato incense burner, Corrento (1990); vase, Corenta (1990); oil lamp, Luce for 91 (1991), *by* Takenaka Works Co., Ltd.
Gwathemy Siegel buffet plate, Tuxedo (1984) *by* Swid Powell
R. Simprini & M. Cavanzi, sofa Tatlin (1989), *by* Edra SpA.
Borek Sipek egg cup and side plate, *by* Koninklijke Porceleyne Fles; candelabra, Simon (1988), *by* Driade SpA.
Ettore Sottsass vases, Piogge Torrenziali, Una Volta, Quello Che Sento; Me Stesso, Fastosi Progetti (1992), *by* Ceramiche Flavia for Design Gallery Milano; table Bharata (1988), *by* Cav. G. Bitossi & Figli; buffet plates, Renaissance; Medici (c.1985), *by* Swid Powell
Philippe Starck stool, W.W. (1990), *by* Vitra; colander, Max le Chinois (1987), *by* Officina Alessi
Matteo Thun vase (1982), *by* Porcellane d'Arte San Marco srl
Oscar Tusquets Blanca decanter, Victoria (1990), *by* Driade SpA.
Shigeru Uchida table clocks, Dear vera 1 and Dear Vera 2 (1989), *by* Alessi; clock, Dear Moris (1989), *by* Acerbis International; armchair, Nirvana (1981), *by* Chairs Design
Masanori Umeda tray, Star (1985), *by* Nichinan Corporation; armchair Getsuen (1990), *by* Edra SpA.
Ann Wahlstrom vase, Labyrinth (1992), *by* Kosta Boda
Hiroko Watanabe boxes, Meditation Box (1991), *handcrafted by the designer*
Windigo desk top organizer (1991), *by* Windigo
Todd Wood gardening tools (prototype) (1990)
Leonid Yentus floor lamp, Plant (1992), *handcrafted by the designer*

FRANCE

Musée des Art Décoratifs, Paris

James Brown vase (1990), manufatured *by* Société des Amis du Musée National d'Art Moderne
Bülow-Hübe cup and saucer, My Favorite Cup (1987); spoon, My Favorite Spoon (1989), *by* Royal Copenhagen
Achille Castiglioni water, wine, whisky and liqueur glasses, carafe and champagne flute, Ovio Service (1983); glass, Paro (1983), *by* Danese
Marco Colombo, Mario Barbaglia table lamp, Dove (1985), *by* Italiana Luce
Claude Courtecuisse seat (1967); table (1967), *by* Ondulys; seat, Apollo (1969), *by* Mobel Italia; seats, Solea and Soleo, *by* Cattaneo
Christian Daninos armchair, Bulle (1969), *by* Formes Nouvelles
Massimo Iosa Ghini carafe, Gervais (1992)
Shiro Kuramata armchair (1983), *by* Ishimaru & Co.
Jean Leppien table, Toile de Septembre (1968)
Enzo Mari carafe, Trinidad (1969); spoon, Kurili (1973); pencil case, Lampeduza (1967); paper knife, Giglio (1985) plate, Aran (1961); ashtray, Griglia (1973); ashtray and waste paper bin, Lipari (1971); spoon, Java (1970); container, Java (1970); bowl, Tongareva (1969) ; box, Citera (1960); goblet Vetro (1991); goblet, No 61 (1991); vase, No 120/200 (1989); desk blotter, Filicudi (1985); vase, Camicia (1961); pencil case, Ventotene (1962); pencil case, Malta et Montechristo (1960); desk, Malta et Montechristo (1960); coatrack, Tricorno Tre (1980); vase, Tortiglione (1969); letter tray, Salina (1985); pencil case, Salina (1985); wallet, Salina (1985); ashtray, Delos (1980); wallet, Mastaba (1987); paper-clip container, Mastabe (1987); letter tray, Suva (1987); waste paper bin, Chio (1987); pencil case and wallet, Lipso (1987); egg-cup, Hamaï (1972) *by* Danese
Bruno Munari bowl, Tongareva (1969); ashtray, Cipro (1974); wallet, Corsica (1962); picture frame, Corfu (1962); knife, Maldive (1960), *by* Danese
Philippe Starck teapot, Ti Tang (1992), *by* Alessi Officina
Christophe Pillet chair, Slow Love (1992), *by* XO
Pete Sans, chair, Sillon Coqueta (1987), *by* BD Ediciones
Philippe Starck lamp, Ara (1988), *by* Flos; armchair, Richard III (1981), *by* Baleri
Oscar Tusquets armchair, Gaulino (1986)
Massimo Vignelli table, Metafora, *by* Casigliani

GERMANY

Kunstmuseum Düsseldorf im Ehrenhof

R Weiss coffeegrinders (1965/1967), *by* Braun

Vitra Design Museum, Weil am Rhein

Mario Bellini Tereride-prototype
Maurice Calca desk, Boomerang
Joe Colombo lamp. KO 27
Coop Himmelblau, Vodöl-prototype
Frank O Gehry 2 x Easy Edges Wiggle Table; Easy Edges Rocking Chair; Suz Chair, Experimental Edges; 5 Knoll bentwood chairs
Alessandro Mendini sofa, Maracatu
Gaetano Pesce lamp, Airport; preliminary model of UP 5-6 La Mama
Ettore Sottsass sofa, Califfo and other pieces; table lamp, Edison; lamp, Tahiti
Robert Wilson, Einstein Chair
Marco Zanuso, Richard Sapper chair, Lambada

THE NETHERLANDS

Museum Boymans-van Beuningen, Rotterdam

Gijs Bakker garden seat (1993)
Bofinger children's chair (1971)
Braun hair dryer (1970s)
Luigi Colani ballpoints and pens (1982), *by* Pelikan Nederland
Mieke Groot vases (1993)
Donald Judd cupboard (1984), *by* Janssen cv
Jan Konings and Jurgen Bey Holland chair (1993)
Barbara Nanning Holland objects (1993)
Jan Siebers mirror, Timide (1991)
Wilma Sommers chair (1993)
Esther Stasse containers (1992)
Jan van der Vaart Holland vase (1993)
Maria van Kesteren Holland containershape (1993)

Stedelijk Museum, Amsterdam

Pieter Aartsen, .Gerrie Babtist Gispen chair, Plano 3 (1994)
Ron Arad chair, Eight *by* One (1993); shelves, Mini Bookworm (1993)
A. Castiglioni lamp, Toio (1962) reissue (1992); lamp, Parentesi (1970) reissue (1992)
Donald Judd chairs and table (1993)
Arno van Leeuwen chair, ditto (1992)
Formsürsorge chair, Thor (1993)
Piet Hein Eek, cupboard (1993); chair (1993)
Friso Kramer redesign of chair, Rebolt (1993)
Ralph Krämer party cutlery, Mon Filio (1993)
Ingo Maurer lamp, Flutterby (1993)
Tejo Remy Milkbottle Lamp (1991)
Ian Scoley sinks and taps, Aqualine (1993)
Henk Stallinga lamp, Watt (1993)
Maarten Vrolijk curtain fabrics, Lotus, Jorge, Vicia, Contura, Furore (1993/94); carpet, Flower Power (1993); carpet, Who Shot Bruno? (1993)
Richard Walraven candle holder, Staircase (1993)
Kees Winkelman/Marcus Engeli candle holder, Spirelli (1994)

NORWAY

Nordenfjeldske Kunstindustrimuseum, Trondheim

Ingegerd Råman candlesticks, *by* Skrufs Glasbruk AB.

Oslo Museum of Applied Art.

Emil Abry desklamp, Jac (1991), *by* Luxo-Jac Jacobsen
Junichi Arai shawl (1992)
Bodum, Denmark 17 items of tableware (1980s - 1993)
Jan Digerud vase (1991), *by* Alessi
Tias Eckhoff chair, Tomi (1985), *by* Tranås
Sigriod Eckhoff, wellington boots, Cherox Flash (1992), *by* Viking A/S
Ellinor Flor vase (1991), *by* Alessi
Helly Hansen A/S sailing jacket, trousers, bag and floating-vest, Ocean Racing (1993)
Ulf Hanses thermal flask (1987), *by* Boda Nova
P. Hartwein electrical toothbrush (1991), *by* Bruan
Isao Hisoe tablelamp, Picchio (1992), *by* Luxo-Jac Jacobsen
John Houghton desklamp, FL-24 (1991), *by* Luxo-Jac Jacobsen
Willy Johanson drinking glass, Jumbo (1960s), *by* Hadeland Glassfactory
Jordan toothbrushes (1960s -1993)
H. Kahlcke foodprocessor, Multipractic electronic VK 210 (1984); coffee machine, Aromaster KF 43 (1984), *by* Braun
Jan Lunde Knudsen chair, Rondo (1963), *by* Karl

Sorlie & Sons
Jean Lanvin sunglasses (1977)
Luxo-Jac Jacobsen desklamp, T 88; desklamp, Luxo- L-1P (1961)
G.A. Muller blender, Multimix MX 32 (1962), *by* Braun
Dieter Rams record player, TC 45/2D (1964), *by* Braun
Rosti, Denmark, 23 items of tableware (1960s - 1993)
Philippe Starck toothbrush (1991), *by* Fluocaril
Transplastic SA, Madrid, picnic set (1970s)
R. Ullman shaving machine, Flex Control (1989), *by* Braun
Hilde Vemren vase (1991), *by* Alessi
Yves Saint Laurent sunglasses (1978)

POLAND

Muzeum Narodowe, Poznan
Andrea Anastasio glass, Moribana (1991)
Ergonomi Design Gruppen, Bahco tools
Marianne and Knut Hagberg children's furniture (1988)
Jan Hampf telephone receiver, Topic (1990)
Hans Hollein table, Schwarzenberg (1981)
Ettore Sottsass bookcase, Carlton (1981)
Swedish textiles (1980s)
Selection of tableware from Ikea, Kosta Boda, Orrefors (1980s)

Muzeum Narodowe, Warsaw
Zbigniew Horbowy glassware, (1987), *by* Inco
Wanda Zawidzka-Manteuffel vase, (1964-75); glass, (1970-71), *by* Irena

SWEDEN

Nationalmuseum, Stockholm
Åke Axelsson chair, Cello (1992), *by* Källemo
Älghult Glassworks three-piece service for Nord Form 90
Karin Björquist coffeecups (1993); teacup (1993), *by* Gustavsberg
Jonas Bohlin table, from the Triptyk series (1988), *by* Källemo
Gunnar Broman, Hans Brindfors, Göran Aneer, Bengt-Ake Jöhnsson, Bosse Asp and Bengi Ehm bottles for Absolut Vodka (1981), *by* Limmareds glasworks
Kerstin Danielsson bowl (1994)
Lena Bergestad Jonsson jug (1992)
John Kandell chair, Camilla (1982); chair, Schablon (1987); stool, Pax (1988); pilaster shelf (1989) *by* Källemo
Matias Ljunggren chair, Cobra (1991), *by* Källemo
John Melin and Anders Österlin, printed fabric for Nord form 90, *by* Borås Wäfveri
Nord Form 90 trays; oilcloth; set of knifes, forks, spoon and teaspoons
Jonas Osslund chair, Decapo (1991)
Ingegerd Räman 5 glasses, jug and two bowls (1993); candlestick, Samuraj; candlesticks; decanter and glass; glass and two bowls, Lilla Servisen, *by* Skruf Glassworks; stoneware pot (1991)
Rörstrand, service for Nord Form 90, Diamant
Barbro Spinchorn embroidery, Vatten Mellan Scenar (1964)
Pia Wallén blacket, Krux (1991)

Röhsska Konstlöjdmuseet, Gothenberg
Elisabeth Alvarsdotter rag and straw rug (1992)
Maria Åström fabric, Lemon; fabric, Sea Pie (1990s), *by* Ljungbergs Printing
Olle Baertling fabric, Denise (1954 reprinted 1990s), *by* Ljungbergs Textile Printing
Hertha Bengtson vase (1990s)
Karin Björquist salt celler (part of the Novel ceremonial Tableware) (1992)
Torun Bülow-Hübe cutlery (1990s)
Helen Dahlman decorative textile (1993)
J.M. Fruelund pot, Otter
Funiko Fujinaki bowl, Japan
Wolfgang Gessl salad cutlery (1990s)
Ulla Grytt tapestry, Poppy (1993)
Gullaskruf candlstick
Hamada tea mug, Japan
Erik Höglund glass cup (1990s); drinking glass (1990s)
Björn Hultén chair, Sally Brown (1990s), *by* Gärdsnäs
Berit Johansson bowl, Jugend (1993-94); wine glasses, Atmosphere (1993-94); tumblers (1993-94); glass carafe (1993-94)
Professor Helen Kuma pictorial bobbin lace (1990s)
Landqvist & Sjoholm plastic handle, Purepak
Ralf Lindberg chair, Tati (1990s); chair, Elle (1990s), *by* Gärdsnäs
Mashiko Nagui tea bowl, Japan
Annica Norberg, horse-hair fabrics (1989), *by* the Department of Arts and Crafts and Design, Gothenberg Univeristy
Sigurd Pehrson, candlestick (1990s); stainless steel disk
Ingegard Räman vase; cup; mug (1990s)
Jane Reumart stoneware bowl; fibreglass bowl

SWITZERLAND

Museum für Gestaltung, Zurich
Heinz Baumann 2 belt-fixed cupboards, Nomad (1991), *by* Möbelmanufaktur hz.baumann
En soie, selection of fabrics (1992-93)
Fabric frontline, selection of fabrics (1992-93)
Frog Design stereo system, Basalt (1992), *by* Studer Revox AG.
Alfredo Walter Häberli and Chritophe Marchand chest of drawers, Zehn Hoch (1992/93), *by* Schreinerei Oswald
Robert and Trix Haussmann chest of drawers, Manhatten (1987); shelves, Janus (1992), *by* Röthlisber AG
Ralph Krämer, cheese knife, Picado (1992), *by* Pott GmbH
Carl Pott selection of cutlery (1965-1976), *by* Pott GmbH
Alexander Schaffner cutlery (ca. 1965), *by* Pott GmbH
Silvio Schmed bookshelf (1992), *by* Röthlisberger AG
Karin Wälchli selection of fabrics

UK

Conran Foundation
(1993 collection selected by Ross Lovegrove)
Apple Newton Notepad, *by* Apple Computer
Arosa garden table
Bamboo chopsticks, Japan
Mario Bellini Persona Pen, *by* Lamy
Andrea Branzi peppermill, Twergi (1991), *by* Alessi
Achille Castiglioni sofa, Hilly (1992), by Cassina SpA.
Antonio Citterio chair, Compagnia delle Fillipine (1992), by B&B Italia
Joe Colombo cutlery and cup for Alitalia
Peter Cook, mineral water bottle, Cook, by Vittel
Stephen Copeland lamp, Ios Task , by Details/ Steelcase
Compangnolo, cyclists' water bottle
Geoff Cottle, Naim Audio Equipment, by Naim Audio
Gardena, gardening system
Frank Gehry chair, Crosscheck (1992), by Knoll International
Richard Gilbert stanley knife, by Stanley Tools
Gillette, shaving gel container
Grainger Hardware, Workshop chair
Grcic and Brandoloni coathangers and stand (1992), by Progetto Oggetto (Cappellini)
Grosfillex, garden chair, Miami
Zaha Hadid carpet, manufacturer by Vorwerk
Makio Hasuike console table, Dama (1992), by Fiam
Hozelock Garden Hose
Michiko Koshino cigarette lighters, by Sarome
Roberto Lazeroni bed, Tomber dans le Vide (1992), by Ceccotti
Ross Lovegrove stainless steel cutlery
Angelo Mangiarotti oil and vinegar set, Olpe, by Colle Cristalleria
Enzo Mari cheese grater (1989), by Zani & Zani
L.E. Mason Co., Weather Tite Light Switch
Alberto Meda, Paolo Rizzato, Lola Light, by Luceplan
Merker Solingen, razor
Miske Miller salt and pepper set (1989), by Keith Munro
Muji aluminium mug
Muji toothbrush
Nannini, spectacles, Rialto
Oakley, Sports sunglasses
Olympus Design, Mju Cameras, by Olympus
Steve O'Neil wet suit, by Vent Design
Plysu watering can
Potente door handles, by FSB Design
Price Pfister, Oakland taps
Renault Design, car Renault Twingo (1992)
Sainsbury's, Sainsbury's Tupperware
Sapporo, beer can
Selle Royal, bicycle saddle
Ettore Sottsass cutlery, Nuovo Milano (1986), *by* **Alessi**
Specialisation, Cyclists' Helmet
Stanley, slide action bolt
Philippe Starck tray, Voici Voila, *by* Alessi
Superbox, In-flight plastic cup
Vimar, light switches
Tommee Tippee, Pur baby bottles
Wilkinson Sword, seed dibber

Design Museum

No acquisitions made

Victoria and Albert Museum, London

Furniture:

Ron Arad chair, Little Heavy (1989); bookcase, Mortal Coil (1993), *by* One Off Ltd; chair, Soft Little Heavy (1989), *by* Moroso SpA.
Garouste and Bonetti chair, Barbarian (1981), *by* Néotù
Peter Karpf stacking chairs, NXT-01 (1991), *by* Swedese Mobler AB
Produkt Entwicklung Roericht (Burkhard Schmitz, Franz Biggel) office chair, Picto (1988-92), *by* Wilkhahn, Bad Münter
Martin Szekely pedestal table, PL (1983), *by* Néotù
Allison Thomas stool, Tutti Frutti (1990), *handcrafted by the designer*

Tableware:

Jane Beebevase, Olympia (1992), *by* Dartington Crystal Ltd.
Karin Björquist Nobel Service (1991), *by* Rörstrand
Alan Caiger-Smith bowl (1993), *by* Aldermaston
Morison S. Cousins bowls, Thatsa; Concept (1991-92); bowls, One Touch; Wonderlier (1991), *by* Tupperware
Anna Dickinson and Neil Wilkin vase (1993)
Geoffrey Eastop vase; dish (1983)
Eva England glasses hand decorated by Arbe Lindblom (1982-83), *by* Orrefors
Hilary Green bowl (1991), *by* Dartington Crystal Ltd.
Clare Henshaw, bowl and glass, Visible Voices (1992-93); vase, The Marriage 2 (1991)
Martin Hunt teapot (1966); jug (1966); coffee pot (1966), *by* Bing and Grondahl; dishes, Asia (1992), *by* Queensbury Hunt
Liz Lowe dish, An Eye for the Past (1990); vase, Future thoughts (1993)
Charles Meaker, Genova Bowl (1990), *by* Dartington Crystal Ltd.
Alessandro Mendini wine glasses and wooden boxes, Esimio; Garbato and Gentile (1992), *by* Venini
Simon Moore, bowl decanters, jar, jug and candlestick (1994)
David Pearce bowl (1993)
Professor Claus Joseph Riedel decanter, jug and various glasses, Sommeliers; Bruxelles, *by* Tiroler Glashütte
Frank Thrower, vase Roman Medium Ripple (1970s); vase, Flare Medium Ripple (1970s); vase Estruscan Medium Ripple (1970s); decanter and goblet, Sharon (1970s), *by* Dartington Crystal Ltd.
Oiva Toikka and glass blower Unto Suominen jug, Sonja (1992), *by* Nuutajärvi Glassworks
Professor L. Tomaszewski coffee service, Dorota (1962), *by* Cmielow
Susan William-Ellis coffee service, Magic City (1993), *by* Portmeirion Pottery
Rachel Woodman vase (1993); decanters, jugs and galsses (1988-91), *by* Dartington Crystal Ltd.

USA

The Brooklyn Museum, New York
Michael and Morison Cousins telephone handset, base support and wall mount (1993) by Warner Communication
Michael Cousins and June Lee Magic Stat Thermostat (1989), by Honeywell Inc.
Michael Cousins hair dryer, Pro Max Compact (1978) by Gillette and Co.
Frank Gehry chair and ottoman, Power Play (1991) by Knoll Group
Jack Lenor Larsen keyboard textile, Cabaret (1985); rain textile, Nimbus (1990); almond textile, Mimosa Sheer (1992)
Peter Todd Mitchell wallpapers, wallpaper design and textile designs (1949-1962).
Bean Bag Chair (1965)
Enzo Mari letter opener (1962) by Danese

Cooper-Hewitt Museum, New York
Mario Bellini cassette deck, Natural Sound Stereo Cassette Deck TC800D (1975-78), *by* Yamaha
Neil Bottle fabrics, Accademia; Fantasia. Galleria (1993), *by* Warner Fabrics
Agnes Bourne sidechair, Tao (1988)
Lois Bryant fabric, Departure III (1990)
Colombo and Barbaglia light, Tabla (1993), *by* Italiana Luce
Morrison S. Cousins canisters and bowls including, Thasta; Wonderlier; One Touch (1992), *by* Tupperware
Cousins Design, Heller Bag Recycler (1990), *by* Heller; Dixie Cup dispenser (1976); thermostats, Honeywell Magic Stage (1989)
Tias Eckhoff cutlery, Maya (1961), *by* Norsk Stalpress
Emma Gismondi Schweinberger umbrella stand, Dedalo (1966), *by* Artémide
Glendon Good screen, Poseidon (1993), *by* Abraxas
Trude Guermonprez, woven samples for buildings in California (1963); dyed hangings, Alter Ego and Weft Face (1970); hanging, Starlight (1974); hanging, Victoriana (1975)

Jack Hokanson, razor, Wally (1992), *by* Hoke 2
Beppe Kessler fabric (1993), *by* Taunus Textildruk Zimmer
Katherine Krizak screen, Shaker (1993), *by* Cappellini SpA.; kitchen knife, Mezzalune (1990)
Lisa Krohn and Christian Dufay light, Squeeze (1992), *by* George Kovacs Lighting Inc
Susanne Lind fabric (1993), *by* Taunus Textildruk Zimmer
Alistair McCauley, fabric, Pastoral Villa (1993), *by* Warner Fabrics
Ulf Moritz fabrics, Saturn; Paradisis, Galaxis Star' Carolina (1993), *by* Sacho Hesslein
Hauke Murken table, Last Minute (1993), *by* Moorman Mobel GmbH
Sheila O'Hara fabric, Sea Saw, (1991), *by* Muller Zell GmbH
Marca Pasanella napkins (1990s)
Dieter Rams and Dietrich Lubs wristwatch, AW 10 (1992-93), *by* Braun Aktiengesellschaft
Said Shohreh fabric (1993), *by* Taunus Textildruk Zimmer
Paul Simmons fabrics, Odrnamental; Grand Acanthus (1993), *by* Warner Fabrics
Matteo Thun cutlery, Balance (1993), *by* Wurttembergische Metallwarenfabrik Aktiengesellschaft
Norman Vincent Sukkar chair, Square (1992-93)
Renate Weisz, screen printed lengths, Scriptura Dekor; Kalligra Dekor; Papyra (1993), *by* Zimmer + Rhode
Renate Weisz fabrics, Poema; Poesia; Fabula (1993), *by* Zimmer + Rhode

The Denver Art Museum
Franco Albini, Franca Helg bowl, Ciotole (1971), *by* San Lorenzo srl
Filippo Alison Samovar, Vesevo (1985), *by* Sabattini Argenteria SpA.
Emilio Ambasz television, Handkerchief (prototype) (1992), *by* Brionvega SpA.; office chair, Qualis (1989), *by* Tecno SpA.
Andrea Anastasio vase, Amma (1991), *by* Memphis Extra
Archizoom and Paolo Deganello chair, AEO (1973), *by* Cassina ApA
Archizoom seating, Superonda (1966-67), *by* Poltronova Srl
Gae Aulenti table (1965), *by* The Knoll Group; lamp, Patrocio (1975), *by* Artemide SpA.; lamp, Pipistrello (1965-66), *by* Martinelli SpA.
Luigi Baroli folding screen, Cartoons (1992), *by* Baleri Italia srl
Mario Bellini, lamp, area 50 1974, *by* Artemide SpA.; television, Best 15 (1990), *by* Briovega SpA.; armchair, Break (1976), *by* Cassina SpA.; calculator, Divisumma 18 (1972); typewriter, ETP 55 (1985-86), *by* Ing. C. Olivetti & C. SpA.; office chair, Figura (1979-1984), *by* Vitra; settee, La Bambole (1972), *by* B&B Italia SpA.; typewriter, Lexikon 82 (1972-73); calculator, Logos 59 (1975); computer, Programma 101 (1965), *by* Inc. C. Olivetti & C. SpA.; television, Sider 20 (1972), *by* Brionvega SpA.
Giandomenico Belotti side chair, Spaghetti (1979-80), *by* Alias srl
Cini Boeri seating, Serpentone (1971), *by* Arflex
Cini Boeri and Tomy Katayanago armchair, Ghost (1987), *by* Fiam Italia SpA.
Andrea Branzi armchair, domestic Animals (prototype (1985), *by* Zabro
Anna Castelli-Ferrieri stacking units (1969), *by* Kartell SpA.
Achille Castiglioni lamp, Gibigiana/52 Red (1981), *by* Flos Inc. tumblers and carafe (1983), *by* Danese srl; goblets, Paro (1983), *by* Danese srl; lamp, Snoopy (1967), *by* Flos Inc.
Achille Castiglioni and Pier Giacomo Castiglioni lamp, Arco (1962), *by* Flos Inc.; armchair, Sanluca (1961), *by* Bernini SpA.; lamp, Tolo (1962), *by* Flos Inc.
Achille Castiglioni and Pio Manzù lamp, Parentesi, *by* Flos Inc.
Livo Castiglioni and Finafranco Frattini lamp, Boalum (1969-70), *by* Artemide
Antonio Citterio office chair, Famiglia AC 2 (1988), *by* Vitra Inc.
Joe Colombo lamp, Alogena (1970), *by* O-Luce srl; armchair (1964), *by* Kartell SpA.; storage trolley, Boby (1970), *by* Bieffeplast SpA.; side chair, Universale (1965-67), *by* Kartell SpA.
Tony Cordero lamp, Ecate (1990), *by* Artemide SpA.
Donato D'Urbino, Jonathan De Pas and Paolo Lomazzi armchair, Blow (1967), *by* Zanotta SpA.; seating, Joe (1970-71), *by* Poltronova srl
Ricardo Dalisi centerpiece, Coppa reale (1993-1994), *by* Edizioni Galleria Colombari
Constantino Dardi teapot, Principesa from the Turandot service (1990-91), *by* Cleto Munari Design Associati srl.
Antonio Da Ros vase 1964-65), *by* Gino Cenedese e Figlio
Gabriele de Vecchi teapot, Emisfera (1985), *by* Argenteria Gabriele de Vecchi
Laura de Santillana platter, Ninfee (1989), *by* EOS design nel vetro srl
Aldo Rossi, Luca Meda armchair, Teatro (1982), *by* Molteni & C
Lino Sabattini fish dish, conch-Table (1973; gravy boat, Estro (1976-77); tureen (prototype) (1990), fabricated by Sabattini Argenteria SpA.
Valerio Sacchetti pitcher, Agilulfo (1984), *by* Fratelli Cassetti SpA.
Roberto Sambonet ashtrays (1992), *by* GFR; cooking set, Enter Line (1964), *by* Sambonet SpA.; cups (1981), *by* Cleto Munari Design Associati
Denis Santachiara sofa, Lumiere (1989), *by* Zerodisegno srl
Richard Sapper oval casserole (1984-86), *by* Alessi SpA.; lamp, Tizio (1973), *by* Artemide SpA.;
Richard Sapper, Marco Zanuso television, Black 201, *by* Brionvega SpA.; telephone, Grillo (1965-87), *by* Siemens
Luca Scacchetti urn, Helsinki (1989), *by* Mangani Ars
Afra Scarpa, Tobia Scarpa lamp, Pierrot (1990), *by* Flos Inc.
Carlo Scarpa table, Doge (1969), *by* Simon International SpA.; flatware (1977); carafe, Interno d'Oro (1978), *by* Cleto Munari Design Associati srl
Ettore Sottsass lamp, Ashoka (1981), *by* Memphis srl; Asteroide (1968), *by* Poltronova srl; centerpiece (prototype) (1989), *by* Alessio Sarri Ceramiche; table, Le Strutture Tremano (1979), *by* Studio Alchymia; lamp, Limante (1977), *by* Vetreria Vistosi SpA.; candlestick, Malide (1986); centerpeice, Murmansk (1982), *by* Memphis srl; cabinet, Nirvana (1966), *by* Poltronova srl; centerpiece, Schiavona (1972), *by* Vetreria Vistosi SpA.; table, Tartar (1985), *by* Memphis srl; typewriter, Valentine I-47 (1969), *by* Ing C. Olivetti & C SpA.; lamp, Valigia (1977), *by* Stilnova; vase, Yantra Y-37 (1970), *by* Poltronova srl
Ettore Sottsass, Hans von Klier typewriter, Praxis 48 (1965), *by* Ing C. Olivetti & C. SpA.
Studio 65 seating, Capitello (1971), *by* Gufram Industria Arredamento
Superstudio table, Quaderna (1970-71), *by* Zanotta SpA.
Kazuhide Takahama lounge chair, Suzanne (1965), *by* Gavina for Knoll International
UFO lamp, Paramount (1965-75), *by* Lapo Binazzi
Massimo Vignelli dinnerware (1964), *by* Heller Inc.
Massimo Vignelli, Lella Vignelli flatware, Ciga (1979), *by* Calegaro
Luciano Vistosi lamps, Bissa and Bissona (1972); bowl, Dodolo (1972), *by* Vetreria Vistosi SpA.
Marco Zanini vase, Simeon (1991), *by* Venini SpA.
Marco Zanuso record player, GD 145 (1974), *by* Brionvega SpA.

Metropolitan Museum of Art, New York.
Raymond Loewy cabinet, DR2000 (1969)
Lucie Rie 3 pots, (1970s)
Bertil Valien 'Map III' (1993)
Gino Valle clock, Cifra 3 (1969)
Mary Zeran flatware, (prototype) (1991)

Museum of Modern Art, New York
Achille Castiglioni hanging lamp, Brera (1992), *by* Flos
Alberto Meda, Franco Raggi and Denis Santachiara table lamp, On Off (1988), *by* Luceplan SpA.
Stephen Peart, Raymond Riley, David Shen adjustable keyboard (1993), *by* Apple Computer, Inc.
Gerrit Rietveld pew for Cornerstone Church, De Hoop (1963), *by* de Boer and Son.
Reiko Sudo fabric Stratus for the Cloud Series (1993), *by* Nuno

PHOTOGRAPHIC CREDITS

The publisher and editors wish to thank the following photographers for the use of their material in this book.

Takashi Abiko *tx 33-4*
Marco Angeretti *f 15-16, 46*
Studio Aleph *l 51*
Shima Akira *tx 16*
Yoichi Aoyagi *p 107*
Masanao Arai *tx 17-31*
Aldo Ballo *f 29, 30, 32*
Naomi Baumgartl & Raffaele Celentano *l 27*
Federico Brunetti *p 67-71*
Nicolai Canetti *p 97*
Bitetto Chimenti *f 2, 74*
Donald Cohen *t 4*
Charles Duprat *t 18*
Rick English *p 1-2, 15, 36*
Nancy Faulker *f 84*
Larry Friar *p 89, 101, 104*
Mitsumasa Fujitsuka *t 7, 26, p 98*
Axel Gnad *l 42*
Leon Gulikers *f 113, t 9*
Alfred Hablützel *f 86*
Yuki Higuchi *tx 11*
Christoph Hitsch *p 96*
Frank Horvat *f 126*
ITA *f 103*
Timo Kauppila/Indav *t 22*
K. Knoblich *f 91*
Satoshi Kosaka *f 83*
Peer van der Kruis *t 15, t 24-5*
Athos Locce *t 10*
Chiaki Maki *t 12,13*
Hans van der Mars *f 27, 88, 101. l 18, t 28, tx 10, p 93*
Sue McNab *tx 14, 15*
Trevair Mein *f 35*
Nacasa & Partners *Inc. l 52*
Paul Newman *l 5*
David Nufer *t 13*
Guido Pedron *f 75, 77, 80, 81*
Marino Ramazzotti *f 11*
Stefan Rohner *f 52*
Carl Florian Ruppel *l 31*
Katsuji Sato *tx 1*
Rei Sato *t 2, 12*
J.-C.Schulten *l 43*
Mikio Sekita *p 39*
Albi Serfaty *f 129, 130*
Michael Sieger *t 19-20*
B J Sorensen *p 43*
Hendrik Stängle *f 54-8*
Station 1 *f 98*
Shinichi Sumikawa *p 110*
Terry Sutherland *p 9, 12, 15*
Swatch SA *p 81*
Isao Takahashi *t 23*
Toshinori Toshima *p 102*
Frank Thurston *f 51, 105, p 49*
Nick Turner *p 87, 90-1*
Tom Vack *f 128, l 19, 25, 26, 28*
Reven Wurman *t 3*
Martin Y Zentol *f 99*